A Prodigal Daughter
James Roth

Golden Pheasant Publishing

ISBN: 9798876119193

Central Tokyo JR Train Lines

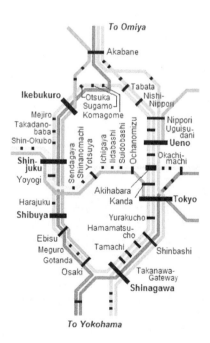

Blank Page

Preface

I got the idea for this novel long, long ago. The idea was that a brother and a sister, seeking to escape a small town in northeastern Japan, use different means to do so. She is clever, attractive, and wily. She seduces the manager of a sushi distributing company where she works, becomes pregnant, and has him marry her. Her husband is from a well-to-do family and has graduated from a prestigious university. She acquires the good life she had wanted, living in a nice house in a Tokyo suburb and is able to buy fashionable clothes. Of course, the marriage never had a chance of working out. She becomes unhappy. She seeks love and finds it, beginning an affair. She wants to marry her lover, but she first needs to divorce her husband.

Her brother chose a different route to escape small town Japan: he joined the yakuza. He ends up in Tokyo as a soldier for a yakuza clan. One evening he botches a hit on a rival gang member and is booted out of the clan. He begins to work as a private investigator. His clients are mostly the wives of wayward husbands who want to know what their husbands are up to. One day his sister comes to him, asking for his help. She wants him to find a girl to seduce her husband, so that she can get some photos of him with her and she can secure an easy divorce. In Japan, it isn't so easy for the wife of an executive at some major companies to divorce. A divorce reflects poorly on the executive, and, in Japan, appearance is what matters, all too often. So the husbands prefer to go on with the appearance of a successful marriage, as do many wives.

The relationship between this sister and brother—she is older—borders on the incestuous. He is a very possessive, how a jealous lover might be, when she tells him she's in love. When she was unhappy, he was perfectly fine with that. Nonetheless, he finds a girl to seduce her husband, gets the photos, and that is when everything goes sideways. Her good intentions, to be happily married, begins a chain of events that neither of them could anticipate, ending in tragedy for many.

I wrote the first draft of this novel in maybe three months, while in Zimbabwe during the COVID years, after my contract as an English Language Fellow in the U.S State Department's EFL Program came to an end. At that time, COVID in the U.S. was on the rampage but there were no cases in Zimbabwe. Moreover, I was having a good time there, riding a motorcycle up into the mountains and playing golf, also writing. I had, for the first time in my life, the time to write and took advantage of it.

I thought the best way to tell the story was as a mystery, using a police detective as the narrator. He pieces together the events of the story, which lead back to him and his wife and prodigal daughter. As I read somewhere, the best detective stories aren't about solving a murder. They're ones that are about the detective, and that is the case with this novel. The mystery is only a means for the detective to reflect on his life and marriage, Japan and Japanese society, and this is what is central to the story. You can contact me at 2contact.j.roth@gmail.com. I welcome readers' observations and a discussion of the novel.

Prologue

I picked Yuji up in Kabuki-cho at a video arcade near a sex shop, just where Nobuyuki had told me he'd be. He was playing the video game Divine Fantasy, a sad thing. He was old enough to be my father, but I didn't let him in on how sorry I felt for him. I just went ahead and did what Nobuyuki had paid me to do.

After Yuji had finished the game, he smiled to himself before looking up and seeing me. I forced myself to pucker my shiny red lips and say, "You won a favor!" He stared at me the way an otaku does, so I had to go on and force myself to say what I knew I had to, "Wouldn't you prefer the real thing?"

Poor Yuji, I thought, maybe he's only been with his wife.

I was wearing some heart-shaped fashion eyeglasses with a red frame, what Nobuyuki had told me to do. My lips were a red as shiny as the frames. I was one of those idiot girl video game avatars come to life, and I hated myself for it.

"Maybe we should go to a hotel?" I said.

The love hotel Nobuyuki and I had picked out was the Amour, in that area of Kabuki-cho where the love hotels are lined up side by side to the end of the street. They all have flashy neon signs out front or on the roofs that make couples think they are going to a carnival, and I suppose they are, but one for adults. I'd been in more of these hotels than I cared to remember, here in Tokyo and down in Fukuoka and even a few between the two cities, I'm ashamed to say.

The Amour was a hotel I'd wanted to visit for quite some time, way back to when I was a high school student and first learned about the pleasures of boys, but it was too old-fashioned for them. The boys said it was for middle-aged women whose breasts hung down to their knees. They wanted a room with video games and AI generated spaceships or soccer matches. Boys! I'm past them now. Long past them.

I liked the Amour because the look of it took me out of Japan and back in time. A miniature of the Eiffel Tower is near the entrance, and the facade is made up like a building painters might have lived in long ago. You know, a bit run down but charming. But all that had nothing to do with why Nobuyuki had wanted me to take Yuji there. The reason was that it was across from a Family Mart convenience store, where he wouldn't look out of place standing at the entrance holding a camera.

When Yuji and I passed Nobuyuki, he let the cigarette in the corner of his mouth fall to the street, ground it out with the tip of a shoe, and then picked it up the butt and put it away in a trash bin in front of the store. He was that kind of man, respectful, even if he liked to pretend he was otherwise. It was only then that he raised the camera and took the photos his client wanted. My job was done. I could've run off then, but on the way to the Amour Yuji and I had talked a bit about life and the distance between us narrowed. He'd got to talking about the sushi company he worked for and the pressures he felt put on him by the president for his section to increase profits. I began to feel closer to him. I had pressures on me too.

Yuji and I slipped past the wall hiding the Amour's entrance and went inside. He booked the expensive Monet room, without me even having to ask for it. It was like he knew who I was, him picking that room. I was thrilled.

He put a ten thousand yen note under the slot in the smoky glass window. An old woman's hand took the bill. We started off toward the room, but the old woman called out, "Sir. Your change."

Yuji returned to the window and took the change.

As we were making our way to the Monet room, a couple came out of another room. The man—or was he still a boy?—was about twenty-five or so, wearing jeans and a white dress shirt. He gave me a good going over as we passed each other. He reminded me a bit of Pirate, scrawny and full of himself, a boy-man girls should steer clear of. His girl elbowed him a good one in the ribs. He deserved it. I'd wanted to, the way he'd looked at me.

We came to the Monet room. Yuji tapped the key card against the door lock, a green light flickered, and we went inside.

What a delight that room was. It was just what I'd wanted, like a room in one of those French painter's ateliers. Against one wall were fake windows. 3D images were in the windows, to make the street scene below them look real. Lining the street were bistros and sidewalk cafes.

I turned around and saw that Yuji's eyes were now totally on me. I had power, and it thrilled me. I'd take him to a private place far away from the stresses he felt, and if he were any good I'd go along on the journey.

I took off my glasses and set them on a counter by the television. I then unbuttoned the first two buttons of my frilly blouse to get Yuji started, but even then he didn't know what to do, and so I took his hands and had him undo the other buttons. Then I slipped the blouse off and tossed it over a painter's easel by a sofa. He stared at my body, as if it were something a person in a museum would admire. I had more to show him, though. I turned around, for him to undo my bra, but I wasn't prepared for his fingers being as cold as icicles. I shivered.

"I'm sorry," he said. "I . . . I've . . ."

"Don't think about it," I told him. "Things will come naturally."

I stood on my toes and kissed his neck. It was like kissing marble, he was so nervous. I'd see that he warmed up to me.

"Relax," I told him.

I then put his hands on the waist of my red dress and got him to undo the hasp. It fell to the floor. I stepped out of it. He finally then caught on to how a man should be and put his thumbs under the waistband of my panties and peeled them off. There I was, ready for him. He stared at me in wonder. No, he'd never been with a girl, I thought, only his wife. I was happy to be there with him.

I reached out for his belt and undid it and his pants dropped to the floor. I saw then that he was a man. He wasn't going to be a disappointment.

He searched for the switch to dim the room lights but it took him a while to find it. He was still a bit nervous. I suppose I was too. The first time is always that way. I was about to pull off the ridiculous blue wig I'd been wearing, but he took me by the wrist.

"Please," he said. "No."

"I'm not an Avatar in Final Fantasy now," I said.

"Please."

He looked so pitiful that I couldn't stop myself from giving in to him, but I didn't like it, not one bit, him not wanting to see me for who I was. I'd get him to think differently about me, I decided.

He was good for two rounds. I taught him some new tricks, and he thanked me. After the second round, when we were lying in bed together, he said, "I haven't been that strong since my honeymoon in Hawaii."

"You poor darling," I said. It was the way I talked to customers, and I hated to be that way, playing a role, but I couldn't help myself. It was who I'd become. Then Yuji surprised me in a way that I could never, ever have imagined. He said, "My wife put you up to this. Didn't she?"

"What are you talking about?" I said.

"That man with the camera," he said. "He's my brother-in-law."

That threw me. "What man?" I said.

"You know."

"No, I don't."

"I think you do. If my wife can take a lover, why can't I? A divorce will ruin me, you know?"

"I don't know what you're talking about," I said, lying. His bad marriage was something I didn't want to talk about. My customers told me about their bad marriages, and I was sick of them using me as a counselor, so I said, "We had a good time."

"I love you," he said.

I don't know why some boy-men have to go and ruin sex by saying that, but too many do. I forced a smile.

He said, "I'm sorry."

"Sorry for what? We had a good time."

"Really?"

"Stop feeling sorry for yourself," I said.

We lay there for a minute or two longer before he said, "My company." He paused, having trouble going on with what he wanted to say, but then he came out with it, first saying, "I shouldn't be telling you this."

I was foolish enough to ask, "Why keep whatever it is a secret after the good time we had? You'll feel better if you tell someone."

"It's too dangerous."

"You work for a sushi company, you said. How could fish be dangerous?"

"I don't want to involve you."

"But we had a good time. Go on, tell me."

He started to breathe heavily, he was so stressed. How could I not feel something for him? I calmed him down by running my fingers through his hair. He took my hand and looked me in the eyes and said, "The time I spent here with you was the happiest two hours of my life."

Two hours was how long he'd rented the room for.

I got to thinking about his company, how he was worried about involving me in something dangerous. I knew danger. I felt I was in danger every time I met Pirate, that one day he wouldn't be able to control himself, he was so drugged up with *shabu.* We'd get into a fight that was more than words. But I needed him. He'd gotten me hooked. Junko. I should've known what she was up to.

I thought about telling Yuji about Pirate but held back. I didn't want to burden him with my troubles. He was having a hard enough time telling me what his were, so I thought the best thing to do to get it out of him was to make him think I was leaving. I said, "I should be going."

"Boyfriend?" he asked, what I should've expected him to say.

I told him, "How could you ask such a thing, after the good time we spent together? No. I'm a hostess. It's hard work, you know, dealing with the likes of men who come to me to unload all their problems. I'm sick of it. Just sick of it. I want to go home one day." I saw that he took that personally, so I calmed him down again by saying, "I'm not talking about you. You were great."

"What, you want to go home?"

"I mean, I want a home to go to, one where I feel welcome."

"I know what you mean. I have a home, but it doesn't feel that way. What's the name of the club where you work?"

"The Nankaitou. It's near Tameije-sanno Station," I told him. "Visit me one evening."

"I don't know. I might cause trouble for you."

"Talking with men, pouring their drinks, lighting their cigarettes. It's my job, sucking up to them. You'd be different. I like it, you talking to me."

"Maybe one day. Can we keep on seeing each other this way? That might be better. We could meet at a coffee shop sometimes and maybe even just talk. I need to talk."

I wasn't sure about that, but when his eyes filled with tears I thought of my father and how he might have been like that, longing to see me again. Yuji then mumbled, "You must know a lot of men? You don't have time for me."

"No. They're only customers," I said.

"Do you think we could spend the night together?" he then asked. I didn't think he'd had it in him to ask me that, the way a man would. He'd just burst out with it.

"Tonight?" I asked.

"Please," he said. "Please?"

"To spite your wife? Is that why?"

"No. No! Of course not. I feel so close to you. Really."

"What about your wife?" I asked. "I don't want to get you in trouble with her."

"Why should I care about her? She's going to divorce me anyway. I'll tell her I had to work late and am going to take a room at a hotel. It wouldn't be the first time. She'll be happy to have the house to herself."

He leaned against the headboard. His white, hairless

chest looked like a moon.

"I'll spend the night with you," I said, "but I have to call in first, tell my boss I've got plans for tonight."

"Won't I be getting you in trouble?"

"That's sweet. No, my boss doesn't ask questions of her girls. She'll understand."

Yuji put a hand on my thigh and smiled. His touch was now warm and gentle, a nice thing in a man. Pirate's touch was like a robot's, metallic. The way he did it was like one, too.

I'd been sitting on the edge of the bed, preparing to leave, but Yuji pulled me over onto him and we lay there for quite a while, looking up at the fake, twinkling stars in the ceiling. The feeling of the two of us lying there together was so peaceful. I had experienced that with Junichi long back, but only him. Thinking of Junichi, I pulled off that ridiculous blue wig and flung it onto the floor but no sooner had I done so than I realized I'd made a mistake.

Yuji saw the scar. He touched my forehead, where the scar was, right at my hairline on the right side of my head. "How did you get that?" he asked.

"It's nothing," I said.

"Tell me."

"A car accident," I said. Thinking of that accident, I had to hold back tears.

"But you're fine now?"

"I broke my right leg. My hip hurts now and then."

"How did it happen?"

I wasn't about to tell him the truth about the accident, so I made up a story.

"Sorry," he said. "Such an unfortunate thing shouldn't happen to a girl as cute as you."

"You didn't have to say that," I told him, "about me being cute."

"I wanted to."

"Okay, then, if it makes you feel better."

He smiled the way a man who's with a girl he cares about is supposed to smile, to my delight and surprise. Seeing that look, I became curious about his worries. I asked, "What is it with your company and those dangerous fish? Go on, tell me. You'll feel better."

He looked at me, his lips trembling, and after he'd gotten himself pulled together managed to mumble, "The yakuza is pressuring me to do something I shouldn't. I've never told anyone about it."

I thought he might break down right there into sobs of fear. I couldn't have that. So I said, "Didn't telling me make you feel better? Come on, now. Cheer up."

He stopped his sniffling and looked at me and got control of himself. The poor man. "It did," he said. "I needed to tell someone."

I knew from my father all about the yakuza and the pressures they put on company men who didn't have it in them to stand up to their threats. But I'd never expected the yakuza to have anything to do with fish.

Yuji mentioning the yakuza kept me thinking about my father and mother. Oh, how I missed them. I knew I could arrange a chance meeting. Yes. I could. But what to say? Could we begin again as if nothing had happened? No. I couldn't admit that I'd been wrong. There will be time. There will be time. For now I had Yuji. I said, "We'll talk some more the next time we meet, but, please, I'm not wearing a silly blue wig."

"Just now and then, if you don't mind? Please?"

"Never again. Never. Accept me for who I am or don't

A PRODIGAL DAUGHTER

accept me at all."

"Sorry," Yuji said. "I want you to be who you are."

He was a kind man, kinder than I could ever have imagined. But what a mistake it was, continuing to see him. What a terrible mistake.

17

CHAPTER ONE

My name is Kawayama Tomoyuki. I am a homicide detective with the Tokyo Metropolitan Police, and I have a story to tell, but it has less to do with the crime my team and I solved than it has to do with me and the shame I have felt for several years. That shame, the assignment of it, is something that I hadn't come to terms with until I wrote this story. In the West, there are psychologists and counselors who help people in situations that I found myself, even ones in police departments, from what I've heard; but we don't have that kind of culture in Japan. We keep our emotions hidden, and this eats away at us at times. Every culture has its failings, and this, I now know, is one of Japan's. I am, or was, a prisoner of Japanese culture. I faced the shame as stoically as I could, in the spirit of a samurai warrior. I'm proud of that bushido spirit, even if I know how damaging it can be. Many Japanese self-destruct, confronting shame by wearing the proper face to get through the day. No one really knows who they are. Some men resort to alcohol and carousing hostess bars to ease the burden of shame. Women have affairs. Or they drink, too. They're called "kitchen drinkers."

The person I needed to confess to the most to relieve my shame was my wife, Mizuko. We've been married for more than twenty-five years. She needed to know what I learned while my team investigated, and solved, the murder, but I just didn't have it in me to tell her until after the killer was found dead in a flophouse in Osaka.

But a brave man who has the bushido spirit took the fall for the murder, admitting to it because of the shame he felt.

I thought before confessing to Mizuko that she might leave me after I told her what I had learned. I don't know how I could have kept on if she had. If that is love, then I love her. Such a thing may sound odd to a Westerner, for a man to realize he loves his wife long after they have married, but such a marriage isn't so rare in my generation. Ours was an arranged marriage, what is called an *omiai*; we were both told by our parents that love would come in time, which it did. So perhaps this is a love story I'm telling you, but certainly not one found in cheap novels or sentimental television dramas involving young people in which the story ends with a marriage. Marriage is really a beginning. Those cheap novels and sentimental dramas are fantasies. A real marriage is not a fantasy. You'll learn about my marriage as you read about the investigation of this murder, which I've done my best to put down as accurately as I know how.

Before I begin the story, I first need to provide you with some background information that will help you to understand Tokyo. Tokyo has twenty-three wards. One is Shinjuku. It is where the murder took place. My desk is in the Shinjuku Police Department building, on the west side of South Shinjuku Station, one of the busiest stations in Japan. It's a station that is used primarily by commuters. I'm one of them. I take the Chuo express line, which has cars that are color-coded orange. The line connects Tokyo Station, where the line terminates, with the suburban towns west of Tokyo. The train makes a stop at South Shinjuku Station, where the cars often empty but fill right back up, before continuing on. The police building is only about a five-minute walk from South Shinjuku Station.

My commute begins at Yotsuya Station. Mizuko and I have a traditional Japanese house made of wood and shoji screens not far from the station. We are fortunate in that regard, living in a house and not a massive building of flats, where so many Japanese live. We are fortunate to even have a small garden. In it there are a few pines and maples and one cherry tree, called a *sakura* in Japanese, 桜.

The Shinjuku Police Department building is not far from Tokyo's municipal building, which is where many companies have their headquarters in tall, steel, glass towers. A man involved in the murder, but not the killer, worked in a company headquartered in one of those imposing towers. It's likely that we might have seen each other on occasion on our walks to our respective stations. He took a train out of Seibu Station, a private train line not far from South Shinjuku Station.

On the ground floors of these corporate towers are coffee shops, restaurants, and expensive clothing stores. The office buildings are separated by expanses of green in which there are pines, cherry trees, and maples. This isn't the Tokyo that many foreigners imagine when they think of the city: the shoulder-to-shoulder throngs of people crossing busy intersections, such as the one so often seen on YouTube and on social media sites in front of Shibuya Station, farther south on the Yamanote Line, which circles Tokyo.

The Shinjuku that most foreigners imagine is eastern Shinjuku, where the murder took place. Eastern Shinjuku has pachinko parlors, peep shows, brothels, hostess and gay bars, illegal gambling dens—many popular restaurants—and, conveniently located to all these, love hotels, rows of them on the streets near Seibu Station, the station I mentioned earlier, that the man involved in the murder commuted to and from. Seibu Station serves commuters who live in the western suburb bedroom communities, which is where this man lived with his wife and children in a large, modern Western-style house.

The love hotels near Seibu Station are in an area called Kabuki-cho, Japan's most well-known pleasure district. The love hotels there are kitschy but quaint. Some of them have little ponds out front. Koi swim lazily around in the ponds, which have lily pads and reeds; an electronic recording of frogs and crickets make the hotels seem far, far away from the whish of trains and clatter of pachinko balls, just what lovers are after.

All of the hotels have entrances hidden behind walls, on which there is a lighted display of the rooms that are available. After a couple has decided on a room, they slip around the wall and enter the hotel and pay for their stay, a few hours or the night, by slipping some money under a slot in an opaque pane of glass. It's all very private. The rooms in these love hotels are as clean as the ones in the Keio Plaza Hotel, one of the best hotels in Tokyo. It's in western Shinjuku, not so far from the Shinjuku Police building. Mizuko plays jazz piano in the hotel's main bar. From time to time I go to the Keio Plaza to have a drink and listen to her play, and when she's finished we take a taxi home after the trains have stopped running, which is around midnight.

One day in October after a typhoon had passed through the city, the weather turned pleasantly cool;

the feel of autumn was in the air. My boss, Chief Inspector Saito, called me into his office. I had started out the day as I had most, by leafing through newspapers, the *Mainichi*, *Yomiuri*, and *Asahi*, my favorite, which, I knew from experience, had reporters who were interested in discovering truths, unlike the other two, which I consider to be tabloid scandal sheets, more pictures than copy, but helpful, nonetheless, to a detective who needs to keep up on social trends and what actor or singer is in the news for having an affair or having been arrested for using marijuana, cocaine, or methamphetamine—*shabu*—which is the drug of choice for yakuza thugs, company men, and, regrettably, the young, who often become bored with their corporate jobs or see no future for themselves. A detective never knows when they might need to rely on some information a reporter has dug up to solve a crime, and that was the case with this murder. A reporter from the *Asahi* helped me put together the pieces of this murder, why it happened and who the killer was.

"Good morning, Kawayama," Chief Inspector Saito said.

"Good morning, sir," I said.

"Sit," he said. He liked to order detectives around, to show his authority, but it really meant little, how he acted; it was just the face he wore to get through the day. I'd seen him break down and cry too many times to believe that his gruffness meant anything, even if his appearance, that of a rugby champion with cauliflowered ears and mangled fingers, did promote the image of a tough cop. I have to say, very honestly, that his breakdowns into fits of sobbing, tears flowing down his bulldog cheeks, were not without some justification and understanding, if a person has any humanity in their heart. I remember one case we went on in which a pretty high school girl, about to head off to Tokyo University to study Japanese literature, had been raped and beaten unconscious. The rapist had placed her body on the Odakyu line, a private line that serves the southwest suburbs. The train severed her body. Who wouldn't shed a tear over that? The rapist was convicted and sent to Abashiri Prison up in Hokkaido, Japan's northernmost island, where the winters are long and harsh. When he was hanged, most Japanese rejoiced. We Japanese still carry out death sentences by hanging. The long drop snaps the prisoner's neck. A majority of Japanese support it. Killers who have upset the equilibrium of a civil society deserve the death penalty, I believe.

I think Chief Inspector Saito started off with some small talk about Chinese fighters penetrating Japanese airspace, down in the Okinawa area. Threats from China had become a weekly occurrence. Our F-15s had intercepted the Chinese fighters and escorted them out of our airspace. Like many Japanese, Chief Inspector Saito feared China's growing military and economic power. China had relegated Japan to the number three economic spot in the world. We'd been proud of our rise from the ashes of the Pacific War to become the number two economic power, and for a while some had even thought, foolishly, that we would overtake the United States. It was the same kind of foolish thinking that had preceded our attack on Pearl Harbor and the consequential destruction of most of our cities during the war, turned to heaps of ash by B-29s dropping incendiary bombs.

As Chief Inspector Saito was talking about China, I looked over his head at the park. I saw the tops of maples, and the sight of the trees made me think of the changing of the seasons, when the maples turn blazing reds and oranges. Mizuko and I always take a trip to a *ryokan*, a traditional Japanese that has a hot spring, *onsen*, that time of year, to enjoy the sight of the changing colors of the leaves, called *kouyo* in Japanese, and also to soak away our stresses in the sulfur water of the baths. The waters loosen our neck muscles, our shoulders and thighs, and bring us closer together. Husbands and wives, even if the attraction is there, a distance between them can't help but creep in at times, and a trip to a mountain *onsen* helps to bring them back together.

I believe I was thinking of dining on some fresh mountain vegetables, tofu, and charcoal-grilled *ayu*, a sort of freshwater smelt caught in mountain streams, when Chief Inspector Saito growled, "Are you listening to me, Kawayama?"

"Yes, sir," I said, "absolutely."

"The war was long ago. The Chinese and Koreans need to move on the way we did, stop blaming us for their shortcomings."

"We did invade their countries, sir."

"And we've paid billions in repatriations, not to mention that Honda and how many other Japanese companies have set up factories in China and are not employing those peasants who would otherwise be in a rice paddy feeling mud squish up between their toes. They should be thankful for our factories being there, not protesting and demanding apologies. My grandfather died in China in the war, you know."

"You're right, sir, the Chinese should be thankful." I didn't dare mention to him that more than ten million Chinese had died during the war and our occupation of their country, or that some of our doctors had performed vivisections on Chinese, to learn what weapons were most effective. Few Japanese talked about that part of our history. It was too shameful to do so.

"A girl was found dead in a love hotel in Kabuki-cho," he then said. "Terrible. Awful. Go see what happened. Ms. Nodoka and her forensics team are already there. It's the Amour."

I knew of the Amour. It's a quaint hotel that has a model of the Eiffel Tower at the entrance and some fake garret windows on the second floor, all to make it look very French, something out of *The Sun Also Rises* or resembling a bohemian painter's studio. I may be a police detective, but I'm a well-read one, having studied English and American literature at Waseda University.

Chief Inspector Saito had remained sitting in his big chair. He seemed to me to be holding back a tear. Then I thought, Who wouldn't? I think it was Edgar Allen Poe who said something about the death of a beautiful girl being poetic. I assumed, rightly, that this girl was beautiful, because of the circumstances of her death—in a love hotel—and that she might have been a prostitute. But what did any of this matter, really? What mattered to me was that she had been a couple's daughter. Mizuko and I have a daughter. Her name is Tomomi.

CHAPTER TWO

I left Chief Inspector Saito's office and went back to my desk, which was in a room full of other detectives. Phones were ringing, and the detectives were answering them, saying things such as, "This is a matter for animal control," "You need to contact your nearest *kouban* if you're calling about the theft of a bicycle," and, "Your neighbor's son didn't come home last night? Ask her about him."

This room of detectives wasn't a scene from an American police drama, in which detectives have tattoos and beards and shout obscenities at each other. There were no drunks or suspects in a cage in a corner of the room. The atmosphere was very corporate, indistinguishable from an office in Sumitomo Life Insurance, with the exception of a few uniformed officers, men and women, who had sidearms, revolvers in a holster that were connected to their belts by a lanyard. The plain clothes detectives were dressed in dark suits and white shirts and silk ties. The undercover detectives who dressed in jeans and ragged shirts allowed their beards to grow, their department was on another floor.

I went to the desk of Detective Izuka, whom I had worked many cases with. He is thirty-seven, married with two children, and is beginning to feel the grind of being a very small cog in a giant bureaucratic machine. Like me, he had held aspirations of being someone of importance when entering the police force. He had ranked as a 7th *dan* in the kendo ranking system, one rank below the highest. Police usually take the higher rankings. But the paperwork involved in being a police detective had ground him down. He'd about given up on kendo and was now preferring young, available women to relieve the stresses—and often boredom—of the job. I said to him, "A girl was found dead in a love hotel in Kabuki-cho."

"Again?" he asked.

"Yes," I said. We'd worked a case involving a murdered girl the year before. The married man she'd been meeting had killed her when she'd attempted to blackmail him. She'd hired a private investigator to take some photos of them entering a love hotel. A few days after her murder, the man committed suicide, hanging himself in a business hotel in Omiya, a city north of Tokyo, out of shame. Adultery played a part in this murder, but in a way I couldn't have imagined.

Detective Izuka bowed his head. His daughter was ten, his son eight. He'd come to Tokyo from Toyama prefecture, an agricultural area on the coast of the Sea of Japan, to be another Dirty Harry. I'd had the same aspirations, or fantasizes, to look some criminal in the eye, point my .44 magnum at his forehead, and growl, "Are you feeling lucky, punk?" Unlike me, however, Detective Izuka did have the build of a Japanese Clint Eastwood, albeit a shorter version. I look anonymously corporate. I wear less than fashionable eyeglasses.

Detective Izuka is ruggedly handsome, has broad, square shoulders, a pronounced chin, and his eyes have a playful glint. All these qualities must have helped him out with women, those he was sexually drawn to and those who were either suspects in a crime or witnesses to one. He had a soft touch when it was needed, beguiling out of them honest answers that helped us in our investigations.

Detective Izuka stood, and, as we were walking to the elevator, put on his jacket. "Know anything about her?" he asked.

"Nothing."

"Men," he said. "They don't know how to treat a woman."

This was ironic, coming from him. I said nothing. Maybe she wasn't a prostitute but a scorned lover who'd taken her life, but the possibility that a man had murdered her was more likely. Women don't usually kill themselves in love hotels. They have a reputation they want to protect.

We got into the elevator and took it down to the basement parking garage, where a black and white Toyota squad car was waiting for us. The driver was a police officer in uniform.

He drove out of the basement garage into the daylight and headed in the direction of eastern Shinjuku and came to a railroad trestle that is often used as an establishing shot in news stories foreign journalists file on the peculiarities of Japan and the Japanese, ones about vending machines that sell high school girls' used underwear, gropers on trains, and square melons that go for over ten thousand yen, around a hundred U.S. dollars, and are packaged in handsome cedar boxes.

These loony stories about the fringes of Japanese society aren't accurate representations of the country, because life in Japan, for the most part, is rather boring. Trains run on time. Children wear pressed uniforms to school. Women use bicycles to go shopping. Sales people are welcoming, enthusiastic, and deferential. But none of this would attract an audience. And so those who know Japan only by what they've read of the country or seen on YouTube or the news really have no idea what Japanese life is really like, with the exception of the occasional deadly earthquake or mudslide, when boredom turns to utter panic in a second. That's closer to the reality of life in Japan.

The trains were whizzing past on the trestle, one right after the other, which does make for an eye-catching backdrop for a reporter, and just past the trestle, at night, there is the neon blitz of eastern Shinjuku and Kabuki-cho when night falls.

On this morning the street scene was more commonplace. The sidewalks were filled with commuters rushing off to their companies, carrying bags. Others were stopping off to have a coffee in one of the many coffee shops there. We're a coffee drinking people, make no mistake about that. Tea, yes, plenty of that as well, but coffee is the drink of choice of many, including myself.

In the alleys of Kabuki-cho, crouched under staircases, were those Japanese the country had turned its back on—wizened drunkards rummaging through spent liquor bottles in the bins behind bars and restaurants. They pour out a few drops of liquor into a plastic cup and drink it down. As long as they remain out of sight, we Japanese put up with them. Some social workers now and then try to steer them to shelters, but they're rarely successful. Living among urban outcasts, that's their group, the way being with other police is my group.

The driver guided the Toyota along lanes in Kabuki-cho, passing bars and restaurants and girly arcades, peep shows and brothels, the photos of many of the girls plastered to the walls near the entrances; many of the photos, however, were taken from porn magazines or videos and had nothing to do with the girls inside, who'd come to Tokyo from other prefectures, often from the agricultural north, where there were few good-paying jobs. The touts would come out at around noon to lure in the lunch crowd of weak-willed men who couldn't hold out until returning home or had no girlfriend or were just too stressed from work to put in the effort to find someone. A simple financial transaction between a man and a woman was so much easier for them. Unlike Westerners, mostly Americans, we Japanese tolerate prostitution. Yes, it's morally wrong, but a gray sort of immoral wrong that many of us have engaged in, including myself a few times as a university student before I met Mizuko.

The driver guided the Toyota along a street, passing a Family Mart convenience store and onto a street lined with love hotels—Blue Moon, Liberty, Starlight, and Lemon Tea, which brought back memories. Mizuko and I had been to it a few times before, and even after, our marriage. We'd also been to love hotels in other parts of Tokyo as well to take a break from the city. They're often strategically located near train stations. Do I feel shame for this? Hardly. It's who we are as humans. We have desires, and in Japan there is little private space. The hotels serve a purpose. But now and then there are drug overdoses resulting in deaths and quarrels between lovers. The manager's only recourse then is to call the police, or, sometimes, the yakuza, who often have a hand in the running of these hotels, promising protection, which they do deliver. The yakuza? I wish they didn't exist. But they do, on occasion, have a place in our culture, by enforcing order in ways that the police can't, and if you continue to read this story of mine you'll learn how I availed myself of their services.

The driver stopped the Toyota in front of the Amour. A police van was there, and members of a forensics team were going to and from it, into the hotel, whose manager was at the entrance, an old man, maybe seventy-five or so, who was smoking a cigarette and looking quite doleful, either because of the bad publicity or his honest contrition. It was impossible to know which.

Detective Izuka and I got out of the car. We were met by Ms. Nodoka, chief of the forensics team. She nodded, issued a professional "good morning," and then added, "Murder."

"How?" I asked.

"Strangled," she said, "with a charging cord for an iPhone." Ms. Nodoka was always very taciturn, didn't waste time with banter, the way some of my male colleagues do. She deserved to be the head of a forensics team one day. "I'm judging she was killed sometime early this morning," she said. "She still has color in her cheeks."

"Any identification?" I asked.

"Jiyumi Harajuku."

"Sounds like an alias," I said.

"My impression as well. The ID looks forged."

Detective Izuka said, "Your new hairstyle is very becoming."

Ms. Nodoka had had long hair, to her shoulders, and now it was short, a bit boyish, brushing the tops of her ears. Her complexion was an elegant, unblemished white.

She glared at Detective Izuka but said nothing, which said plenty. She was too smart to fall for his insipid flattery, unlike the younger women he was successful with.

Harajuku was a station on the Yamanote line, near the Meiji Temple. Young people gather near the station on weekends, the girls in all kinds of elaborate costumes, often in a doll or video avatar motif, and the young men in black leather and bracelets with spikes, how the owner of a pit bull might dress his or her dog. This aspect of Tokyo life, of young Japanese gathering near Harajuku Station, had been the subject of many foreign journalists' stories, to the point that there was no longer a story in the story, and so they had moved on to search for another strange aspect of Tokyo life. Bloggers had already written about love hotels and included videos and maps to Tokyo's more interesting ones, including even reviews of the bed, so stories of love hotels were no longer of interest to foreign reporters.

Ms. Nodoka said, "I have work to do." She went back into the hotel.

"She's getting a divorce," Detective Izuka said.

"I didn't even know she was married."

"I like her new hairstyle."

"She's too intelligent for you."

"I need a change of pace."

"You'll be heading for a divorce if you don't watch yourself."

"My wife would be lost without me."

"Don't flatter yourself," I warned him.

I went over to the manager, who was standing by

the window where couples look at the lighted board of rooms that are available. The manager was working his way through another cigarette. He had ground out the first one in a pocket ashtray he carried around in a trouser pocket. He bowed and handed me his *meishi*, business card. Even managers of love hotels have business cards. His name was Tanaka. I showed him my ID and asked, "What do you know about this?"

"I don't know a thing, sir," he said. "Nothing. Nothing at all. I wasn't here at the time, you understand. Nothing like this—"

I said, "You're not a suspect. We just want to know what you know."

He nodded his head, then said, "Mrs. Kikuchi was at the front desk last night and this morning. Shall I call her?"

"Is she inside?"

"She's distraught, the poor woman. She's a widower, you understand, living on her husband's life insurance."

"Not too distraught to talk," Detective Izuka said.

"No, no. She's willing. But she's an old woman who watches TV dramas all night. It's a boring job."

"Take us to her," I said.

Detective Izuka and I, following police procedure to prevent the contamination of evidence, put on white cotton gloves before entering the hotel.

We followed Mr. Tanaka into the small lobby, where there was a kitschy model of the Eiffel Tower beside the opaque pane of glass the receptionist sits behind. Beside the window there was a door. Mr. Tanaka opened it and in a tiny room there was an old woman with hair dyed brown sitting in an office chair. A small television was on a shelf beside her. She was a bit stout and looked to be a drinker. Her cheeks were red and her lipstick a medicinal pink. Many of these front desk clerks drink their way through the night as they watch television dramas. She stood when Detective Izuka and I showed her our badges and bowed. I told Mr. Tanaka that we'd call him if we needed him, and he walked off.

"Please take a seat," I said to Mrs. Kikuchi.

"May I serve you tea or coffee?" she asked. Next to the television there was an electric kettle, tea pitcher, and cups, and tucked away behind the cups a small bottle of *shochu*. It's a Japanese drink made of rice and barley and other grains that is stronger than sake, over twenty-five percent alcohol, that has recently become popular with young women. Why? I have no idea. When I was younger, women thought *shochu* was an old man's drink. None of them would've been seen drinking the stuff.

"No, thank you," I said and remained standing.

"We'll be quick," Detective Izuka said. "We just want to ask you a few questions."

"There were two of them," she said.

That was fairly obvious.

"How old was the man?" I asked. "Could you make a guess from his voice?"

"I'm so sorry," she said. "You're sure you don't want some tea?"

"No, thank you," Detective Izuka said. He added, "Was he young, middle-aged?"

"Customers here, they don't talk."

I could've guessed as much. I hadn't when Mizuko and I had visited a love hotel. Anonymity was why people went to love hotels.

"About what time did they arrive?" I asked.

"I think around six. The news was on. I like Yomiuri. What about you? NHK is too dull."

"So they were planning to spend the night?" I asked.

"The man paid for the night. That true crime story was on TV, about the woman poisoning her husband for his life insurance money. That's why I remember the time."

"What room did they take?" I asked.

"The Monet room," she said. "It's very French, even has an artist's easel as decoration and windows that have views of Paris street life. It's like going to Paris, I'd say. Very romantic."

"Nice touch," Detective Izuka said.

I said, "Did he have a dialect? From Tohoku or Kansai?"

"No. Standard Japanese, very educated and polite, from what I recall. Yes, that's what I'd say. Educated. And a bit shy. I think he and that girl have been here before, but I can't be sure about that."

"You didn't see either of them?"

"Of course not! I'm no snoop. Mr. Tanaka would fire me if I were a snoop. What couples do, that's their business. That's why they come here."

Detective Izuka and I looked at each other. Was their affair a long-term one? Company men do take lovers who are young enough to be their daughters, and these women, well, they take the men for a ride, having them buy them expensive designer clothes and bags, perfumes, and the latest model smartphones.

"Married," Detective Izuka muttered, reading my mind about the man.

"The girl never said anything?" I asked.

"No. Girls are shy."

"You said he was polite?" Detective Izuka said, "but that he hardly spoke. Why do you say he was polite?"

"Well, I got the impression he was. I think he was the man who forgot to take his change a while back. Sometimes drunks show up. They're not so polite. Their breath smells of beer. He wasn't like that. His hand was shaking when he took the change."

I asked her for her ID card and wrote down her address and asked her for her telephone number. "Please don't come to my home," she said. "I live with my daughter, and, well. . . She doesn't know I work at a place like this. It would be so embarrassing."

"We'll call first," I said.

"Thank you." She bowed.

Detective Izuka and I went back out into the hallway, where Mr. Tanaka had been waiting, smoking away. I asked him if he had a maid on duty, and he said he did and that she had been at the hotel all night. It turned out that she was the one who discovered the body. Her name was Mrs. Oita.

"We need to talk to her," I said.

"She's in the linen room, waiting. She's an old woman, too, all broken up over this. It's never happened before."

"I wouldn't think it has," I said.

"Mrs. Oita, she's kind of a mother to some of these girls, when the men leave them in the room crying. She's a comfort to them. She enjoys listening to their stories and offering advice."

"Take us to her," Detective Izuka said.

The linen room was at the end of a dimly lit corridor, along which there were doors to the rooms where the action took place. We passed the room where the woman's body had been found. The forensics team was in it, collecting evidence, and a photographer was taking photos. The flash from the camera was like summer lightning.

We came to a door at the end of the corridor. Mr. Tanaka knocked on it.

"*Hai*," Mrs. Oita answered.

Mr. Tanaka said, "There's a couple of police detectives here who'd like to talk to you."

"Please," she said.

Mr. Tanaka opened the door.

Mrs. Oita was a robust little woman with a wide face and gray hair, very grandmotherly; she was the kind of wholesome woman almost any girl would immediately open up to after a man has dumped her. She was sitting in a wooden chair beside a shelf of towels and bed sheets. There were also boxes of Okamoto condoms on one of the shelves in red little packets decorated with hearts. The better hotels put condoms and Meiji chocolate samplers on the pillows. I think some Meiji executive, after a romp in a hotel, got the idea to furnish the hotels with chocolates to promote the company's sweets.

Detective Izuka and I showed Mrs. Oita our badges and introduced ourselves. She stood and nodded. Another chair was in the room. She offered it, and the one she had been sitting on, to us.

"That won't be necessary," I said.

A canned Boss Black coffee was on a little table beside a small television. She looked at the coffee and said, "You know that old ad with Ei-*chan*. I like him. What about you?" She was referring to Yazawa Eikichi, the so-called Mick Jagger of Japanese rock music, who must have been king when she was young. The suffix -*chan* was usually used to refer to young girls. Using it to refer to him made him seem charming and innocent, which he probably was. I guessed that the younger generation wouldn't have recognized him if he were walking across that crowded intersection in front of Shibuya Station. The young, I suppose, would think he was an old pervert on the prowl if they saw him in Shibuya, where bored young girls congregate, attracting porn scouts and drug dealers.

"Yazawa Eikichi makes good ads," I said, to loosen her up.

"Doesn't he, though? But he's getting on in years now. I need coffee to get me through the night. Tea doesn't do the trick."

"About what happened in the Monet room," I said.

"It's terrible. A tragedy. The poor girl. No girl should come to her end that way. No. Makes no difference to me who she was. You'll catch the killer, won't you?"

"That's why we need to talk to you," Detective Izuka said.

"But what can I tell you?"

"Maybe you saw the man," I said. "Or the girl? Or saw someone enter the room?" That's the way some of the older, more traditional Japanese are, assuming responsibility for a crime they had nothing to do with. She added, "The couples that come here don't want to be seen, you know?"

"Quite," Detective Izuka said.

"But I can tell you this." She leaned forward. "It's not only men and women who come here. Now and then it's two men."

"You don't say?" Detective Izuka said.

"They like the décor, I believe, those kinds."

I didn't want to point out to her that she had just contradicted herself, that she actually did take a peek at who was coming and going from time to time, and put her on the defensive, and so I said nothing. Detective Izuka knew to do the same.

I said, "Perhaps you could relate to us how you came upon the poor girl, what time it was, what you remember. Just speak freely, please. Don't think we're here to judge you."

"It's only because I need the money that I work here," she said. "I've tried to get work at good hotels. But, I know what those youngsters who do the hiring think —'that old woman, she won't hold out.'" She drank some of the Boss Black coffee. "I've still got it in me, the drive to work."

"I understand," Detective Izuka said.

"And what time was it, about, that you found the girl?"

"A few minutes past seven this morning, I'd say, just as I was about to finish my shift. I knew right away what had happened. I watch Crime TV. I know things. A girl on the floor, naked. What else could it be but . . ."

"Did you go over to her, to see if she was, well, alive?" Detective Izuka asked.

"I did. But I knew immediately that . . . Her eyes were open. She had this lonely stare."

"Do you think she was one of *those* girls?" Detective Izuka asked.

"So what if she was? They have it tough, you know, dealing with all kinds of men. They're sellers of spring."

She seemed to be speaking from experience, which explained why she had ended up as a maid in a love hotel, more than the hiring policies of legitimate hotels.

The word for prostitute, when written in traditional Japanese, is 売春婦, *bai-shun-fu,* a woman who sells spring.

Japan has a long history of women working in what we call the water trade. Some of these women are prostitutes, but most are what are now called hostesses who work in clubs. There are plenty of these clubs in Kabuki-cho and other pleasure districts in Tokyo. These pleasure districts are in every Japanese city or town, even small fishing villages, which now have imported hostesses from the Philippines, Japanese girls preferring the status of working in a city. There are soaplands, too, a euphemism for brothels, in these districts. The yakuza run them. Yoshiwara, in the Asakusa district of Tokyo, is one of the oldest pleasure districts. It has a history that dates back centuries. It was a refuge for samurai, merchants, artists, and bureaucrats. They were all equals there, once they set foot in their favorite brothel.

"Who will inform her family?" Mrs. Oita asked.

"A police officer will," I said. I didn't know just how wrong I was about that then. No one told her family. The police never could find her family. Japan's secrecy laws are strict. When a person disappears, we refer to them as the evaporated. There's not much the police can do to help the family track the person down, and so those mothers and fathers who have children who've run away have to rely on private detective agencies, but even they have difficulty finding out who the family is. It's the result of the Pacific War, these strict secrecy laws we have, because before and during the war the government could track down anyone who was opposed to the war and throw them in prison. Or see that they disappeared. Permanently.

"We'll find whoever killed her," I said.

"I hope he ends up hanging from the end of a rope."

"He will," Detective Izuka said.

"So what did you do then, after you realized she was dead?" I asked.

"Screamed," Mrs. Oita said.

"Of course."

"Anyone with a heart would."

She finished off the can of coffee and set it down. "I could do with another," she said.

Detective Izuka said, "I'll get you one."

"There's a machine in the lobby," she said.

He left and Mrs. Oita and I looked at each other. I saw in her eyes a woman whom I could pour out my soul to, all those dark secrets that I hadn't told anyone, those secrets that have brought me to tell this story. "I have many experiences here," she said, "but nothing like this. You can't imagine the stories I've heard. Truth really is stranger than fiction. There were even some men who got left behind and cried like babies. They weren't very experienced with women. Men aren't as strong as they make themselves out to be. I try to get them and the girls back on their feet by lending them an ear. They always thanked me. Sex. It's supposed to be pleasurable, now, isn't it?, not turn one to tears."

"Yes, it is," I said.

"I remember when I was young . . ."

Detective Izuka then entered the room and handed her a can of Boss Black coffee.

She nodded her head. "Thank you. I need it to get me through the night," she said, repeating herself, the way so many of the elderly do. She went on, "I have terrible backaches. Terrible. A morning bath fixes me up."

"You'll be home soon," I said, "enjoying your bath." I said to Detective Izuka, "We were just discussing the complications of life."

"There are many," he said.

"Making up rooms, that's not all I do, you know. Anyone can do that. I was telling Detective Kawayama that men aren't as tough as they think they are. Women, they're the tough ones."

"I wouldn't know," Detective Izuka said.

She looked at him incredulously.

"My wife is tough," I said.

"Women have to put up with so much more than you men. You wouldn't know what it's like to be groped on a train."

"So what did you do after you screamed?" I asked.

"Why, I ran out of the room and told Mrs. Kikuchi."

"How long were you in the room?" I asked.

"Not more than a minute. How could I stay there?"

"I understand," I said.

"You didn't see anyone all night?" Detective Izuka said, "not even hear anything from the room?"

"Do you think I'd keep this job if I went snooping around? People nowadays have cameras in their phones. I don't want anyone to think I'm that kind of person."

"Maybe they were regulars?" I said.

"Could be," she said. "But I tend to my own affairs. I'm not a snoop."

"You've been very helpful," Detective Izuka said.

"Don't flatter me," she said. "I didn't tell you anything of importance." She drank some of the coffee. "I like my coffee black," she said, "not that syrupy sweet stuff. A woman has to be strong to take on this job."

"Detective Izuka wasn't flattering you," I said. "You've been helpful."

She nodded her head.

We left her there with her can of Boss coffee and went down the hall and came to the Monet room. It was made to resemble a painter's garret room, except for the space over the bed, which had a fake night sky of twinkling fake stars. Two pillows were tossed onto the floor. On a stand beside the bed were two Okamoto condom wrappers.

The bed faced a row of fake garret windows that had holograms of a Paris street, bistros and bakeries and newsstands and sidewalk cafes. People were crossing streets dressed as they had back in the nineteenth century, in overcoats and long dresses and bonnets. In some of the windows there were horse-drawn carriages. What a Japanese sense of detail and ingenuity the room had for the benefit of two people out to indulge in their fantasies.

The girl's body was in a corner, beside the artist's easel, over which hung a pair of her jeans and a boy's white dress shirt. She was naked to the waist, lying on her side. The girl's Louis Vuitton handbag, rather small, no bigger than a bento box—lunch box—had a thin strap with a gold buckle and was on a counter near the bathroom door. The bathroom had, as all of these love hotel rooms do, a tub that was big enough for two people.

Across the room from the girl was a table that had flimsy legs made of wire in a French style. It had a couple of bottles of Kirin beer on it and a dish of peeled edamame shells. An ashtray as well was there, but no cigarette butts were in it. This came as a disappointment. I'd been hoping that there might be a butt there, as an indicator of what brand of cigarette the man smoked, then I saw two balls of tissue—I assumed used condoms—in a trash bin beside the bed. They'd have the DNA evidence we needed. So would the beer bottles and edamame shells. The killer had been sloppy. Maybe he'd killed the girl in a fit of rage. Some men are that way. They think they own the woman who agreed to sleep with them, particularly a woman who is a seller of spring because they paid for her.

Detective Izuka, looking at the condoms wrapped up in tissue, said, "I'll leave it to Ms. Nodoka's team to collect those."

She'd heard him and turned and shot him a cold stare. In return, he smiled. She went back to work.

She and a photographer and a couple of men in her team were still gathering evidence. I knew they'd get to the condoms soon enough. One man was dusting for fingerprints; another was on the bed, holding a magnifying glass and tweezers, gathering strands of hair and placing them in a plastic bag. We'd have plenty of DNA evidence, but none of it mattered, in the end.

Detective Izuka and I went over to the girl's handbag. I asked Ms. Nodoka, "Can we examine the contents?"

"We've dusted it," she said.

I opened the bag and laid what was inside on the table —a bottle of nail polish, red, fake finger nails, those kind with gem stones in them, tampons, a packet of tissues, a cigarette lighter in a silver case but no cigarettes, a bit odd, and a bottle of Gaiac 10 perfume. Detective Izuka said of the bottle, "Expensive stuff. Has a musky, arousing fragrance."

"You'd know," I said.

"Only sold in Daikanyama, I think."

Daikanyama was a very exclusive shop in Shibuya, catering to young, stylish—and wealthy—women.

The girl also had an expensive titanium Zebra fountain pen, a small bar of handmade soap from a shop in Akasaka, tweezers, three tubes of lipstick, all subtle reds, and a cosmetics kit made of bamboo that included a small mirror. Her purse was very supple, elegant goat skin. It had in it more than thirty thousand yen, some change, an ATM card from Sumitomo Bank, and a JTB charge card. The name on the cards was Harajuku Jiyumi 原宿自由美. The Jiyumi was the kanji for beautiful freedom, 自由美. Harkajuku was the same kanji for the train station, 原宿.

I looked at the fake ID card. She was born in the Japanese Heisei year 10—1998—on September 12th; her address was in Bunkyo Ward near Iidabashi Station. The rent there had to be too high for a young girl like her, unless she was sharing the place with someone, so that stood out as a possible lead, that she had a roommate or lover; or maybe she had a company man who was paying the rent. These girls often did. Then there were forgers I knew that I could lean on to provide me with information about who had forged her ID, to find out, maybe, her real name, but I wasn't holding out for that. A forger probably didn't even know her real name if she had wanted to become one of Japan's evaporated. She was also carrying in that Louis Vuitton bag a pack of Okamoto condoms. Then there were twenty or so of her *meishis*. On them were her name and phone number framed by two Japanese cranes, like those on a JAL airliner. She was a traditionalist. No Hello

Kitties or bunnies on her *meishi*.

"She must've had quite the client list," Detective Izuka said.

"Her telephone is missing," I said.

I looked in every pocket of her bag but it wasn't there.

"A girl like her with no phone. Impossible," Detective Izuka said.

"I'll have IT trace it," I said. "We do have her phone number."

Looking at the girl, Detective Izuka said, "Such a pitiful end."

"I've never known you to be sentimental," I said.

I looked over at her body. She was shapely. I could tell that, even if she was lying on her side, her back to us. A towel was draped over her bottom. Strange, I remember thinking, how the killer had had that kind of respect for her, to cover her with a towel. Her youthful breasts were flattened out on the parquet floor. She had a long, elegant neck, the kind French painters would have admired. Sadly, red ligature marks from the charging cord disgraced that neck. Yes, there aren't too many things more poetic than the death of a beautiful girl.

While looking for her phone, I had pulled out a receipt for a restaurant bill at a sushi shop, one for a pair of Prada shoes, one for a taxi fare, and a lottery ticket —Ichiban Kuji. We could easily trace the lottery ticket back to where she had bought it. Most important of all, I found a payslip from the Nankaitou Club. Nankaitou, written 南海島, means south sea, *tou* means island, *kai* 海 sea, *tou*島 island. These clubs are where lonely men go to be pampered by young, heavily made-up women who often wear evening gowns. The women pour their drinks and light their cigarettes and do a lot of listening, the way a psychologist does. It's tough work, listening to these arrogant men, who are often wealthy department or section chiefs with clout and managerial responsibilities. They use these hostesses to talk about things they might not risk telling their wives because their marriages are so sour. The Nankaitou Club was in Akasaka, one of the more affluent neighborhoods of Tokyo. This girl had class.

I handed the payslip to Detective Izuka.

"She must've been freelancing," he said. Some hostesses did sleep with customers they got along with. It's a normal thing, when men and women meet and drink. I wouldn't call that selling spring.

Over by the front door was a woman's lavender Montbell windbreaker, and in the shoe rack a pair of high-top Keds, which my daughter Tomomi had worn when she was in high school. Seeing them, a shudder of memory of her in her school uniform rattled up my spine.

"Remember when those long socks were the rage?" Detective Izuka said.

Tomomi had never gone in for them. She said they made a girl look dumb and puffed out her legs to the shape of *daikons*, a Japanese white radish.

"The girls used glue to hold those long socks up," Detective Izuka said.

"How many pairs have you rolled off a girl's legs?"

He said nothing.

"Just remember, you have a daughter," I said.

He groaned.

The photographer said to us, "I've finished," and left the room.

We went over to the girl and knelt. A black charging

cord was resting a meter or so away from her head, which was turned to one side. The side of her face was pressed onto the parquet floor. She had a thin, elegant nose, unusual in Asian women, but some are born with them, very straight and Romanesque.

Death hadn't quite set in. Her cheeks were a youthful pink. She had a scar just below her hairline. I thought of her parents, who she was, how she'd come to be in this room, and with whom? Why had he—and I was certain that it was a man—strangled her? What could she have done to provoke him to do such a thing? I doubted that she had done much of anything other than what she'd gone to the room expecting to do. Maybe he had beaten other girls. Maybe he was a psychopath. It was reasonable to think so. I thought that we'd have to go through arrest records and try to narrow down who he was, if the girls he'd beaten had filed a report. But I wasn't optimistic about that. They wouldn't want to be shamed by being in a love hotel with him.

I continued to stare at her. I just couldn't understand why, after this man had gotten what he'd wanted from her, he hadn't just walked out of the room, as other men did when their desire was quenched. She looked like the kind of girl who would satisfy any man. She was indeed cute, even in death. And then a feeling of nausea knotted up in my gut. I feared that I might have to make a dash for the toilet. You see, the girl lying at my feet was my daughter Tomomi.

CHAPTER THREE

How can a father describe the feeling of discovering, at his feet, his murdered daughter? If there are words that can describe such a feeling, I do not know them. What I felt was the way I felt on occasion when I rose too quickly and blood drained away from my brain and I thought I might lose consciousness and pass out.

Several times I'd played out in my mind what I would say to Tomomi if we happened to meet by chance somewhere in Tokyo, if she had even remained in Tokyo, because Mizuko and I really had no idea where she'd run off to. I knew that if I did meet her I'd admit my mistake, ask her to come home, and offer my support in whatever she chose to do with her life. Tomomi was a free-spirited girl, unable to fit in in a company office or even as a university student. She had bridled against the pressures to conform and fit into our society. The name she had taken, Jiyumi, beautiful freedom, was evidence of who she was.

Tomomi was such an ordinary name, one thousands of Japanese girls had. Written in Japanese, Tomomi means beautiful friend, 朋美, but Tomomi hadn't had any close friends that Mizuko and I were aware of. For a Japanese girl, she was very unusual in that regard. She had made snide comments about her classmates, how they had empty heads like that of a bell pepper. Mizuko had tried to be her friend, but Tomomi had seen her attempt as a way of exerting control, I suppose, and that had driven her even farther from us. You see, Mizuko had lost her only sister when she was sixteen. Mizuko and her sister, Mamiko, had been best friends, and I don't believe Mizuko really ever recovered from her death. A drunk driver ran her down on her bicycle when the two were on their way to high school one morning. The man, a construction worker, after a night of drinking, had fallen asleep and driven through a red light. Mamiko died right there in front of Mizuko. Mizuko's family was living in Kisarazu in Chiba prefecture then, on Tokyo Bay, but they were originally from Shinjo, a small town in Yamagata prefecture in northeastern Japan, the Tohoku area. Mizuko confessed to me how she'd felt about her sister and why she'd wanted to name our daughter Tomomi, as a way of connecting with her sister.

Mizuko and I had often wondered if our son Satoshi had known something about Tomomi leaving us, but doubted that he had. The two weren't particularly close. Satoshi was an app developer nerd who could spend all night reading manga, while Tomomi was interested in about every book, song, and person who was contemptuous of modern Japanese life. She had once been the lead singer in a girls' punk band, the Little Nipples, that had garnered some success in Shibuya clubs, but the band never left the club circuit or made any recordings that were financially successful.

I suppose the band had been too iconoclastic for many Japanese, and the name was misleading. It suggested that the members of the band were adult video actresses who were drumming up interest in their videos. Mizuko and I had both thought about asking the girls in the band, which had broken up by the time Tomomi ran off, if they knew anything about her, but hesitated. The girls might get in touch with her, driving her farther away from us, and so we thought the best thing to do was to be patient and wait out her period of rebelliousness. A year became two, then three, and I started to accept that she had given up on us. Mizuko didn't. She prayed for Tomomi's return every morning before our *butsudan*, Buddhist altar, lighting incense and ringing a brass bell before placing her hands together and bowing to pray for her return.

Tomomi saw herself as a bohemian, or, at the least, a girl who wanted to live the life of one, hanging out in cafes and bars, discussing the meaningless lives of those who trudged off to work each day, commuting on trains. I believed that that was why she had ended up in the Amour, which had the French bohemian appeal she craved. She had often talked about wanting to go to Paris and discuss with others, what else, the ideas of Sarte and de Beauvoir.

I knew how she felt. I had been an aspiring Bohemian back in my student days, until I became weary of that lifestyle—living in six mat rooms that had grimy windows and no bath, only a toilet, which required the tenant to go to the local public bath. There are still plenty of them around in Tokyo, but their numbers have decreased significantly since I was a student. The baths have become more modern, too, a cross between an onsen—hot spring—and a traditional public bath, called a *sentou*, 銭湯. The modern baths have restaurants, and there are several different kinds of baths, even a sauna. Some of the baths are outside, called a *rotenburo*, 露天風呂, whereas a traditional *sentou* only has two baths, one a different temperature than the other, and places to sit in front of a mirror to wash and shave.

I'm digressing. I want to tell you about the night Tomomi, Mizuko, and I had an argument over her future. Mizuko and I wanted her to take the university entrance exam, even if she chose not to attend a university.

Mizuko said, "An education is something to fall back on. Suppose you can't make it as a singer?"

"Singer? Do you think I could spend time with those dimwit girls? One is already planning to marry her loser boyfriend, the fool."

"We're just asking you to take the examination," Mizuko continued. "It's not too much to ask, is it? Considering all we've done for you? We didn't protest you being in that band."

"What an embarrassment, the name," I said.

"Worried about your career, father? That the Little Nipples will embarrass you and hold up a promotion?"

"That was unnecessary," Mizuko said. "He supports us by going to do a job that causes him a great deal of stress on occasion. But he's dedicated to his work. He's responsible. He puts in long hours riding the trains."

I said, "I'm just trying to look out for you. Life is full of surprises. You need to be prepared for them, and an education will be your insurance policy."

"Take our advice," Mizuko said.

"You're young," I said, "too young to understand how decisions you make now might affect your life later on."

"I understand how a career is a death sentence." She grinned. As the lead singer in the band, she had shaved off the hair from the left side of her head. The hair on the right side hung down to her shoulder. It was tinted green and its edge was as sharp as a knife blade.

"Satoshi is off to university. He didn't like it at first, but now he sees the need," Mizuko said. Satoshi was attending Tohoku University in Sendai.

"He's living with his dimwit girlfriend, you know," Tomomi said, "and she's not going to a university. She works in a kennel, washing dogs."

"Don't insult his girlfriend," I said. But the truth was that I wasn't too happy about who he was living with. I thought he could've done better, maybe found another app developer.

Tomomi went to the front door and put on a pair of black leather Dr. Martens and tucked her skinny jeans into the tops and opened the door and walked out of our home and off in the direction of Yotsuya Station, a MontBell backpack hanging from a shoulder.

Mizuko said to me, "Don't worry. She won't be gone long. She forgot her telephone."

Her telephone was resting on the kitchen table. Mizuko and I laughed nervously.

"Want something to drink?" Mizuko asked.

"A sake," I said, "cold. What's on TV?"

CHAPTER FOUR

Tomomi's room, as we say—not a flat or apartment —was in a modern building not too far from JR's Iidabashi Station, which had a connection with the Nanboku subway line she could take to Tameike-sanno Station, near one of Tokyo's more affluent neighborhoods, Kojimachi, where the Nankaitou Club was.

The building was made of blue bricks, was solid and earthquake proof. It had balconies where residents could air their futons and dry their laundry. Some of the newer places don't allow for that. The airing of futons and drying of laundry, the management feels, is an eyesore that lowers the value of the property. The building had a functioning security system with a camera. A person had to have a code to enter the building or call up someone on an intercom to be let in. It was twelve stories, squeezed in between a 7-Eleven and a preschool.

A police van was at the curb, and at the entrance was the manager, a woman in her late thirties wearing a black business suit. She bowed deeply, a sign of contrition and sorrow. Detective Izuka and I nodded our heads and continued on inside the building, to the elevator, entered it and took it to the twelfth floor, the top floor, the one Tomomi's room was on.

The forensics team was going through Tomomi's clothes and some documents. One man came out of her room carrying an Apple laptop. I wondered if there were photos of Mizuko and I on that computer. I would've known when I entered her room if she'd had some on display in her room, but no one on Ms. Nodoka's team said anything to me or gave me a strange look. It sounds selfish, I know, to admit that I was worried about myself, and Mizuko, but I was. If that makes you think that Tomomi was right to run off, I'm willing to live with that. Sometimes I think I gave her reason to.

What I feared most before going to her room was that someone would discover I was her father and I'd be taken off the case. Chief Inspector Saito would then assign me to a backwater job handling evidence in a windowless basement vault while detectives who might have made jokes about Tomomi and her father investigated her murder. I couldn't have that. I wanted to find her killer. I was determined to do so. And it wasn't because I wanted to relieve my shame and guilt. I wanted to do it for Tomomi. And Mizuko.

Detective Izuka and I put on white cotton gloves, took off our shoes, left them in the *genkan*—entrance— and stepped up onto the floor of Tomomi's room. Ms. Nodoka and her team had already gone online to try and find out if Tomomi had a social media site—Facebook, Instagram, Twitter, or Line, the preferred texting app, rather than WhatsApp—but they couldn't find one. Mizuko and I had tried to track her down that way but failed. Tomomi really had wanted to become one of the evaporated, and had, well, until her death, done a fairly good job of it. But there still was her telephone and her internet account that we could use to learn something about her and maybe who she had gone to the Amour with.

On the drive to Tomomi's room, I'd made a call

to Chief Inspector Saito, and he assigned a team of detectives to do the necessary legwork of talking to people who worked in convenience stores, restaurants, and love hotels in Kabuki-cho and also to ask those who worked in Shinjuku and Seibu stations if they might have seen her with a man. The women there working in the newsstand kiosks, they don't miss much. In that regard, I was still an old school detective who believed in eyewitness accounts and the piecing together of bits of information to track down a killer.

Ms. Nodoka called me over to a small desk and said, "Take a look at this." She was holding Tomomi's bankbook from Sumitomo Bank. Her account showed a balance of over a million yen, about eight thousand U.S. dollars at the exchange rate of the time.

"She was doing better than I am," Detective Izuka said.

"It's a lot of money," Ms. Nodoka said, "for a hostess."

"What else was she doing?" I asked.

"That's your job to find out," Ms. Nodoka said.

"We will," Detective Izuka said. "This guy's a sicko."

Detective Izuka and Ms. Nodoka looked at each other for a period of time that was just a little longer than what was normal between a man and a woman who are colleagues. And then Ms. Nodoka gathered herself and said, "And this. We found this." She held up a syringe that she had bagged and a small plastic vial of a white substance that we all knew was *shabu*.

"How could she have so much money and be a user?" Detective Izuka asked.

I had the same question.

The coroner's report stated that Tomomi had been injecting *shabu* between her toes, a popular way to go about it with women. I thought then, seeing the

syringe and the *shabu,* that I had to get in touch with
Satoshi, find out what he knew about his sister's habits,
if anything. Tomomi, until the day she left home, still
regarded her brother as a manga otaku who knew little
of girls. When she'd known him, he had looked the part
of an otaku. His eyeglasses, cantered always to one side,
were smeared with thumb prints, and his hair was a bit
dirty and always unkempt. As a student, he'd lived off
instant ramen and soba. But as he neared graduation
from university he became more professional looking,
even if he did remain unassuming and shy, looking a bit
nerdish. I have no idea how he had worked up the nerve
to get a girl to take up with him. Maybe she'd pitied him,
the way she pitied the dog's she groomed in that place
she worked. Tomomi had never given in to sloppiness,
even as the lead singer in that punk band she belonged
to.

I had wondered if there would be some men's
shoes in the *genkan,* but none were. What there was,
was an earthquake preparedness bag containing a
bottle of water, some canned meats, juices, bandages,
antiseptics, and a rope ladder. The 2011 Tohoku
Earthquake up in Miyagi and Fukushima prefectures
had shaken all Japanese out of their complacency.
Mizuko and I kept three of the bags in our home, one in
our bedroom, one in the entrance, and the other in the
kitchen. There was a bit of irony seeing that earthquake
preparedness bag in the *genkan* of Tomomi's room.
She'd been prepared for what most Japanese prepare for
but not for what was coming her way in that love hotel
room. Maybe she'd been too sure of herself. She'd always
been one who thought she could handle any man.

Tomomi's room had a small living area and bedroom,

partitioned off by fusuma—sliding doors—a kitchen, bath, and Western toilet; all of the rooms were very tidy. The bed was made, the plates and cups put away, the bath tiles sparkling. Her lotions were all lined up on a glass shelf. Her toothbrush and a tube of paste were in a holder. She was her mother's daughter. On a dresser in her living space there was a cedar jewelry case containing some earrings, ones made of mother of pearl and zircon, and one from her punk days that was a safety pen. A bottle of that expensive perfume, Gaiac 10, was on a dresser. In the drawers of the dresser were some white silk panties that had ribbons on them and under them one of those two egg vibrators, pink, that women use. Detective Izuka balanced the wires coming off the device and the two eggs between a pen and held the thing up.

"I've never been with a woman who needed one," he said.

"Put it back," I told him. "It's got nothing to do with why we're here."

He gave me a suspicious stare before placing the vibrator back in the drawer. We'd been on other cases where we'd made inappropriate jokes, so he had to have sensed that I felt differently about this one.

Seeing the vibrator, I was reminded of the times Mizuko and I had been on our futon and heard the rattle of one a few times coming from Tomomi's room. But what could we say? Tomomi was in high school then. We had an idea that she had lost her virginity as a high school student, if not earlier, in middle school. She was changing boyfriends every few months. Once Mizuko had gone into her room after an earthquake struck, knocking over some books in our room, to see if Tomomi's room needed to be straightened up, and found the vibrator. Mizuko said, "We can't stop her from growing up."

"Did you, when you were her age?"

"Times are different. We can't go poking around in her sex life. She'll hate us if we do."

"She already hates me."

"She doesn't hate you."

"She better not get pregnant," I said. "If she does, she's having an abortion."

"I also found some condoms," Mizuko said.

"Then she has some intelligence," I admitted.

"She'll grow out of this, become responsible."

"Let's hope so."

Detective Izuka and I continued to search her room. In a closet there were several pairs of jeans, some in that ragged style that is fashionable, and several pairs of shoes, some running shoes, three pairs of high heels, some pumps and sandals, a pair of Dr. Martens, and one pair of geta, the wooden clogs that Japanese wear when they go to an *onsen*. She also had some kimonos that she kept in cedar boxes. I couldn't believe she had spent her money on them. Some man must have given them to her, maybe the man who'd seen that she had money in her bank account.

On a shelf beside a stereo there were a few books on astronomy, and one on, of all things, meditation— a surprise to me, considering her petulance—that she would be interested in a form of Zen Buddhism. In a small refrigerator were some cans of Asahi Black beer, a bottle of Nihonshu, a container of tofu, a carton of milk, a piece of chocolate cake, take out yakitori, and an assortment of vegetables—tomatoes, onions, carrots, and bean sprouts. Then there was a package of *nato*, fermented soybeans that most Westerners can't get past the smell of to even taste.

Detective Izuka said, "I wouldn't have expected a girl who used *shabu* to have a supply of carrots."

Next to a flat screen television was the small desk, and on the desk a tablet of paper that had some notes and phone numbers written down on it in a recognizable hand. I used my phone to take a photo of it. Her room was still a crime scene, and we couldn't remove any of the potential evidence. In a notebook in a drawer there were some names and phone numbers, and I took a photo of them as well. Then I saw an official Japanese ID card among the papers. Before taking a look at it, I told Detective Izuka, "Why don't you go through her shoes, see if she's hiding something in them?"

He looked at me. "Really?"

"You know how girls are," I said, "when it comes to hiding things. You'll discover this when your daughter is older."

"How is your daughter? Was it one of her tricks, hiding things in shoes?"

He'd never met Tomomi, never even seen a photograph of her. We Japanese, we keep our profession and family life separate. You won't find photographs of a man's wife and children on the desks of most men and women. We're private about our family lives, many of us, and don't share these photos of our sons and daughters and wives with the people we work with but only close friends.

"Tomomi is fine," I said. I almost broke down, saying that.

He went into her bedroom, and when I heard him

rattling Tomomi's shoes around and saw that no one on the forensics team had their eye on me, I took out the ID, quickly glanced at it, and saw that the surname on it was Wada. Who was my daughter? Why did she have Wada as a surname? I put the ID away in a coat pocket. I didn't want anyone to have it. It was for me to find out who she was.

Detective Izuka came back into the room. "Nothing," he said, "but foot powder residue."

After an hour or so Detective Izuka and I left Tomomi's room and returned to the Shinjuku police building to brief Chief Inspector Saito but not before I had him issue an order for detectives to question all the people in the building where Tomomi lived and those who worked in the shops nearby, to find out if anyone had seen her with a man. It turned out that a 7-Eleven clerk had. The man was a few years older than her and was, in the clerks words, "a dirty guy, scrawny like a mongrel dog that hasn't eaten in a few days. They came here now and then to buy beer or ice-cream, sometimes ramen or potato chips. He liked those shrimp tasting ones. Girls! The choices they make. The two didn't look like they would have anything in common." This clerk, who had the face of a cherub, was a married woman who lived a few blocks away. She said that the man had sprouts of unseemly whiskers coming off his chin and his hair hung over his ears. He was always wearing dark glasses. She'd seen the two of them arguing a few times outside the shop. "It was always quite a stir," she said. "People kept their heads down when they walked past them. Once or twice I wanted to call the police, it was that bad."

The man, the way the clerk had described him,

sounded like a *shabu* dealer.

To help us find out who he was, I turned to a detective in the narcotics division for assistance. He said he'd do his best to track him down.

Back at my desk, the first thing I did was an internet search to learn about the secret life my daughter had led. Why was the surname on her national ID card Wada? I discovered that she had evidently gone to Fukuoka, a major city on the island of Kyushu, Japan's western most island, after leaving us. She had taken up with, then married, a third rate music producer named Junichi Wada. He was forty-six at the time. She was eighteen, just old enough to legally marry him. He'd been married twice before to singers who'd had a few hits but hadn't lasted in the very competitive Japanese music industry. I think she married him because he was the iconoclastic loser type that she found attractive. It couldn't have been for money, because he didn't have much. He had debts, loans he'd taken out on his Nissan Skyline, the mortgage on his house, and the equipment for a recording studio—which he had fallen behind on with the payments, and gambling debts to the yakuza. He was borrowing money from personal loan companies at nearly twenty percent interest to pay off these debts.

One Sunday afternoon, when they were returning from a trip to an *onsen*, the bands of an approaching typhoon were causing waves coming off Hakata Bay to lash the highway. Junichi lost control of the Nissan, and it broke through a guardrail and rolled down some rocks into the bay. Junichi was knocked unconscious and drowned. Tomomi suffered a concussion and a broken leg, just below the knee of her right leg. She managed to get out of the car and make it to the shore, where those who had seen the accident offered her shelter and called an ambulance. She spent a couple of weeks in a hospital. Because Junichi hadn't even been keeping up on his life insurance payments, Tomomi received nothing. She didn't even inherit his home. He had designated his oldest son as the beneficiary in his will, but that didn't come without a cost. The son had to keep up with the mortgage payments. Tomomi did get some survivor benefits from the government, but not enough to have a million yen balance in her bank account.

Sometime after the accident, when Tomomi could walk again, she must have come back to Tokyo. She'd gained a reputation in Fukuoka as a gold digger, even if Junichi turned out to be a deadbeat loser. Her reputation must have made it difficult for her to land a job, and that might have been why she returned to Tokyo. Why she hadn't chosen to go to Osaka or Nagoya, maybe even Kobe or even farther away, up north to Sapporo, I don't know. No one would have known her in those cities. But Tokyo? Even if the metro area is around thirty-five million, there was always the possibility that she'd come across someone she knew when either on the street or passing through a station. Both Mizuko and I had met classmates that we hadn't seen in years in train stations and on sidewalks. I like to think that Tomomi wanted to be close to us again, and that is why she had returned to Tokyo, but that might just be hopeful thinking on my part. She did live nearby. The Nanboku line even made a stop at Yotsuya Station, where I caught the Chuo line every morning. It's even possible that we could have been in Shinjuku Station, as busy as it is, at the same time, passing close by the other without realizing it. I like to think that we could have patched things up between us if we had met. But what does it matter now, that kind of thinking?

Maybe it had been pride that had prevented her from getting back in touch with us. It pains me to think so, that she wouldn't have ended up in that hotel room if we had met, even by chance. The odds just weren't in our favor, as it turned out.

CHAPTER FIVE

The Nankaitou Club was a short walk from the Tameike-sanno Station. Its location was very strategic. Company men, referred to in Japanese as *salarymen*, can pass by it on their way to catch a train, have a drink with a hostess, maybe put a hand on her thigh, even suggest they go off to a hotel together, and if the hostess refuses, they can stumble to the station to catch a train home to be with their disinterested wives.

The club was on the seventh floor, toward the front of an embarrassingly uninspiring gray concrete building. The names of the clubs were all listed on signboards, up the side of one of the corners of the building, and would come alive at night when the restaurants around the station were doing a good business. But Detective Izuka and I were a bit early for the signs to be bursting with yellow, blue, and pink neon.

We got out of the police car and went into the building and took the elevator up to the Nankaitou. Ms. Nishikawa, the owner—or mama-san—met us at the entrance. We'd called her ahead of time to tell her about Tomomi. She was wearing a blue kimono. Her hair was pulled back in a bun. She was maybe in her early fifties, old enough so that the skin around her jaw line and along her neck was beginning to wrinkle and sag. But she hadn't let her body go. She was tall and willowy, rare for a Japanese, a more common characteristic among Chinese, and I immediately felt a sense of strange relief that Tomomi had worked for her rather than for a greasy man who managed a skin shop for gaijin in Roppongi. Tomomi, in spite of being a member of a punk band, had remained a traditional Japanese girl, which pleased me immensely.

I couldn't, at first, picture Tomomi in the Nankaitou at a table with a wealthy business executive, dressed in a fine kimono, dutifully pouring his drinks and lighting his cigarettes while having to listen to his dull stories. She had always made fun of hostesses, saying that prostitutes were more honest about how they earned their money than a hostess. But I suppose the reality of having to make a living—and having no means to do so other than her intelligence, wit, and looks—changed her mind about the life of a hostess. I knew she'd be popular, particularly with those men who appreciate a hostess who makes some witty remarks. Even so, it was work, those witty remarks of hers. She would've preferred not to be there, but to be off somewhere living the life of a nineteenth century impressionist painter's mistress or model in the South of France. That's being Japanese: putting on one face, doing one's job while wearing that face, and keeping their feelings about doing their job to themselves, until they went out drinking with friends and cut loose with the pressures, bitterness, and anger that had built up inside them. The salarymen who came to visit the hostesses were there for exactly the same reason, to let loose with what they couldn't say at work to their bosses, subordinates, even their wives.

Detective Izuka and I introduced ourselves, showed our badges, and gave Ms. Nishikawa our *meishis*.

She bowed deeply, a display of contrition, and said, "Please come in."

No customers had showed up yet. A barman in his thirties, wearing a white shirt and bow tie, was polishing a black marble counter-top. He smiled and nodded. He had square shoulders, a broad chest, and an actor's distinguished good looks. Behind him on mahogany shelves were bottles of various whiskeys that had name tags hanging from the necks by little gold chains, like necklaces. It's a tradition in these clubs that customers buy a bottle of their favorite spirit for an outrageous price and keep it there.

Ms. Nishikawa showed us to a booth in a corner. The seats were fine leather. The tables were a black marble, matching the counter-top of the bar, and were trimmed in a shiny stainless steel.

The barman came to the table.

"Coffee for me," I told him.

"I'll have the same," Detective Izuka said.

"I'll do whatever I have to assist you," Ms. Nishikawa said. "I'm so sorry."

"Do you know anything about her parents or family?" Detective Izuka asked.

"I didn't pry, and she didn't volunteer anything. She was a responsible girl who did her job. That's all I expect from my girls. Sometimes I make the mistake of hiring girls who can't escape being who they are. They can cause me trouble. But not her."

Referring to Tomomi as Jiyumi was something I had trouble accepting.

"How was Jiyumi different?" I asked.

"Charm," she said. "A girl has it or she doesn't. She must've been born with it, the way some girls are born with double-lidded eyes."

Ms. Niskikawa had double-lidded eyes, the kind that

have folds, unlike so many Asians. The Koreans have made an industry of turning a woman's natural Asian eyes into those double-lidded ones.

"Charm isn't so easily explained," Ms. Nishikawa said. "With Jiyumi, her charm had to do with her independence, the challenge she presented the men, her intrigue, a hint of risk, even danger and certainly mystery. She always seemed to be in control, a very intoxicating quality in a woman."

"Did you ever think that Jiyumi Harajuku wasn't her real name?" I asked.

"I knew it wasn't, of course. What girl would have a name like that? But who am I to poke around in her personal life? Girls come here to escape their pasts, and I try to help those I can. The direct deposit into her bank account went through. That's all that mattered."

"You really have no idea what her real name was?" Detective Izuka asked.

"No. If a girl does her job, that's all I care about. Jiyumi did her job."

"She might have had a man on the side," Detective Izuka said.

Even if I had asked that question in other investigations, it now seemed crude and disrespectful to do so.

Ms. Nishikawa said. "If it didn't interfere with her job, I can't judge. Men and women, when they meet, things like that happen. She did call in from time to time that she had plans for the night. Maybe she was seeing someone."

"Do you know the names of her regulars?" I asked. "Maybe she was seeing one of them?"

"No. Sorry. That was none of my business."

"You want to help us find her killer, don't you?"

"I don't know anything about her venturing into Kabuki-cho to meet a man."

"We need names," I said.

"A list."

"I'll talk with the other girls and Mr. Sawahara." She nodded to the bartender. "I'll have a list ready for you by tomorrow."

"Email it to me," I said.

"In a love hotel in Kabuki-cho," she said. "That's a place for company men, not young girls."

"We'd like to know why she was there, too," Detective Izuka said.

"Jiyumi had no patience for men her age. She called them men-boys. If he was one of her regulars, why would they meet in Kabuki-cho when there are hotels nearby? He was probably older."

"A father figure," Detective Izuka said.

Ms. Nishikawa smiled. "That's a stereotype," she said, "about young women and older men."

"She had her secrets, as we all do," I said.

"You're a kind of philosopher," Ms. Nishikawa said.

"He's read too much fiction," Detective Izuka said, "watched too many American detective movies from the fifties and sixties, the noir kind, in black and white that have long shadows and back alleys."

"I like those, too. The movies nowadays are all flash."

"Aren't they, though," I said. "But those movies back then, the killers ended up dead. They had a moral to them."

"I can only imagine the things you've seen," Ms. Nishikawa said.

"If only you could see what I've seen with these eyes,"

I said, paraphrasing that line from *Blade Runner* that Roy says to his maker, Eldon Tyrell. But Ms. Nishikawa didn't catch the allusion. It didn't matter. Few did. Detective Izuka did, because he'd heard me say the same thing before. Many times.

The barman brought us our coffees and Ms. Nishikawa her green tea.

We kept up the formalities. Detective Izuka and I said, "Itadakimasu," a polite phrase which sounds totally unnecessary when translated into English—"To receive"—before drinking our coffees.

"No rivalries between her customers?" I asked.

"I wouldn't know," Ms. Nishikawa said.

"Give it some thought," I said. "Maybe some incident will come to you."

"I'll do my best."

"Were any of your other girls jealous of Jiyumi?" Detective Izuka said. "You know how girls are, if one is more popular than another."

"I don't allow for that."

"Couldn't it be that they talked with each other," I said, "outside work?"

"I wouldn't know. I suppose. Girls are girls."

She had the barman bring over a framed photo from behind the bar. He set it down on the table. In the photo Tomomi was there beside Ms. Nishikawa. Another girl was on the other side of Ms. Nishikawa, and another standing before her. Tomomi was smiling brightly, her face as radiant as a sunflower. She was wearing a youthful blue kimono that had lilies embroidered on it. Her hair was long but held up off her neck, to show off what we Japanese think of as the most beautiful part of a woman's body, the nap of a woman's neck, the *unaji*.

I recalled Tomomi wearing a kimono one New Year's Day, but with a pair of black Dr. Martens. We had all gone to the Suga Jina Shrine that day. Tomomi had caught some critical stares, which hadn't bothered her. They had probably even validated, in her mind, her style, as it was a threat to them, a protest against Japan's repressive culture.

"Is this a recent photo?" I asked.

Ms. Nishikawa said it was.

I took out my camera and snapped a photo of it.

"What was the make of the telephone Jiyumi had?" Detective Izuka asked.

I might have walked out of that club failing to ask this, the most obvious of questions, I was so twisted up inside. I wasn't sure, looking back on that day, how I'd managed to hide what was inside me. Maybe it was being Japanese, keeping that face a police detective is expected to wear.

"Sorry," Ms. Nishikawa said. She nodded her head.

"There's no need to apologize," I said.

"Does it matter, her telephone?"

"It might," I said.

"It was missing," Detective Izuka added.

Ms. Nishikawa said, "I can't imagine her without a telephone."

My mind wandered and I thought back to that day Tomomi had stormed out of our home, swearing she would never return, but leaving her telephone on the kitchen table.

Tomomi didn't come home that night. Or the next. We were sure that she was with a friend. But we didn't bother to try and track her down or to call Satoshi and ask him if he knew where she was. We thought that showing our indifference to her rebelliousness was a better strategy. And it was. By the weekend she was back home, that telephone of hers, a Sony-Erickson, firmly in her grasp. "Next time you run off," I told her, "don't forget it."

"I won't," she said.

And she didn't. That was when she claimed to be pregnant but didn't know who the father was, all to provoke me, which had worked.

I slapped her.

She smiled back at me. "Thank you, Father," she said. "Thank you, thank you!"

I'd done exactly what she'd wanted me to.

She'd already had a bag packed and went into her room and retrieved it and walked past Mizuko and I, to the front door, and out onto the street, turning for Yotsuya Station.

"You didn't have to strike her," Mizuko said. "Why?"

"You heard her."

"You're a policeman. Can't you control yourself? She's not pregnant."

"She was laughing at me."

"So what if she was?"

"What are we going to do this time?" I said.

"Wait," Mizuko said.

We did. For years. The next time I saw Tomomi was in the Amour.

Ms. Nishikawa brought me back to my job when she said, "Junko was close to Jiyumi. She might know something."

"A friend?" I said.

"Another hostess. The two were close. They went out together from time to time, even shared taxi rides home."

"You know more than you think you do," I said.

"She'll be arriving soon," Ms. Nishikawa said.

I must have been staring at the photograph of Tomomi with the other girls and Ms. Nishikawa, because she pointed at one of them and said, "That's Junko."

"All your girls are attractive," Detective Izuka said.

"I'm more interested in character," she said. "I had my troubles when I was younger. It's not just a girl's looks that matters. This is hard work, the psychology of allowing a man to fantasize about you, but not allowing it to get out of hand as some girls do, ending up. . . Sorry," she said. "It's still a shock."

A silence fell like a curtain, and it was then that I realized that the barman had put on some jazz, Miles Davis's "Kind of Blue." Ms. Nishikawa ran a classy club. The music sent me into another direction. I thought of Mizuko in the Keio Plaza Hotel, at the grand piano in the main bar, playing jazz standards three nights a week. I knew that I would be there this evening, the toughest day of my life, sipping a bourbon.

"I like your place," Detective Izuka said.

"Maybe there's a girl here you'd like to talk to?"

"Shrewd."

She smiled wryly, as did Detective Izuka, in reply.

About five minutes later Junko Atada showed up. She was older than Tomomi, nearing thirty, a bit rounder in the hips, and had a gentle, maternal face. She was a few centimeters shorter than Tomomi, around one hundred sixty or so, the height many men find attractive, because their diminutive stature empowers them. A woman who is taller than them is a threat. Junko was wearing jeans and a purple jumper. Her long, straight hair was down and lay splayed out on the jumper.

When Ms. Nishikawa had Junko come to our table. Detective Izuka and I stood.

Ms. Nishikawa said, "These are police detectives, Junko." She introduced us. "They would like to ask you a few questions about Jiyumi." Junko stiffened up, the way people who are hiding something do when police detectives show up unexpectedly to question them. I was immediately suspicious of her.

"Is something wrong?" she asked.

"Please sit down," I said.

She sat across from us, very tentatively, bracing herself for the news she knew was coming. And when it did—Ms. Nishikawa told her—she cried.

"What happened?" she asked. "Why?"

"That's what we want to find out," Detective Izuka said.

"Maybe you can be of some assistance to the detectives," Ms. Nishikawa said.

"I'll do whatever I can," Junko said.

"Do you know what telephone she owned," Detective Izuka said, "the make?"

"An iPhone," she said.

"Color?"

"Black in a red leather case. Why is that important?" I told her.

She started to cry again. Ms. Nishikawa brought over a packet of tissues, and Junko took a few and blotted her tears.

"Who would do such a thing? Who?" She said, talking more to herself than to us. But she knew. What an act.

"We're going to find out who," I said. "Maybe you

know something. Possibly one of her regulars was too fond of her?"

"They all treated her like a daughter," she said.

That hurt. I knew that girls talk and suspected that Tomomi had told Junko about her father and how she had run away from home. She then looked at Ms. Nishikawa, who said, "Excuse me. I need to prepare for tonight." She went over to the bar and started to talk to the barman.

"I suppose I should tell you this," Junko said. "She mentioned to me a few times when we were out drinking that she was doing some work for a private investigator."

"Work?" I asked.

"I suppose you'd call it that."

"Escorting?" Detective Izuka said.

"No. No. Nothing like that. It was something else. She was very secretive about it, but she told me it paid well."

"Is this P.I. a customer?" Detective Izuka asked.

"If he was, she didn't tell me. Jiyumi did tell me the work had something to do with . . ."

"What?" I asked.

"You know, that sort of thing."

"Sex," Detective Izuka said.

"That's embarrassing, the way you put it."

"I can't help myself."

"You don't know anything about this P.I.?" I asked. "His name?"

"She said he was missing part of a finger."

"A yakuza?" Detective Izuka said.

"She didn't tell me."

"He was missing the digit of a finger. I don't think he lost it working as a carpenter," I said.

"I don't know why she'd take her chances with a man like that. Can you protect me from him?"

That was an odd thing to say. Why did she think she needed police protection?

"Maybe he knows about me?" she then said. "Maybe Jiyumi told him."

"You've got nothing to worry about," Detective Izuka said.

"How do you know?"

We didn't know, of course.

"Why are you afraid of him?" I asked.

"You two are here asking me questions about him, aren't you?"

"Call us if you see a man missing a digit prowling around," I said.

"Don't go home alone," Detective Izuka said, "or to a hotel with a man you don't know well."

"I don't like the way you talk."

"A lot of women don't. I lack charm." Detective Izuka smiled that beguiling smile of his. Junko grunted. Not many women grunted back at him when he smiled.

"Jiyumi knew a lot of men," Junko said.

"Ms. Nishikawa said as much," I said.

"I think you do all right for yourself," Detective Izuka said.

"You've got a sweet tongue."

"It's his nature," I said.

"I feel sorry for his wife."

"How do you know I'm married?"

"I know."

Junko took her hands, which had been at her sides, and put them on the black slab of marble and looked at the nails. They were blood red. A few had fake diamonds in them.

"Nice nails," Detective Izuka said.

Junko looked up at him. "Thank you," she said. "I wasn't sure about the color."

"Does Ms. Nishikawa pay off the yakuza?" I asked.

"You can't ask me that question!" Junko said.

"You said Jiyumi was working with a P.I. who had a digit missing. Maybe Ms. Nishikawa knows this man?" Detective Izuka said.

"Maybe she does pay off the yakuza. It's not unusual, you know, for people in this business to have to pay them off. Or don't you know that? They do what the police won't—provide a harmonious work environment. They're not all bad."

"Of course," I said. I despised them, but she did have a point. Too many Japanese shop owners paid them off, to avoid the scandal and publicity that would follow if they didn't.

"Perhaps you could go to a yakuza for protection?" Detective Izuka said, "if you feel that way?"

"They do know how to treat a woman."

She must have known something about a particular yakuza that I didn't. Many of the ones I knew trafficked in women and ran adult film companies.

"A girl learns a lot in a job like this. Lots. Men can be real fools. If a girl wants to know about men, she should work this job."

"This P.I.," I said. "You don't know anything about him. Nothing? His name? Why he hired Jiyumi?"

"How many times are you going to ask me that question?" she said. "No." She looked at her fingernails again.

"Men will like the color," Detective Izuka said.

Detective Izuka and I kept on staring at Junko but said nothing. She couldn't couldn't hold out for more than a minute and said, "Jiyumi did tell me that this private investigator had a tattoo of a tiger on his back. He was born in the year of the tiger. She adored tattoos, thought about getting one herself, but could never decide on the design. She was lost to herself much of the time, even when she was with customers or me. She was a thinker, you understand, who had an artistic streak, a sort of philosopher. She was the lead singer in a punk band called the Little Nipples. I heard them once in a Shibuya club. She put on such a show! What a great singer and dancer she was. The boys, they all fell in love with her straight off."

Detective Izuka said, "How would Jiyumi know about this tattoo if she wasn't sleeping with him?"

The corner of her mouth turned up ever so slightly. "Maybe he told her," she said. "Those yakuza are always bragging about their tattoos."

That was a lie. They never bragged about their tattoos. They kept them covered.

Detective Izuka said, "I think she was giving this P.I. something on the side, as a bonus for whatever she was doing for him."

"Maybe they went to a hotel now and then."

"She wouldn't sleep with a man for money."

"A hostess with principles," Detective Izuka said.

"Apologize."

Detective Izuka only smiled. "So what if she was giving him some favors," Detective Izuka said.

"You're being disrespectful. She's dead."

"We're just doing our jobs," I said

"I used to respect the police."

Detective Izuka said, "Nice place, this club. If I could afford the drinks, I might become a regular."

"Jiyumi would've kept you drinking. She knew how to listen to men like you."

Detective Izuka said, "You're making all this up about Jiyumi working for a P.I.."

"Why would I do that? I want you to find the man who killed her."

"Then tell us who this P.I. is," I said.

"I honestly don't know his name."

Detective Izuka and I looked at each other.

"You've got to believe me. Please."

Detective Izuka said, "Try to remember his name."

She looked at her fingernails, back up at us, and said, "Jiyumi did let it slip out when she came to work late once that she'd been in Kabuki-cho with a man."

"We know," Detective Izuka said. "That's where her body was found. Was it sex work?"

"No," Junko said. "It wasn't that."

"She was found in a love hotel," I said.

"That man she was with was someone she could talk to she told me once."

"Who was he?"

"A man with money," she said, "a salaryman. That's what she told me. He was very kind to her."

"Sure," Detective Izuka said.

"You have no respect."

Detective Izuka said, "I'm just doing my job. I'm telling you the truth. He was a salaryman. I'll tell you the truth about me, because you'll probably find out anyway. I'm ashamed to say it . . . I was once . . . I worked as an actress."

"That sort of actress?"

"I thought it might lead to me being a real actress."

"For some girls it does turn out to be a career path," Detective Izuka said.

He was right about that, strangely; there were girls who'd been adult entertainment actresses who'd gone on to be celebrities and TV personalities, but not many. I wanted to know more about this salaryman and asked, "What company did this salaryman work for? Did she tell you that?"

"No. But here's what's odd. The P.I. had something to do with them meeting. That's all I know. Really."

Now I understood, or thought I did. I knew of cases like this. The P.I. was using my daughter to blackmail this salaryman. Sometimes the blackmail attempt failed and the man was the one who ended up dead, by his own hand, he was so shamed by what he'd done.

Detective Izuka said, "These P.I.s, they're always on the lookout for girls to work scams for them. Maybe you were jealous that he went for Jiyumi, not you? That's what I think. She was making all that big money."

"You're wrong. Wrong. How can you think such an awful thing?"

Detective Izuka said, "I don't like it when young women are found dead in a love hotel."

"Okay," Junko said, "I'll tell you this." She leaned over closer to us. "She was hooked on *shabu*. That's why she needed some extra cash . . ."

"Really?" Detective Izuka said.

"She might've even been dealing it."

"And who might've been her supplier?"

"I wouldn't know."

"You aren't a user?"

"No! You two aren't like the police I know. You're not

kind and respectful at all."

"We're real ones, not those actors in cheap TV dramas or movies," Detective Izuka said.

"I'm not a user, but I can understand if a girl does use it. This job—don't get me wrong, I owe a lot to Ms. Nishikawa, her taking me on—but it's hard to get through the night sometimes without a little help. What's a girl to do?"

"Of course not," Detective Izuka said.

"I don't care what you think."

Detective Izuka and I both knew she was lying. She used *shabu*. But what did it matter if she did? So many young women did.

Just then two more of Ms. Nishikawa's girls came in. We told Junko we'd had enough questions for her, that she'd been very helpful, that we'd be in touch if we needed her to answer more questions, and to call us if this P.I. came snooping around. She nodded her head and went off through a door by the bar, I guess to change into an evening dress or kimono.

We questioned the other girls after they'd had their cry and a packet of tissues had piled up on the table. One of the girls, Akiko, who had short hair and was as tiny as a little bird, said after she'd stopped her sniveling, "Junko knows all about Jiyumi."

I knew as much. Junko hadn't told us everything she knew. We'd wait and get what she knew out of her. She'd talk. People who are keeping information from the police in a murder case often do.

The other girl, Takako, was a little taller than Akiko. She had divided her hair into two girlish ponytails tied up in red, polka-dotted ribbons. She reminded me of the kind of girl seen in manga porn, and that was how she probably intended to present herself, considering the business she was in. She said, "Yes, Junko and Jiyumi were good friends."

"They went to Tokyo Disneyland together back in the spring," Akiko said.

"Was it April or May?"

They were looking at each other.

"It doesn't matter," I said, "the month."

"You're sure about that?" Detective Izuka said.

"Oh, yes. Junko showed us a photo of them all together."

They looked at each other and nodded in agreement.

"The two of them and a man went there, but we never asked about him. He was the sort of man a girl doesn't want to get too close to or know about."

"He was scary looking," Takako said.

"Maybe a *shabu* dealer?" I asked.

"Maybe," Akiko said.

"We didn't want to know."

"It's better not to know sometimes," Akiko said.

"He looked like he could do with a good shower."

They chuckled for a while, then caught themselves.

"Junko said he came on some free tickets to Disneyland. I think Junko wanted to make us feel jealous that she'd gone there for free."

"So what if she went there for free? We weren't jealous."

"We get offers every night to go there."

"I would've never thought that Jiyumi would be interested in Disneyland," Akiko said.

"I can picture her stepping on Mickey Mouse's toes, just for laughs. Maybe that's why she went, to make fun of it all."

Akiko said, "Jiyumi had a wonderful sense of humor."

"We heard," Detective Izuka said.

"She made us laugh and laugh, the way she made fun of men."

"Not you, the police," Takako said, "but our customers."

"We didn't take it that way," I said.

"She mocked the ones who thought they were someone special behind their backs. But she had a soft spot for the weaklings who were inexperienced with women."

"Did she mention a salaryman she was seeing?"

"No."

"Sorry. Do you think he did it?"

"We don't know," I said.

"It's such a pity. She could've been a singer, not a dumbell hostess."

And then, without any warning, the two of them started to cry again.

"It's not right," Takako said, sniffling into a tissue. "Jiyumi was special."

"You'll find whoever did it?" Akiko asked.

"We will," I said.

"I don't think it was one of her customers," Takako said. "They all adored her."

"They're going to take it hard. That's for sure. None of them would do a thing like that."

"Junko mentioned a private investigator that Jiyumi was working with. Do you know anything about him, or what she might have been doing for him?"

"Really?"

"That's news to us," Akiko said.

They both nodded their heads.

"She did have her secrets," Takako said. "We knew her name wasn't Jiyumi."

"A girl learns not to pry in this job. It might get you in trouble. I wonder what her real name was."

Tomomi really had evaporated. I looked at my watch. "You two probably need to dress for work," I said.

"I hope you can make it through the night," Detective Izuka asked.

"Maybe Ms. Nishikawa will close down for a few days," Takako said.

"It would be a nice gesture," I said.

"If we have to work, we'll put on a face."

"Don't we all," I said, "put on a face."

They squeezed each other's hand.

Detective Izuka and I went to the bar and thanked Ms. Nishikawa, who told us she wasn't going to open for a few days.

"I should've thought about that earlier. Maybe we'll have a private ceremony."

"You don't know anything about a private investigator who was one of Jiyumi's regulars?" I asked, "or a salaryman she was sleeping with?"

"What? No. No."

"The P.I. had a digit missing from a finger," Detective Izuka said.

"I would've remembered him. No. Definitely not. I don't allow those types in."

We thanked her and left the club and went to the bank of elevators down the hall and waited for a car to arrive and as we waited Detective Izuka said, "Junko knows more than she's letting on to."

"You must be a detective," I said.

"I know liars."

"Let Junko stew away in her guilt," I said.

"It will gnaw away at her. She's weak."

The elevator door opened, and two girls and their customers got off. The girls were all giggles and the customers all smiles. They walked off toward a club. The girls were wearing these glittery silk evening dresses and had caked on the makeup. One had this sparkling tinsel, like stars, on a cheek.

Detective Izuka said, "Do you think this P.I. killed her? Or was it this salaryman?"

"The P.I. killing a girl he was using to blackmail suckers? Hardly. Maybe the salaryman."

We took the elevator down to the street level and went to the police car and got in it, and the driver took us back to the police station. It had already been a long day, but I wasn't finished with my work.

I wrote up a report and printed it and stamped it with my seal. By that time it was nearing eight at night. I didn't want to return home. All day I'd been busy with the investigation, and that had held me together; being alone in our home, well, I knew I'd crack. I just couldn't be in that empty house feeling Tomomi's spirit. I would hear the ringing of the brass bell that Mizuko struck every morning before our *Butsudan* and smell the incense she lit. I thought of Tomomi's room. We hadn't made any changes to it.

There were no childish silly cute things in her room, no Hello Kitty kitsch. No pictures of Korean boy bands. Her closet was a mix of jeans, flannel shirts, Montbell mountaineering clothing, school uniforms, and leather jackets and pants that had silver studs. There were those Dr. Martens, too. She had an Apple laptop, but we didn't know the password and weren't sure we wanted to know her secrets. On her dresser there was a bottle of cheap perfume she'd bought at a 100 yen shop and on a bookshelf a few novels—one was *The Stranger.* She also had an MP3 player and some vinyl records by Blondie, The Pretenders, and the B52s, which she listened to from time to time on an old TEAC turntable of mine.

Mizuko and I were at first a bit alarmed by her tastes in movies and music, but we always told ourselves she would pass through that stage, as Satoshi had passed through his obsession with manga, some that were rather sexually explicit and depicted young girls in very unrealistic ways, disproportionately large breasts and large, innocent eyes.

No, I couldn't be in that home without Mizuko. That would be too much for me. And so I decided to go over to the Keio Plaza Hotel to listen to her play.

CHAPTER SIX

The walls of the hotel's main bar are red brick. The red brick at first seems out of place, not very Japanese, as if it belonged in a foundry, but after a while it makes you feel as if you have slipped back into an earlier time, when brick was a commonly used building material in factories. A person begins to feel as if they are far, far away from their troubles, that there, in this bar in a luxury hotel in one of the world's largest metropolitan areas, they have found, for an hour or so, peace of mind, privacy, solace. Leather chairs are arranged so that couples can sit cozily next to each other, so close that they can whisper something in the other's ear.

Mizuko was at the Steinway grand piano, which was on a dais at one end of the bar. A beam of light fell on her and the piano. She keeps her hair short, to her shoulders, and wears glasses that are set in a burnished, austere titanium frame, very understated and Japanese. Her dress this evening was blue silk, down over her knees, trimmed with white lace. A necklace of pearls hung from her slender, white neck. The light made her glow. I had to tell myself, as I often did when I saw her at the piano, that she was my wife. I had to tell myself this because at that piano she takes on a role that I am less familiar with; she is not the woman who wears an apron while preparing a meal or the woman wearing jeans who rides a bicycle to the nearby market to buy fresh vegetables and fish or wears leather gloves in the garden to plant tulips or trim pines.

My usual table is not one that is popular. It is in a dark corner of the bar, far from Mizuko. I like it because I do not think I'm a distraction to her when I sit there, though she has told me many times that she is too absorbed in the playing of the music to notice anyone in the bar. She says she enters a world in which no one can touch her. I am envious of this feeling. I felt that way from time to time when writing this story, but for most of my life I've been a police detective, and there is little solace for a man in the world of murder investigations and the requisite paperwork.

I sat down, and Chie, a waitress, whom we call older sister, One-san (姉一さん), came over.

"Good evening," she said. "How long has it been?"

She was studying law at Tokyo University, known as Toudai, *tou* for east, 東, Tokyo, and *dai* for university, 大, a shortening of Tokyo University, 東大. She was from Kumamoto prefecture in Kyushu. She missed little of what was occurring in the bar and knew how to talk to people; she had a sharp wit, not so rare among modern Japanese women. Ms. Nodoka had such wit. Westerners who have never been to Japan misunderstand that women are not as discriminated against as they think. There are women airline pilots and shinkansen engineers and police officers. Most of the air traffic controllers are women. So are baseball announcers and news anchors.

I'm sure that every night Chie received several propositions from big shots who had come to Tokyo for business meetings and were staying at the hotel, free of their wives. She may have even accepted a few. Modern Japanese women, they're that way, too, independent. Tomomi aspired to be independent, but without a university education in Japan, it's very difficult to achieve independence. During earlier Japanese eras, about the only positions in which they had power were as courtesans, but then that all depended on their relationships with men, so I can't say that they were independent of them then.

"You're sure you don't want to be a police detective?" I said to Chie.

"Perhaps a prosecuting attorney," she said. "Then we'd be partners." She smiled. She had the face of a primary school teacher, very kind and gentle. She was tall and attractive. No Shibuya orange-haired nitwits who hiked up their skirts were going to find work at this bar.

In Japan, the police and the prosecuting attorney work closely with each other to build a case, unlike other countries, such as the United States, where the prosecuting attorney is an elected official who kowtows to his or her constituency, boasting of their conviction rate. Japanese prosecuting attorneys are a part of the massive bureaucracy. But there is security in being on the government payroll, and stability is a quality that Japanese hold in high regard. Despite the protests that Japanese have of the bureaucracy—including me, I admit—in their hearts they really want the social stability it offers.

"What would you like?" Chie asked.

"A Wild Turkey," I said, "on the rocks. Straight."

"A rough day?"

"You don't want to hear it."

"Maybe you'll tell your wife about it later on." She looked at Mizuko, who was playing "Autumn Leaves," a very appropriate song, considering that *koyou* was near. Mizuko's repertoire is mostly from the fifties and sixties, Bill Evans, Eroll Garner, Mary Lou Williams, Dave Brubeck, Oscar Peterson, and renditions of Miles Davis ballads. Tokyo is famous for its jazz clubs and jazz musicians.

Chie sensed that she had gone too far in her conversation with me, had become a bit too inquisitive, and left me there to watch Mizuko play. Mizuko had entered that world that only she owned. I thought, How can I possibly tell her what I know? How? Not today. But when?

Chie returned, smiled, and set my Wild Turkey down. "Enjoy," she said.

I raised the glass and drank and let the smoky taste and smoothness of the bourbon take hold of me. I felt the release from the day's horror. I sipped the bourbon again. Then again. Soon I was off somewhere where things such as what I'd experienced that day had never happened. There was only beauty and serenity, the release of all emotions, what Buddhist priests would call enlightenment. That's a sacrilege to say such a thing, when one says they have found enlightenment through drink, but there's truth in that sacrilege, so I don't feel guilty when comparing the two.

As Mizuko played, I not only listened to the music, the sound of each note hanging in the air, but also the accompanying whispering and clinking of glasses, the sweetness of a woman's laughter nearby. It all made Mizuko's playing of "Autumn Leaves" more moving.

When she finished playing, she turned and nodded her head. Applause followed, jazz applause, restrained and somehow a part of the experience, no hooting and shouting. No. None of that. Not in this bar. Not in any jazz bar in Japan, and there are plenty, many no larger than a twelve-mat room.

Mizuko saw me and smiled before turning back to the keyboard and striking the first notes of a song that tore at me, "It Never Entered My Mind." It was our song, dating back to the first day we'd met in the lobby of the Palace Hotel, near the grounds of the Imperial Palace, on a chaperoned *omiai*. It was then, when a man at a piano began to play this song that we both opened up and began to speak freely about ourselves, our dreams and the challenges ahead of us. After we'd married, she'd play "It Never Entered my Mind" to settle us down after a quarrel, or just to remind the other of how far we'd come, through the deaths of friends, the illnesses we'd had, the disappointments brought on by my own high expectations for a promotion or the lack of recognition I received from a superior when my team had cracked a case; then there were the confrontations we'd had with Tomomi. Her playing soothed us like a balm.

I couldn't listen to "It Never Entered My Mind" to the end. I just couldn't. It was too much for me. I had to get up and leave. I went to the men's room outside the bar and into a stall and sat on a toilet seat, and it was there, alone, that the tears that had been building up in me all day flowed. I took off my glasses and sobbed and choked and blotted away the tears with a handkerchief. I thought that it was me, really, who had killed Tomomi, because if I'd been more understanding and less controlling as a father—hadn't slapped her— she wouldn't have left home. She wouldn't have ended up working for a former yakuza P.I., blackmailing some salaryman and ended up garroted to death. Her death came down on me with the weight of a millstone around my neck. Thoughts of suicide even came to mind but drifted away just as quickly. I couldn't go through with that, bringing shame to Mizuko. Me? I didn't care about me. I cared about that beautiful woman at the piano playing "It Never Entered my Mind."

I don't know how long I was in that toilet stall sobbing and thinking about myself, that I was a failure as a father and husband. I only know that after a while there were no more tears, and it was then that that millstone lifted just a little from around my neck, allowing me to stand. I left the stall and went to a sink and washed my face and eyes and looked at myself in the mirror, seeing a man who was no longer handsome, who had thinning gray hair and had gained weight, who had become a tad paunchy, who was wearing an anonymous dark suit and white shirt, a man who is part of the crowd of commuters pouring out of the Chuo line at Shinjuku South Station, heading off to his office. Only those who walked with a cane or were blind or hobbled along, stricken by arthritis stood out.

I returned to my table and sat and watched Mizuko, who was now playing "Misty." I raised my bourbon and drank and drank again and when I had finished with it I ordered another.

It was past midnight when Mizuko finished her last set. During her performance, she had taken a few breaks, but had never come over to my table. She had, rather, done her job and spoken with a few guests in the bar, something she had never really liked to do but was obligated to, to make them feel pampered, a necessity in the hotel industry.

After her last set, she changed into a pair of Blue Blue Japan jeans, Merrell walking shoes, and a hooded blue wool jumper. She was, at heart, an outdoorsy type. Her family came to Chiba prefecture when she was in her early teens, when her father got a job with Perfect Enso, a printer and publisher of company documents. He had been perfectly happy in Yamagata among the rice fields, dairies, and mountains, and he and his wife returned there after his retirement.

Mizuko came out to the hotel's lobby, where I'd been waiting.

"Was it such a bad day?" she asked.

How could I answer that question? I just said, "It was bad."

"Will I read about it in tomorrow's paper? Or was it so bad that the crime will make the TV news?"

"Maybe the TV news," I said.

We walked through the lobby, in which there were only a few couples who seemed a bit drunk, probably having spent the evening bar hopping in eastern Shinjuku. A line of Hybrid Toyota taxis and electrics were waiting. A doorman waved to a driver. The driver pulled the Toyota up to us and we got in and the driver closed the door. (In Japan, customers don't close taxi doors.) I told him where we were going, to a side street across from Sotobori Park. We don't give drivers street addresses. There aren't any. The city is divided into smaller and smaller sections, in a grid pattern, and the address of one's home is the smallest grid. Our house was in Honshio-cho, a block away from a community center where Mizuko went from time to time to teach piano to children.

As we were heading home, Mizuko said, "Don't forget about Satoshi."

We had made plans to take the shinkansen up to Sendai to meet our son's fiance on Sunday. I hadn't been looking forward to it. I had a feeling that I wouldn't like her. She hadn't attended a university. She had a certificate from a private school that taught students how to groom dogs and cats and worked in what was called a pet boutique. Satoshi had sent us photos of her. The photos had given me a bad impression of her. Her name was Rei. She had tinted her hair red and was wearing a short skirt, up over her knees. Tomomi had never looked so cheap.

"Try to be friendly," Mizuko said. She turned and looked at me. "If not for yourself, then for me."

"I won't judge her until we meet."

"You always say that," Mizuko said. "But you can't help yourself. You're a police detective. It's in your blood to judge people by how they dress, their hairstyle and wristwatch."

"I judged you before I joined the police," I said, "and I was right."

"Don't flatter yourself, Clint."

I wanted to be Western and tell her she was beautiful, but she would've thought I was mad to say such a thing. It wasn't the way Japanese men my age talked to their wives. "You played very well," I said.

"Was the blue dress fine?"

"Very fine," I said. "You could've made friends with some of the men there, I'm sure, found a rich man, not a police detective."

"I made my decision long ago," she said. "Why risk it all with a stranger?"

"To forget," I said.

"Let's not talk about her. Please."

About ten minutes later, because it was late—there was no traffic—the taxi stopped in front of our home, a traditional two-story wooden one that has shoji screens and fusuma doors. We got out of the taxi and walked up the flagstone path that led to the front door and went inside. We hung up our coats at the door. Then we went to the kitchen. Mizuko was often a bit hungry after her performances. Now and then she had a light snack with a glass of white wine.

She took a bottle of Riesling from the refrigerator, two hard-boiled eggs, and a container of Japanese pickles. She put all of it on a plate and the plate on the kitchen table, a heavy one made of Japanese maple that had visible black knotholes in it.

"Hungry?" she asked.

I had eaten some soba noodles at my desk after our visit to Tomomi's room.

"Perhaps an omelet?" Mizuko asked. "I bought some ham yesterday."

"That'll be fine," I said.

"Today couldn't have been that bad?" she said.

How could I explain?

She made the omelet and served it to me with some shrimp-flavored corn chips. "Don't we have a beer?" I said.

"You don't need a beer. You've had enough to drink."

"You played beautifully."

"You're drunk. You already said that. Eat your omelet."
She put it down in front of me.

I ate the omelet while watching Mizuko peel the hard-boiled eggs, sprinkle them with salt and pepper, and then top them with a shred of pickle. She took a bite. She sipped her wine. Now and then she looked at me and grimaced. This wasn't the first time we had spent a night like this. There had been other hard cases. She had grown accustomed to my moods.

When she'd finished with her eggs and was about to finish with the wine, she said, "Should I draw you a bath?" In spite of her artistic personality, she remained a traditional and kind Japanese wife, one who felt an obligation to look after her husband.

"Thank you," I said.

The bath in our house is something I'm proud of. It's a traditional one, made of Japanese fir.

I got in the bath, enjoying the hot water loosening the muscles in my back and neck, but couldn't stop myself from thinking of the day and, once again, felt guilty that I had caused it all. I tried to tell myself that it had been Tomomi's decision to run away, to involve herself with the wrong people, that she could have come home and we would have welcomed her, forgotten all about our differences, but it didn't matter. Shame and guilt had taken root.

I don't know how long I stayed in the bath, letting the hot water do its work on me, but it must have been longer than usual, because Mizuko shouted,

"Did you drown?"

"I'm fine," I said.

"You know, I'd like to take a bath too."

There were times when we had taken baths together,

and I looked forward to our annual visit to a mountain *onsen*, when we would do just that, but, well, on this night it hadn't worked out that way, us being in the bath together. I don't know why. It just didn't. It seems that marriage is like that, routine dulling the romance until there is only a little sparkle left. We learn to make room for the other in our life and fit their routine into ours, as we both go about our daily lives, and that is marriage, for better or worse.

I got out of the tub and dried myself and put on a robe and went into our bedroom, where Mizuko was also wearing a robe.

"It's all yours," I said.

She went to take her bath.

Long ago, seeing her in that robe, the nipples of her breasts pushing up against the fine silk, she wouldn't have made it into the bath. We would have lay down on the futon together. But that was long, long ago.

CHAPTER SEVEN

The first break in the case came, surprisingly, the next day. I learned of it shortly after I had read a story in the *Asahi Shimbun* about the murder of a girl in a Kabuki-cho love hotel. The story was twelve lines long. Was that Tomomi's life, twelve lines of print in the *Asahi Shimbun*?

The break had to do with the lottery ticket Detective Izuka and I had found in Tomomi's bag. It was a break like many others: the seemingly insignificant leads to the killer. Two detectives, Tsuchida and Morita, were the ones who did the necessary legwork that led them to the kiosk where Tomomi—or should I say the salaryman—bought the ticket.

We called detectives Tsuchida and Morita Laurel and Hardy, because they were as mismatched as those two, one thin, the other portly, and they were somewhat of a comedy team as well. They'd been working together for more than fifteen years. Because of the comedy team antics, there was no chance of them going up the bureaucratic ladder. But they didn't care. They were more interested in solving crimes, and they were good at it.

"He bought the ticket at a kiosk in Seibu Station," Detective Tsuchida, the portly Hardy said. His tie, as usual, was loose around his thick neck, to prevent his face from turning red. The collars of his shirts were always a size too small for him.

"He?" I asked. We were in a conference room. "Who is

'he'?"

"That salaryman," Detective Morita said.

Detective Izuka said, "How many men are stepping out on their wives?"

"Less than a million," Detective Morita said.

They laughed. I didn't.

"The woman who sold the ticket is a sharp granny."

"She saw them take the Kabuki-cho exit."

Detective Tsuchida said, "We're all familiar with these types."

"They're as anonymous as I am on the Chuo line," I said.

"You have dignity, sir," Detective Izuka said.

"Don't flatter me."

"But you do. You're Japanese."

"I should have been born two hundred years ago, when it meant something, being Japanese. Now we're all just a bunch of bureaucrats and slaves to companies."

"I stand out," Detective Tsuchida said, raising the end of his tie and fumbling with it the way Hardy does.

"You don't stand. You roll out," Detective Morita said. "Buddhist priests. They're no better than salarymen. Remember that arson case in which one burned his house down, only his wife was inside dead?"

We all nodded our heads.

Detective Tsuchida had a point there. I knew of one married priest who drove around town with hostesses in a late model BMW coupe. There's money to be made in putting the dead to rest.

One of my favorite Japanese movies is "Ososhiki," about the hypocrisy of the funeral industry.

Many of the women—and they were almost always women—who run these kiosks in train stations were no longer youngsters, but they weren't grannies. Many just want to get away from their husbands, who are retired and clutter up the house with cigarette butts and beer bottles, creating more work for them.

"Let's get back to this case," I said. "Where is this woman?"

"Here," Detective Morita said. "Her name is Mrs. Emi Horiishi."

"We knew you'd want to talk to her."

"Aren't we the clever ones, reading your mind, boss?" Detective Tsuchida said.

"Not that clever," I said.

"We're gathering together all the CCTV footage in the station," Detective Morita said.

"I'll see that you're promoted to Chief Inspector," I said.

"No thanks," Detective Tsuchida said. "I'd have to suck up to those higher-ups with diplomas from good schools. Too much obligatory drinking. I prefer to drink the way I like, with whom I want."

"Maybe our boss will foot the bill," Detective Morita said.

"When the case is closed," I said.

"Where would you like to go? The shabu-shabu or yakitori joint?" Detective Tsuchida said.

"Charcoal grilled yakitori. I know a place nearby. The master grills the meats on charcoal. There's grease dating back to the Showa era on the wall."

"Show me to Ms. Horiishi," I said.

They took me to a comfortable interrogation room, not anything like what you might see in a Western movie, lights in the face, gray table, a two-way mirror. Very harsh. We don't work that way with some witnesses. We want to make them feel welcome.

The room had a well-padded black leather sofa and two matching chairs. A table was between the two. It resembled a reception room at a company.

I knocked on the door, announcing ourselves, and opened the door. Mrs. Horiishi stood and bowed. I introduced myself and Detective Izuka and we handed her our *meishis*.

Mrs. Horiishi was wearing a crisp blue and gray uniform. She also had on a blue head covering, but strands of gray slid from her across her forehead. Her eyes were clear and sharp behind a pair of glasses that had exceptionally large lenses. Her lips were a bright red. She was small, under 150 centimeters, and probably didn't weigh more than forty kilos.

"Thank you for coming," I said. I told her that I was recording the conversation.

"Fine," she said. "Why should that bother me? This is about that murder, isn't it, that I read about in the paper this morning?"

"Perhaps," I said.

"I know you're not going to tell me. I'm used to this routine. The police have come to me before."

Just then a girl who serves tea entered the room holding a tray of three teacups and a tea pitcher. I'd never seen her before. Detective Izuka eyeballed her. She poured the tea, went to the door, turned, bowed, and closed the door behind her. Mrs. Horiishi sipped the tea, leaving on the rim of the cup a print of her lipstick. Then she sat back, her fingers knitted together, resting on her lap, and looked me straight in the eyes. This was a woman who feared little. Detective Izuka and I sipped our teas.

I laid the lottery ticket on the table and said, "I heard you sold this lottery ticket."

She looked at the ticket. "I wouldn't know if it was that particular one," she said. "I was asked if I sold one to a salaryman who was with his girl. I recognized her from the picture in her ID that those two detectives showed me."

"This ticket could be very helpful to us," I said, "now that we know the man bought it from your kiosk?"

"The girl asked him to buy it for her. He would do just about anything for her. I saw how he was looking at her."

Mrs. Horiishi was one sharp woman. Most of the women who work in those station kiosks are. Hundreds of people buy a paper or pack of cigarettes, maybe a canned drink, and aren't patient. They don't have time for a woman in a kiosk to fumble with change or a card reader.

"The man stopped to buy the *Nikkei* from time to time."

The *Nikkei* is Japan's equivalent to the *Wall Street Journal*.

"Was he distinguishable in any way?" Detective Izuka asked.

"Only that he looked unexceptional. You know what I mean, a mama's boy who grows up knowing only studying and his company. I didn't raise my son to be that way. He's a truck driver, but what do I care? He drives from one end of Japan to the other."

"Have you seen this salaryman recently?"

"Last week, before the murder."

"How tall is he?" I asked.

"I'd say about the same as you."

"Is he thin or a bit pudgy?"

"Not really pudgy, but certainly not a man who gets much exercise. Or spends much time out of doors. His face was as white as a ghost's. He always looked dejected and resigned to life when he bought the *Nikkei*, but with his girl at his side his face glowed. Good for her, how she put some life into him. Dead? Why would he do that? I feel for her family. A friend of mine lost her daughter in a traffic accident."

That hurt.

"We don't know who killed this girl," Detective Izuka said.

"Was there anything remarkable about him?" I asked. "Anything distinguishable? A mole on his face, gray hair, the length of his hair, a unique necktie, suit, scar? The brand of his bag? An expensive wristwatch? Wedding ring?"

"An ordinary commuter coming from the western suburbs," she said. "It's hard to believe a man like that would have it in him to kill anyone."

"We don't know if he killed her," I said.

"Hard to believe he'd have it in him."

"Men change when they're with a girl," I said.

"I'm sure you know more about these sorts of things than I do."

"I wouldn't know about that," Detective Izuka said.

She looked at him. "You're no dull commuter. You're trouble."

Detective Izuka smiled.

"Now the girl, she stood out from the crowd," she went on. "She wasn't a loser like so many girls these days, those types that hang out in Shibuya with orange hair. She had a brain. She had the brightest eyes, unnaturally bright and cheerful. She was all smiles, bright as a cherry blossom in April. Or is it March now, because of climate change? I think she was the one who was with him wearing a blue wig. She looked foolish. And she had on these

silly fashion glasses that girls wear nowadays that were in the shape of hearts. They didn't go with her personality, not at all. She was only that way once. If it was her. It could have been another girl then. But it was him, with that girl."

The man had a history of going to love hotels with young girls? That didn't quite fit with the theory I was working with then, that he'd been with one girl, Tomomi, and that this P.I. had used her to blackmail this salaryman.

Detective Izuka looked at me, and I knew what he was thinking, that Tomomi's cheerfulness was from *shabu*. Maybe so. Maybe not. No matter, when a stranger described Tomomi it deepened my guilt. I thought of Mizuko ringing that brass bell and lighting the incense, praying for Tomomi to return, and of myself keeping the truth from her.

"Anything else come to mind?" I asked, "about this man or the girl?"

She thought for a while before saying, "No. Nothing special about him. Oh, he wore those old-fashioned glasses, plastic and steel, the ones Prime Minister Obuchi wore. He kind of looked like him as well." Prime Minister Obuchi was famous for lack of inspiration. He had been Japanese prime minister from 1998 to 2000. He died of a stroke, while in office.

She then sniffled, snatched a tissue from a box on the table, and wiped her nose.

"If you see him again," I said, "contact us. We're going to put your kiosk under surveillance."

"How exciting!" she exclaimed.

"Detective Izuka here will tell you how the set-up works."

"This is the most exciting thing that's ever happened to me in all my years of marriage." She'd probably had an *omiai* that hadn't turned out well. Many didn't.

Detective Izuka laughed.

"You mustn't tell anyone about this," I said.

"No. I wouldn't dream of it. Never. I want that girl's killer caught."

"I think that's enough," Detective Izuka said. "Come with me and I'll explain the set-up."

We all stood.

"I hope I've been of some help."

"You have," I said.

Both Detective Izuka and I thanked her again. Detective Izuka stayed with her in the room, to tell her how the surveillance operation would work.

Detectives Tsuchida and Morita had been waiting for me outside the room. They both had obsequious smiles.

"We're putting her kiosk under surveillance," I said, "and one of you will take the first shift."

They looked at each other and did a rock, paper, and scissors, to decide on who would do what. Detective Morita lost. "Damn!" he said.

I said, "Is there a camera near the entrance to the Amour? Maybe at that Family Mart across from it?"

"Indeed there is," Detective Tsuchida said, grinning.

"And you didn't tell me this earlier? Why?"

"Isn't an eyewitness more important?" Detective Morita said.

He had a point. I thought, a Family Mart in Kabuki-cho, a place as far removed from family as one of those Kabuki-cho basement peep show arcades. I'm sure this Family Mart was well stocked with beer, sake cups, chips, Meiji chocolate bars, and condoms.

"See if the camera caught the two together," I said.

"We're already on it," Detective Tsuchida said.

"Alternate shifts between surveillance and going through the video," I said.

"I can taste the charcoal grilled *yakitori* now," Detective Tsuchida said. "We'll have this creep within a week."

"Because you want some free *yakitori* and beer?" I asked.

"A sense of duty, to the girl's family," Detective Morita said. He was speaking ironically, and I didn't like it much, but I couldn't say anything. It was the way they often spoke when working a case. I hadn't said anything to them before about the way they spoke.

"You never stop with one glass of beer," Detective Morita said to Detective Tsuchida.

"Neither do you."

They laughed.

"Get to work," I said.

They both saluted me in a silly way and walked off.

Detective Izuka came up behind me and said, "They'll never get promoted."

"They don't want to," I said.

"What about you?"

"It's not something I consider anymore," I said. He looked at me, a bit surprised, and I added, "Do you want to make chief?"

"Too much politics," he said.

"There you have it," I said.

I returned to my desk and less than an hour later, while I was writing out the interminable reports, I got a call from Detective Morita. He'd been going through security camera videos in Seibu Station. He said, "I have something you might want to take a look at."

Detective Izuka and I went to a room especially designed for viewing CCTV footage. The computer allowed the operator to run the footage forward or backward at a slow speed and print out frames.

A large screen was against one wall. Detective Izuka and I sat while Detective Tsuchida operated the computer. We watched footage of Tomomi—or was it Jiyumi?—walking up to Mrs. Horiishi's kiosk with a man who was as ordinary as Mrs. Horiishi had described him. I would describe him as bovine. He had on an anonymous dark blue suit. His shirt was white, his tie, the only thing distinguishable about him, a green paisley print.

It was easy enough for us to track him down. The next morning detectives Tsuchida and Morita went to Seibu Station and caught sight of him as he was making his way through the station and followed him to West Shinjuku, where he had an office in a glass tower but three minutes from my desk. He was a vice president in the procurement division of Pacific Sushi, a major distributor of maguro. A quick internet search gave us his name, Yuji Uno.

CHAPTER EIGHT

Mr. Uno commuted from Tachikawa, a town in Saitama prefecture northwest of Tokyo. A lot of commuters live there. The homes are less expensive than the ones in Tokyo. They are often in a Western style with a yard and garage, but have a tatami room for formal occasions. (The only way I'd been fortunate enough to own a home inside the Yamanote line was that I'd inherited it from my father, who'd inherited it from his father. The house had been in our family for almost a hundred years and had, fortunately, survived the B-29 incendiary raids of the war, when much of eastern Tokyo, what we call *shitamachi*, or the old area, was burned to the ground. More people died during the March raids of 1945 than the bombing of Hiroshima, something few people outside of Japan know.)

Mr. Uno's home was two-stories, made of white siding, and had large, curtained windows, except for the Japanese room, which had shoji screens. The house also had a garage, a garden with pines and maples, and a net for hitting golf balls into. As an executive in a major company, golf was obligatory.

Detective Tsuchida was the one who tailed him home one day and discovered all this and took photos of the house. Then he and Detective Morita began to tail him on his commute, taking photos of him from a discreet distance. We used the photos to show those old women who worked at the Amour, to see if they recognized him. None did, a love hotel being what it is. But we got lucky when we showed them to a shopkeeper on the street the Amour was on.

A university student named Nao Ujiie who worked in the Family Mart across from the Amour recognized Mr. Uno and confirmed that he'd been with a young woman. Nao was a bright young woman attending Waseda University. She found it exciting to work in Kabuki-cho, "where the sin is," she said. "Working here is better than watching a TV drama." She was studying management and thought of working at a Family Mart in Kabuki-cho as a kind of case study of people's behavior, which, being the kind of area it was, revolved around eating, drinking, and sex.

Detective Izuka and I interviewed Nao outside that Family Mart. She said of Tomomi, "She looked out of place here. Most of the couples are middle-aged."

An autumn chill was falling on the city. Neon lights were beginning to come alive. The rush hour traffic of commuters was picking up. We were looking across the street at the Amour, which was back in business. Mr. Tanaka, the manager, was stooped over, under the weight of a watering can, the kind used to water gardens, and was putting water down on the street and scrubbing the asphalt with a brush.

A man and a woman came to the entrance, stood there, studying the lighted photos of the rooms. The man was tall and handsome, had a strong chin and full head of hair. His build was very athletic. He might have been forty-five. The woman was around thirty-five and had long hair, in which there was a sparkling hairband. She was wearing tightly-fitting jeans, a red jumper, and purple running shoes.

Mr. Tanaka had the good sense not to look at them

and maybe run them off as they were studying the room photos. The woman pointed at a photo of a room, and the two of them went around the wall that provided a degree of privacy and entered the hotel.

"They're regulars," Nao said. "It's who humans are, isn't it? As necessary to our survival as water."

"Care to explain?" Detective Izuka asked. He really hadn't wanted her to explain. He was just baiting her.

Nao smiled back at him. "I think you know, detective," she said.

She was holding his *meishi*. She looked at it, at him, then put his *meishi* away in an apron pocket, and smiled at him again. She'd already given us her phone number and address. It wasn't too difficult to predict what was going to happen next with those two.

I showed her the photo of Mr. Uno again. "You're sure it was him?" I asked.

"It was his ordinariness that I remember. Not so many men like him come to Kabuki-cho."

"Thank you," I said. "You've been very helpful."

We turned and had taken only a couple of steps when Nao said, "You're not very good detectives. You didn't ask me about the man who was taking photos of them."

Detective Izuka said, "I was distracted."

Enough flirting, I thought. "Please explain," I said.

"He was right where we're standing, holding a camera and pointing it at them. A person stands out in this area, if they're holding a camera."

This had to be the PIr. Yes, he was working a blackmailing scam with Tomomi.

"Can you describe him?" I asked.

She held up her left hand and gestured that the digit of his little finger was missing.

"You noticed that?" Detective Izuka said.

"He bought some cigarettes, Seven Stars."

"What about his face," I said, "his physique? How old was he?"

"Oh, maybe in his forties, early fifties. It's hard to tell with those yakuza types, the way they drink and smoke and ruin their bodies. But he was small, maybe only one hundred and seventy centimeters tall and very thin. He was wearing a black hat with a wide brim, like detectives wear in old movies."

"He must be on the security camera video," Detective Izuka said.

"I wouldn't know. It feeds into a system at Family Mart headquarters."

She was right about that. I'd get Tsuchida and Morita to go through the videos and find him. It wouldn't be too difficult. We knew the day and time he had been there.

"I'm safe, aren't I? I don't want him to know I told you this, but if he had anything to do with that poor girl's murder, I want you to catch him. I owe her that much."

"Thank you," I said, "but you have nothing to fear. We're not telling anyone what you told us."

"Anything else you might have seen that could be of use to us?" Detective Izuka asked.

"If I think of something, I'll contact you." She took out Detective Izuka's *meishi* and looked at it and the two smiled at each other.

"Do contact us," he said.

This time we turned and left for good.

We walked up the street and went into an entrance for Shinjuku Station and followed it over to Shinjuku South Station, and returned to the police building. I resisted saying anything to Detective Izuka about him and Nao. An air of smugness had come over him. I'd seen it in him before. I didn't much like being around him when he was that way, eager for another tryst, but he was a conscientious detective, and that was what mattered most.

After learning that Mr. Uno had been to the Amour with Tomomi—and that this yakuza P.I. had been taking photos of them—my team and I met and discussed if we should pick Mr. Uno up and confront him with what we suspected, that he was being blackmailed, but decided against this tactic, believing it was too risky. Not many company men would admit to being blackmailed, if any at all. It brings their company—and them—shame. There have been cases in which once it came out that a company man was being blackmailed, because of a connection with the yakuza or a tryst with a girl, he had, out of shame, killed himself. I couldn't have that. I decided that it was better to hold off for a few days, to see if Mr. Uno led us to the P.I.. I suspected that he was continuing to pay him, now even more than before, because of his involvement in a murder.

We were in the conference room again, Detective Izuka, me, and detectives Morita and Tsuchida.

"The killer got into that room when Uno was there," Detective Morita said.

"I've thought of that," I said.

"This P.I. hired him to kill her," Detective Tsuchida said. "He's yakuza or was or has yakuza connections. We know how they are."

"Perhaps," I said.

"Uno isn't going to talk if we threaten him," Detective

Izuka said. "He's not going to shame Pacific Sushi."

We all knew that this was true.

"This P.I. is the key to it all," I said.

Detectives Tsuchida and Morita shrugged. "All those videos," Detective Morita complained.

"You two know the day and time," I said. "You should spot him within an hour."

Detective Tsuchida said, "Uno will talk. He's weak. We need to pick him up."

"It's usually good enough for a court," Detective Morita said, "to get a conviction if the man can be placed at the scene. We have a witness. And Laurel and Hardy will soon have video evidence."

"That's lazy police work," I said, "and we could be arresting an innocent man, damaging his reputation. I want the man who did the deed." There had been several cases in the news over the past ten or so years in which police had coerced confessions out of down-and-out men, who'd been convicted and condemned to death row. Fortunately, lawyers who actually wanted to do something other than suck up a client's money had taken up their cases, seeing that they were set. I wasn't going to authorize an arrest of a man who probably wasn't Tomomi's killer, a man who, I knew, had a wife and two children.

"Don't be so lazy," I said.

They all fell as silent as first graders whose teacher had scolded them.

Detective Izuka grumbled. "What if Uno gets wind of us knowing what we know and goes into hiding? We'll be the ones who answer for that."

"How would he?" I asked.

"We all know there are police on the yakuza's payroll

who could hide him."

"No one in this room is. Are they?"

"But word gets out. You file reports."

"Mr. Uno's not going anywhere," I said. "He wouldn't know how to become a fugitive. All he knows is commuting to work and loyalty to Pacific Sushi."

"He must've heard of Nishinari," Detective Tsuchida said.

Nishinari is a neighborhood in Osaka where there are blocks and blocks of single-room hotels, gambling dens, smoky *shogi* clubs, pachinko parlors, and, bordering all this, a traditional red light district. The brothels are made of cedar and have roof tiles. Paper lanterns hang at the sides of the entrances. It's a beautiful sight, these traditional buildings, if a person can manage to go on what's inside.

Detective Izuka said, "Remember that case involving the adult actress who was sleeping with married actors in Osaka?"

"She was working with the yakuza down there."

"The yakuza were blackmailing the men."

"And one man killed himself when the scandal sheets broke the story," I said. "Remember?"

They all fell silent.

"I won't have it, a man killing himself because we weren't careful in our investigation."

"Reputations," Detective Tsuchida said, "what a heavy burden to bear."

"You shouldn't worry about yours," Detective Morita said. "It's well-known that you're a heavy drinker."

I adjourned the meeting and returned to my desk. It was there that I had done some internet searches and learned that every morning several buyers from

Pacific Sushi went to the Tsukiji fish market in Chuo-ku in central Tokyo to bid on premium quality maguro. Pacific Sushi sold the maguro to sushi shops and classy hotels throughout the country. Mr. Uno was the one who approved all of the company's purchases of premium maguro.

Mr. Uno was from Nara, a historical city famous for its temples and a park where high school girls on their school trips feed deer *senbei*, rice crackers. Tomomi had gone there for her high school trip. "What a bore!" was her response to feeding the deer. "The other girls were all giggles. They made me nauseous! If only we'd gone to Osaka to listen to some decent music." Osaka was an hour away by train. Unlike other Japanese, people from Kansai are boisterous and quick to laugh, even when they're not drunk, and proud of their dialect, which is rough and urban.

"Knowing you," Mizuko said to Tomomi after she'd returned from the trip, "you and a friend did sneak off to Osaka. I won't be angry if you tell me you did."

"Mother! We were like prisoners in that hotel."

I said, "To keep you girls out of trouble."

"Okay. We did go to a club in Osaka. People speak their mind there, not like in the rest of Japan. They have humor."

"They do," I said. "You're right about Kansai people. They're a different breed."

We were at the dining room table, having a dinner of grilled *sanma*, an oily mackerel when it is in season in the fall. Satoshi was there, home for the weekend from his first year at Tohoku University.

Satoshi said, "We can go to Osaka one weekend, take in a show, sister."

"I wouldn't want to be seen with you at a convenience store," Tomomi shot back.

"That's why I invited you. I knew you wouldn't go."

"Take a girlfriend, if you have one. Or are you too afraid to talk to a girl, you otaku. Do you pay for it?" Tomomi, in her high school uniform, grinned knowingly. "I know how boys like you are."

"That's enough!" Mizuko said. "Stop it!"

Tomomi slurped down the last of her miso soup and said, "I'm going for a walk."

"Which boyfriend is it?" Satoshi asked. "You go through plenty."

"Stop it!" Mizuko said again. "Show some respect!"

"*Gochisousama desu*," Tomomi said and stood. It's what we say after a meal, to thank the person who has prepared it. But Tomomi had spoken sarcastically, which had made Mizuko's cheeks flush red. "Go!" she said. "Get out of this house!"

"Gladly," Tomomi said. She picked up a black hoodie to cover the sailor collar of her uniform and made her way to the door.

"Don't wake us when you return," Satoshi said.

"Lay off her," I said.

Tomomi proceeded to leave the house. That wasn't such an unusual dinner conversation in our house, when we were all at the same table. It went better when Satoshi wasn't there and Mizuko and Tomomi had this restrained respect for the other.

On that night, We heard Tomomi return to her room at around two. We hadn't managed to get to sleep before then. The next morning at breakfast, Mizuko told Satoshi to keep his mouth shut, not to ask Tomomi about where she'd been, but to respect her rebelliousness.

"She isn't my sister," he said. "My sister would know her place."

"Listen to your mother," I said to him. "Give Tomomi some space."

He grunted.

Tomomi came to breakfast a few minutes later, saying, "*Ohayo Gozaimasu!*" She looked like she'd had eight hours sleep, her face was so fresh, her eyes so sharp.

Mizuko served her miso soup and a scrambled egg.

"Thank you, Mother," she said. "I'm sorry about my behavior last night. Forgive me." She nodded.

"We're happy you're back safely," I said.

She looked at me and smiled and thanked me for my consideration.

###

When doing research on Mr. Uno, I came across an interview he had given to a reporter for a trade magazine. A grandfather had lived in Oma in northern Aomori prefecture, on the tip of the Shimokita peninsula. The peninsula is well-positioned to have a fleet of fishing boats that can venture out from villages along it into the Tsugaru Strait, which separates Honshu from Hokkaido. It's where the big, sought after bluefin are. The current is strong and there's a supply of sardines for them to feed on. Mr. Uno had spent his summers there with his grandfather, who, by chance, ran a sushi shop in a little town, one that was so famous that people traveled to it from all over the Tohoku region, because of its glowing reputation for serving some of the best maguro to be had.

I also learned that Mr. Uno had a wife named Ayako

and two children, one, a daughter, in high school, the other, a son, in middle school; both were probably headed for careers like their father's, boring ones in prestigious major corporations after graduating from Tokyo or Kyoto university. They'd probably marry into a good family, have two kids, and perpetuate the myth that prestige brings happiness.

Mr. Uno's wife was the interesting one. Whereas he disappeared in a crowd, she stood out. Detective Morita had snapped a photo of her one day, when she left the house to catch a train to Tokyo to do some shopping at Seibu Department store in Ikebukuro. She kept a Facebook page and volunteered as a Japanese teacher at a community center in Tachikawa that a women's group ran. She was from Kesennuma, a small but major fishing town on the Pacific coast in northern Miyagi prefecture. It had been a quaint town surrounded by steep hills that had a deep harbor and fleet of fishing ships, but all that came to an end in 2011, when the Great East Japan Earthquake struck, the most powerful ever recorded in Japan. The resulting tsunami picked up large fishing boats and sent them several kilometers inland. The town was destroyed. The Fukushima Nuclear Plant, down the coast, flooded and, because the diesel auxiliary power unit failed, the reactors lost their cooling and exploded. The area, because of the spread of radiation, is now a "No Go Zone."

Mr. Uno, when he'd joined Pacific Sushi, had worked as an assistant manager at an office Pacific Sushi had in Kesennuma. Ayako had worked there as a secretary. Her father was a laborer in the fish market, unloading the catch—and by-catch—of ship's. It was very odd that he had married a woman from a family of a much lower social status. Seven months after their marriage in Tokyo, their daughter was born. It didn't require detective skills to figure out that she had seduced him, as a way to escape Kesennuma.

"What a class act," Detective Morita said of Ayako. "Why is it that a woman like her marries a stiff like him?"

I told him what I suspected of her.

"Clever woman," Detective Morita said.

"Do you think she knows that her dullard husband was having an affair and being blackmailed?" Detective Tsuchida said.

"I wouldn't think so," I said.

"Why was he bedding down with this young girl when he had a wife like that?" Detective Izuka said.

"She might have become bored with him," Detective Morita said.

"That makes sense," I said. "You've been married long enough to know those things."

"Tail her," I said. "See if she turns up a lead. You never know what she might turn up, considering she seduced her way out of Kesennuma."

"I'm on her," Detective Izuka said.

"You'd like to be," Detective Morita said, "but you never will me."

They glared at each other. Detective Morita was right. Ayako Uno was out of Detective Izuka's league.

Ayako was a woman whom I would describe as elegant. She wore long skirts and expensive wool sweaters and often a necklace of pearls. Her coats were Burberry. Her hair had a natural red tint, as some Japanese women's hair has. She was maybe one hundred and sixty-five centimeters tall. Her face was heart-shaped, her chin quite pronounced. Her nose was sharp and aquiline, a bit crooked. Her nose was her most distinguishing trait.

Detectives Tsuchida and Morita reported to me her routine, which went something like this. She gave foreigners Japanese lessons at a community center on Monday and Wednesday mornings and now and then had lunch with them. She always seemed to enjoy the lunch. She laughed and made gestures with her arms, as if to add an exclamation to whatever she was saying, How interesting! Some of her students were the wives of U.S. Air Force officers and airmen or even off-duty airmen. The Mizukota Air Base was nearby. One of the airmen tried apparently to get closer to her outside one of the restaurants after lunch, and she politely refused and walked off.

On other days she took a train into Tokyo to do some shopping at a department store or specialty shop in Ikebukuro or across town in the Ginza. She looked right at home in the Ginza, mixing with other women who had money. She usually went into the Mitsukoshi Department store to buy something, like a fountain pen or scarf or pair of kid leather gloves.

When Ayako was in town she always had a coffee at Cafe Veloce, a national chain. Veloce is an ordinary place with cheap coffee, served cafeteria style, which didn't fit her, but she had her reasons for going there—anonymity. Veloce is frequented by all types, businessmen and women, students—university and high school—artists, foreigners, and housewives, who usually sit in a group, chattering away; so it was of some interest that, for several days, she never met anyone at a Veloce near the north entrance to Kanda Station, on the circle Yamanote line. She sat at the counter. A few men made passes at her, which she politely rebuffed with a smile. But she did stay on the phone a lot, texting. I wondered who she was texting, certainly not her husband. It was then that I began to suspect that she, too, had a lover, but she never went off to a love hotel, just straight back to Tachikawa. Then she met a runty little man with wavy hair, turning gray, who had an acne-scarred complexion and was missing the tip of his little finger on his left hand.

CHAPTER NINE

"I know him," Detective Tsuchida said. "He was a yakuza loser. Now he's working as a P.I.. His name is Ohashi Nobuyuki. He has an office near Kanda Station."

We were in a conference room again.

Detective Tsuchida continued, "We met up with Ohashi while on an investigation once, to shake him down for information. He was as tight as an oyster. No help at all, the bastard. We were working a missing person's case. A cute high school girl had disappeared. It turned out that she had run away from home for a couple of weeks but got tired of sleeping in train stations and dealing with perverts. One of her friends mentioned that she had worked with him and referred her to him. He said didn't know anything about her, but I never believed him. When he was in the yakuza he worked as a porn scout. Anyway, a week later, she went home."

"What do you know about him losing?" I held up my left hand, wiggled my little finger.

"Atonement for botching a hit on a member of the Watanambe-gumi who was trying to muscle in on his gang's territory. He was a member of the Yamaguchi-gumi."

The Yamaguchi-gumi, though thinned out by the Act for Prevention of Unlawful Activities by Criminal Gang Members, passed by the Diet in 1995, still nibble around the edges of society, preying on whomever, and whatever businesses that are vulnerable to extortion.

The most recent example of this was in the Kanda Station area, where shop and restaurant owners were paying the yakuza rather than going to the police, which only kept them solvent. There's no end to the yakuza in a society where putting on the right face is more important than the law.

"This Watanabe thug was leaning on *izakaya* owners," Detective Tsuchida said.

An *izakaya* is a tavern that serves meals.

"Is Ohashi the one who shot up that izakaya in Shinagawa a few years back?" I asked.

"That's him. Fired three times, hit three different bottles of the best Scotch whiskey. Never grazed the man his boss wanted him to hit."

I held up my hand again, moving my little finger. "And that's how he paid the price?" I said.

"Yes."

"What does a digit mean to these losers?" Detective Izuka said, "if they're allowed to bed down with an adult actress from time to time? That would more than make up for a missing digit."

"You wouldn't have any fingers left," Detective Morita said.

We all laughed, even Detective Izuka.

"Expensive whiskey went to waste in that *izakaya*," Detective Tsuchida said. "That's a crime in itself."

"The owner closed up his place, moved to another location, from what I heard. No one would go near his place after that," Detective Morita said.

I said to detectives Tsuchida and Morita, "Go see Nao Ujiie, see if she can ID Ohashi as the man with the camera standing outside that Family Mart."

"Yes, sir."

"I can pay her a visit," Detective Izuka said.

"She hasn't called you?" I asked. "What else do you know of Ohashi's past?" I asked detectives Tsuchida and Morita.

"He was a bagman. That's as far as he advanced, before he lost his digit. Five or so years back he left the gang."

"Shooting up an *izakaya* does put an end to a career," I said.

"Now he's running his own blackmail scams," Detective Izuka said, "a real entrepreneur. He does have experience in that area."

I knew that wasn't all he did. He provided a service, even if it was on the shady side. The parents of would-be brides often hire P.I.s to investigate their daughter's choice in a husband, to find out about his family, if any member of it has had a run in with the police —shoplifting, drugs cheating on a university entrance exam, been involved in a traffic accident that resulted in a fatality, or perhaps there's even an illegitimate child in another city. Wives also hire them to tail their husbands, wanting to know if they are having an affair. Ohashi hiring Tomomi? That reeked of blackmail but not of murder.

"There's one more thing," Detective Morita said.

Just then that new tea girl entered the room holding a tray of tea. She was around twenty-two or -three, had a round face, and was a little busty in a push-up bra. Her hair was braided, a requirement for working with the police, tied up by a blue ribbon. Detective Izuka eyed her again.

"As pleasant as a daisy," Detective Morita said after she'd left. He sniffed the air.

Detective Izuka remained silent. Detective Tsuchida said to him, "Cute girl, don't you think?"

"I didn't notice," he said.

Detectives Tsuchida and Morita laughed. "One day your wife will find out," Detective Morita said.

"So what if she does? She can't live without me."

"She might surprise you," Detective Morita said, "the way my brother's wife did."

"Knock it off," I said. "What were you going to say about Ohashi?"

Detective Morita said, "Maybe it's a coincidence."

"But maybe not," Detective Tsuchida said.

"What?"

"We did some checking. Mrs. Uno's maiden name is Ohashi."

That set me back. I would have never connected her and that runty P.I. as being from the same family. "Ohashi is a common name," I said.

"He's from Kesennuma," Detective Tsuchida said.

I couldn't speak.

"He's Mrs. Uno's brother."

"You're sure?"

"Sure."

CHAPTER TEN

The next day Detective Izuka and I, after Ujiie Nao had identified Ohashi as the man who had been taking photos of Tomomi and Mr. Uno entering the Amour, went over to stakeout Ohashi's office, Rising Sun Investigation Services, near Kanda Station. We wanted to know what kind of people showed up there before questioning him and, as unlikely as it was, if Mr. Uno went there to pay him off rather than using a dead drop, often a locker in a station.

Ohashi's office was in a building that was very convenient for almost anyone to get to, because Kanda Station is on three major train lines, the Yamanote, the Sobu, and the Chuo. The Kanda area is known for its bookstores, which have a selection of Japanese first editions dating as far back as the Edo period (1603-1867), to modern fiction, to scientific textbooks on astronomy, physics, various atlases, and even oceanography. Several shops have books that are only related to coin collecting. Valuable coins dating back to the Edo period are in the window behind an array of steel bars.

Ohashi's office was in a building between two bookstores. A person in the P.I. business has to present themselves as upstanding—even if what they are dealing in is anything but—to attract customers and being in the Kanda area presents that false front.

Detective Izuka and I stood across from his office, near the entrance to a bookstore that specialized in history books, while watching mostly women—occasionally a man or middle-aged couple—come and go from Ohashi's office, which was on the third floor. From what I suspected, his office was like other P.I.'s offices I'd been in, very clean and orderly, like that of an insurance broker's or one of those personal loan joints that plunges the borrower into debt that they are unlikely to be able to pay back, the interest rates are so high. Yes, these are often yakuza fronts.

Toward the middle of the afternoon, Ohashi left his office and walked a few blocks to a Veloce and sat by himself at a table and had a coffee. He was decked out in pleated, pinstriped trousers and a matching double-breasted jacket, his uniform. He wanted to make a point with his clients—and those on the street—that he wasn't a dull salaryman, I suppose. It was his uniform, those close.

Detective Izuka and I were fortunate enough to find at a table near him. I was hoping that he'd meet someone, maybe even Ayako, or make a telephone call, but he didn't. He didn't even text anyone. He read a sports paper that had advertisements for soaplands and escort services while drinking his coffee. One section had horse racing cards. He began to circle the names of some horses that were racing at Fuchu, Japan's oldest track. After thirty or forty minutes, he returned to his office.

He looked older than his years, forty-three, and turned out to be a chain smoker and heavy drinker, whiskey and *shochu* who paid former actresses, hostesses, and whatever girl would accept his offer to sleep with him. He had a place over by the Sumida River, across from what Japanese fondly call the "Golden Turd Building," the Asahi Beer Hall. But the golden flame that tops more closely resembles something a person squeezed out. The flame does closely resemble a turd.

Ohashi had carefully spaced out the appointments of his clients so that they never met each other. He closed up at a few minutes past five and took the train home. So did we.

Our stakeout of Ohashi's office was after the weekend Mizuko and I had gone to Sendai to meet Satoshi and his fiance. When I returned home, Mizuko was here. She had grilled fresh *sanma*. She'd served it the traditional way, with grated daikon and, as always, miso soup and Sasanashiki rice, from Miyagi prefecture. All the best rice in Japan is grown up in Tohoku.

I mixed some of the sanma with the daikon and ate it. "Oily," I said, "the way sanma should be."

Mizuko, being the traditional Japanese woman in so many ways, modestly said, "It is rather tasty."

"You're an excellent cook," I said. She smiled. She never knew how to take a compliment. She looked away from me. She was wearing the flower print apron that she always wore when she cooked.

I drank some miso soup, ate a pickle, and drank some tea. We ate silently for a while, listening to the Bill Evans album "Portrait in Jazz." We'd listened to it hundreds of times. Then she surprised me by saying,

"That girl who was found murdered in a Kabuki-cho love hotel, is that the case you're working?" She'd put down her chopsticks.

I couldn't lie. We'd lived together long enough for her to know when I was lying. So I had to face the truth. "Yes," I said. I ate some more *sanma*. I drank some miso soup. I looked at her.

"You could've told me," she said. "You shouldn't protect me from all these cases that remind you . . . You're only damaging yourself."

"I was thinking of you," I said.

"Stop thinking of me. Think of us." She looked at me the way a primary teacher does a misbehaving student, and that's how I felt, about seven-years-old.

"I feel sorry for her parents," she finally said.

It was all I could do to prevent myself from choking and starting to weep. "The soup is good too" was all I could manage to say.

"It's the same soup we always have," she said.

"So it is," I said.

"You don't have to protect me," she repeated.

Did she know? I wondered. Was there a way for her to find out? Was she trying to find out, perhaps even hiring a private detective to learn who the girl was? Was I being paranoid? Probably.

"I'm sorry that the chief puts you on cases like this," she said.

"He doesn't know about Tomomi, of course."

"I forgot. Only we do. And Satoshi. I guess. One day she'll return," she said, "and things will be back to the way they were."

I had to change the topic. "Our trip to Sendai worked out," I said.

"Be honest. You don't like Satoshi's fiance."

"She works in a kennel," I said.

"So she loves dogs. What's wrong with that? A lot of people love dogs."

"I know," I said. "I see them walking them every morning, picking up their shit."

"Maybe we should get a dog?"

"Are you out of your mind? Do either of us have the time to look after a dog?"

"It was just a thought," she said. "Maybe when you retire. We can go on walks with it."

"Maybe a real dog that's knee high. Not one of those toys."

"I expected you to say that. I hope *koyou* is beautiful this year. Last year, you remember, a typhoon came through and blew all the leaves off the trees. How disappointing."

I pulled out the skeleton of the sanma and set it aside and ate some of the fish mixed with daikon. Then a pickle and some rice. I drank some tea.

"Where should we go?" she asked, "I mean to what *onsen*?"

"I'll leave that up to you," I said.

"I'll do some research," she said. "What about one in Nagano prefecture? You don't mind traveling a bit, do you? We'll take the train."

She knew how much I liked riding a train through the Japanese countryside. We had a Honda Fit, but we rarely used it, now that there were only two of us. The trains were faster and there was no parking problem. "That's fine," I said. "I'd like to get out of Tokyo for a few days. We haven't been to Nagano prefecture in a few years."

"I'll find one there. The mountains and an *onsen* will refresh us."

"It's the best part of the year," I said.

We finished dinner and continued to listen to Bill Evans, then Charlie Parker, Dave Brubeck, Erroll Garner, Yousuke Yamashita, Ichiko Hashimoto, and Nate King Cole sing "Mona Lisa," "Unforgettable," "L-O-V-E," and "Stardust." Then, as we laid out our futon and prepared for sleep, we put on a track of Miles Davis's "It Never Entered My Mind," setting it to repeat, and lay on the futon, saying nothing, and went to sleep, feeling the warmth of the other.

CHAPTER ELEVEN

The next day Detective Izuka and I returned to Kanda, to stake out Ohashi's office, and that afternoon, at around two, he left his office to go to the same Veloce he'd been to, dressed in his uniform. This time he sat nervously at a table, drumming his fingers. He kept his hand with the missing digit under the table. I suppose he didn't want to upset any of the other customers.

Ayako Uno showed up ten minutes later.

Detective Izuka and I had gotten a table near them, but not near enough to hear what they were saying, the coffee shop was so crowded. But we reasoned that whatever they were talking about was serious, because their expressions were very stern, unlike the others there who were laughing and smiling or perhaps doing some homework with a boy or girlfriend. And then after fifteen minutes or so Ohashi left and Ayako stayed there. Neither one of them had even sipped their coffees. She called someone, and a few minutes later a man about her age showed up. He was handsome the way a Westerner, an actor like Bradley Cooper, is, who draws women to him while making them fearful of him at the same time.

"It's pretty clear who he is," Detective Izuka said of him.

We learned later that his name was Haruto Murata. He was a section chief, *buchou*, for Neptune, a company that made diving equipment.

He and Ayako may have ordered coffees, but neither

of them did more than take a few sips. Mostly, they whispered to each other for ten minutes or so, and then they left together.

Detective Izuka and I split up. I followed Ayako and Haruto, and Detective Izuka went back to Ohashi's office to stake it out. Haruto and Ayako took the Yamanote Line up to Uguisudani Station, where there was a good selection of love hotels. They went to a classy one called Moonbeam, its entrance on an alleyway off a main street. I felt a little slimy for following them there, but it was my job to do so, I reminded myself. Prying into the private lives of people who may not have committed a crime, that goes with police work, and it brings me no joy at all. Some police take pleasure in discovering something lurid to gossip about, but I don't. I didn't stick around, but returned to Ohashi's office. I told Detective Izuka, "I don't think Ohashi was running a blackmail scam."

We both reasoned that he had hired Tomomi to seduce Mr. Uno, so that he could take photos of him entering a love hotel with her. The photos would secure for Ayako a quick, uncontested divorce. Japanese P.I.'s often do this kind of work. Ayako simply asking for a divorce? He probably wouldn't have granted her one. It would look bad to his boss and the reputation of Pacific Sushi, Uno not being able to handle his wife. If he couldn't handle her, he couldn't handle the people he managed. They could have lived out their lives separately under one roof, but a divorce was out of the question for him.

"See anything of interest?" I asked.

"An old woman who used a walker paid Ohashi a visit," he said. "Why would she be hiring a P.I.?"

"It's not for us to know," I said.

"We all have our secrets, I suppose."

I gave him a hard look. "You do," I said, "plenty."

"They can't be secrets if you know them."

"One day your wife will."

"So what if she does?"

"You shouldn't talk about her that way."

"Our marriage has been going downhill for years. I wish she'd take a lover, make it easier on the both of us."

He suddenly took interest in a pair of girls coming our way. They were dressed in jeans and sweaters and had long hair and bright, optimistic expressions. As they passed, there was the bracing scent of sandalwood. Tokyo University wasn't too far away. I thought they were students there. They went into a bookstore that specialized in old literary magazines.

"They're too intellectual for you," I said.

"My tastes are maturing," he said.

I thought, Ms. Nodoka is out of your league, then.

"I think we should pay Mr. Ohashi a visit," I said.

"Now?" he asked.

"We'll wait until he's closing, so that we don't interfere with his schedule."

Detective Izuka looked off in the direction of the bookstore the girls had entered. "One day you'll grow up," I said.

"Like you?"

"Your children need a father," I said.

"I'm home on weekends," he said. "Most weekends."

"Shameful," I said. "It's good to be happily married. It requires some effort but marriage is rewarding."

"You sound like my great-grandfather, from what I remember of him. My father told me when I was old enough to know about what goes on between a man and a woman that he'd had an *omekake-san* until he could no longer afford her. She saved his marriage." An *omekake-san* is a paid mistress. Literally, a woman to hang one's eyes on. Before, and even for a few years after the Pacific War, it was not at all uncommon for wealthy married men to take an *omekake-san* and set her up in her own home and pay her a monthly stipend. All she had to do was be available when he wanted her. Detective Izuka's grandfather had owned an electronics business that went bust after the war. During the war, he'd made money from military contracts. Wealthy men nowadays set up women the way their ancestors did, but fewer wives, even older, traditional ones, tolerate this the way they used to. They file for a divorce and strike out on their own.

The university girls came out of the bookstore and walked past us. The scent of sandalwood struck me once more, and I thought of the times when I was a student at Waseda. It was a Proustian moment. I recalled girls I'd known when I was a student, before meeting Mizuko. We'd had some good times. One of these university girls looked at Detective Izuka as she passed him and smiled confidently. The breeze coming from the traffic on the street blew her hair off the red crew-neck sweater she was wearing. She wasn't anything like the tea girl at the police building, who looked unsure of herself, as if she were new to Tokyo and didn't know her way around, was lonely and easy prey for some men. This girl was thin, small-breasted, and had a few strands of naturally white strands of hair, which made her look all the more intellectual, wise, and cosmopolitan. She seemed to know it, too. Her confidence and even a hint of pride and insolence made me think of Tomomi.

"Heavenly," Detective Izuka said.

At a little past five Ohashi's receptionist, a stout woman in her fifties, whose hair was dyed a dark shade of red, left his office and came out of the entrance to the building. She walked favoring her right leg, as if she had an arthritic knee, and headed toward Kanda Station.

Up in Ohashi's office, I saw him let down a blind over the window.

"It's time," I said.

We crossed the street and entered the building and took the elevator up to the fifth floor, where his office was, and caught him just as he was locking the door. The name of his agency, Rising Sun Investigation Services, was stenciled on the door under the Japanese battle flag.

Ohashi turned around. "What do you two want?" he asked. He knew right away who we were, but we still showed him our badges.

"We want to talk," I said. Detective Izuka and I had worked out a strategy on how to question him on the way to his office.

"That woman you met in the Veloce is out of your league," Detective Izuka started out.

Ohashi smiled sardonically. "You got it all wrong," he then said.

He had retained the rural Tohoku accent of his youth, which made him sound like a country yokel, not the urban tough guy he wanted others to believe he was. He lit a Seven Stars and then tried to push his way past us.

"You're running a blackmailing scam," I said.

"You were taking naughty photos outside the Amour."

"The love hotel where a young woman was

murdered," I said.

He sucked on the Seven Stars and blew a stream of smoke into our faces, the way a yakuza would.

I looked down at his left hand, seeing the missing digit. "We know about you," I said.

"You wouldn't be detectives who were worth a damn if you didn't."

"You're a loser," Detective Izuka said.

"You can't even shoot straight."

"Ever been to the Nankaitou club?"

"I'm not talking to you two out here in the hall."

He pushed open his office door, and we all went inside. He flipped on the lights. The place had, as I'd suspected, a waiting area, like one at a doctor's office. On the receptionist's desk there was a laptop and behind the desk on a stand a printer under a painting of koi in a pond. Many yakuza have koi tattoos, as a symbol of strength.

The door to his office was past the desk. He opened the door and we went inside. The large window Detective Izuka and I were familiar with dominated the room. Just outside it there was a tangled web of utility lines connected to concrete poles, on which there was a sign for his office and others in the building.

The floor was polished hardwood, like that in a temple. He went behind his desk and sat in a black leather chair that swallowed him up. His desk was an imposing maple colossus, clearly meant to intimidate, and it probably had that effect on most of the people who looked over it at him. But in the leather chair, his head resembled a chestnut, which made him look like a kid pretending to be someone he wasn't. On a corner of the desk in a silver tray he had his *meishi*, which had on it an embossing of the rising sun battle flag. Detective Izuka and I took one.

I removed a photo of Tomomi from my coat pocket of her lying dead in the Amour and showed it to him. This rattled him. He said, "No girl deserves that. No. None of them, no matter what they've done. I got nothing to do with that."

"Sit over there," I told him, "if you don't mind." I pointed at a leather chair across from a sofa, a traditional furniture arrangement for receiving clients, who sit on the sofa.

"I mind," he said.

"Detective Kawayama was being polite. Get over there," Detective Izuka commanded.

Ohashi reluctantly pulled himself out of his big leather chair and hobbled over to the chair opposite the sofa. He was not a man who was in good physical shape, which he had brought on himself with the life decisions he'd made. Yakuza, they're heavy drinkers and smokers. Gout, diabetes, heart disease, lung cancer, and strokes from hypertension put more away than the police do.

He groaned when he sat. "Is this an interrogation?" he asked.

"Gout?" I asked.

"You a doctor too?"

Detective Izuka and I had sat on the sofa. "Mrs. Uno is the one we're after," I said, to rattle him, which it did. He said,

"Who's she?"

"We know more than you think we know."

"She has something to do with this girl's murder," I said.

"She's the classy woman you met in the Veloce. Don't

try to con us."

"Am I?"

"You know you are."

"She had something to do with the murder of a girl in a Kabuki-cho love hotel."

"Don't play your stupid police games on me. She had nothing to do with that and you know it."

"So you do know Mrs. Uno?"

"You know I do. You saw us together."

"If she had nothing to do with the murder of this girl, who did?" I asked.

"I'd like to know myself. He's scum, whoever it is."

"You weren't there when the girl was killed. We know that."

"So you are real detectives."

This timeline fit in with what I was thinking, that Tomomi had been murdered after Ohashi had taken those photos of Jiyumi and Mr. Uno entering the Amour their first time together.

"Is Mrs. Uno a client of yours?" I asked. "Her husband was the one in that room when Jiyumi Harakuju was killed. You know that. Don't you?"

He smoked his cigarette.

"Mrs. Uno's husband is a *buchou* at Pacific Sushi," I said. "He was having an affair with Jiyumi Harajuku."

"I don't know anything about that. If he was, go question him about who killed Jiyumi Harajuku."

"You were blackmailing Uno," Detective Izuka said, "and using Jiyumi Harajuku for that purpose."

The upper corner of the right side of his mouth ticked upward involuntarily. Many Japanese have uncontrollable tics and twitches that give them away.

"I run a clean shop," he said. "I don't use girls to

blackmail company men."

"You use them to get photos for their wives," I said. "Is that what you'd call running a 'clean shop'?"

"Those salarymen are the ones who decide to go to a hotel with a girl. How could I force them? They're weak down there."

"But you do hire girls and one of them ended up murdered?"

"I'm not talking. Find Jiyumi's killer, detectives. Or can you?"

"That's why we're here, talking to you, to find out who killed her. You need to have more confidence in the police," I said.

"What have the police done for me? Not a damn thing."

"You must've learned a few tricks about where to find girls to hire when you were a bagman for the Yamaguchi-gumi?" Detective Izuka said.

"That's all in the past." He ground his cigarette out in a cut glass ashtray on a table between us. "I'm sorry about what happened to Jiyumi Harajuku. If I had something to do with that, I would've turned myself in. I couldn't have lived with myself. I'm Japanese."

I almost choked, him saying that, even if it wasn't so uncommon for killers to do just that, even yakuza who'd killed a rival from another gang. It was the essence of *bushido*. I just doubted that he had that spirit in him.

"How did Jiyumi's parents take the news?" he asked.

I wanted to punch him. In a flush of realization, I'd mistakenly thought that he knew I was Jiyumi's father, that he was baiting me, but then it came to me, by seeing the sad expression on his wrinkled gray face and in his watery eyes, that he was really concerned for her, was even feeling guilty and shameful. I certainly hadn't expected him to have that look. We became instantly closer.

"Mrs. Uno hired you to get something on her husband," Detective Izuka said. "Right? Admit it."

He stared back at us.

"We'll get the truth out of her. Women. They crack easy."

Ohashi nervously fumbled a cigarette out of a pack and lit it and took a long drag on it, but this time he blew the smoke across the room, not into our faces. His expression had changed. No longer was he the tough guy. "Mrs. Uno is my sister," he admitted. "I was doing her a favor. You'll find out. So why not tell you now? Leave her out of this. Please." He stood and bowed. What a shock that was.

I came clean with him and said, "We know she's your sister."

"Damn you!"

"We're police detectives," Detective Izuka said, "not one of your hoodlum friends."

"I'm not in the Yamaguchi-gumi anymore. They're parasites. But you already know I'm not one of them. Don't you?"

I saw no need to answer his question. I said, "We won't threaten your sister if she tells us what she knows."

"How can I trust you?"

"You don't have a choice now, do you?"

"Promise me you'll take it easy on her."

"If she cooperates," I said.

"She will," he said. "She's suffering because of what happened. Plenty. She wants to know who killed her as badly as I do."

"Don't do what I'm thinking you might," I warned him.

He looked back at me and said nothing, which said plenty.

"That man your sister met in Veloce," I said. "Who's he?"

"Don't insult me."

"Her lover?"

"My sister's marriage is not a happy one," he said.

"How did you connect with Jiyumi Harajuku?" Detective Izuka asked.

"I was wrong. You're not detectives. Or you're lying and know you are."

"We know. It was through Junko Atada, wasn't it?" Detective Izuka said.

"Never heard of her."

"Strange. She knows you," I said. I held up my hand and wiggled my little finger. "She knows you so well that she says you have a tattoo of a tiger on your back and that you were born in the year of the tiger. She knows you are missing a digit."

"Were you two fucking?" Detective Izuka said.

"I said I don't know her."

Detective Izuka said, "You're lying. She and Jiyumi worked at the same club."

He didn't say anything, just drew on his cigarette again.

Detective Izuka said, "What're you hiding? Out with it!"

Ohashi looked around the room while smoking his cigarette, thinking about something, before saying, "After what I did for Junko, and she double-crosses me and Jiyumi. You're going to find out, so I'll make it easy for you. Junko made some wrong decisions in her life, got caught up in the film industry. I bailed her out. Got her a job in the Nankaitou. The mama-san and I are old friends. She was an actress too, long back. Is that so bad, what I did for Junko?"

"No."

"So she's the one who connected you with Jiyumi Harajuku?" I asked.

"Yes. Ayako told me that her loser husband might go for a girl like her, if she dressed up as a video avatar. He sometimes stops off to play video games on his way to his train. There was an avatar he likes who has blue hair. What a loser, my sister's husband. He knew nothing of real girls. Nothing."

"I'm sure you do," Detective Izuka said.

"Something wrong with that?"

Detective Izuka smiled in reply.

I hadn't expected Ohashi to volunteer that much information, but it made sense that Ms. Nishikawa would help out girls who had a past similar to hers. But she'd lied to us. That surprised me. And she'd done it so convincingly. What an actor she was. What else was she hiding? I had to wonder. But I doubted that if she was hiding something it had anything to do with Tomomi's murder. We all have our secrets.

"What did you talk about with your sister?" Detective Izuka said, "at the Veloce?"

"What do you think? An innocent girl was murdered because of us. That's something we'll have to live with for the rest of our lives." He drew on his cigarette, let out a stream of his smoke, and could no longer hold in what he'd been thinking all along, saying, "I'll kill the sum when I find him."

"That's what you told your sister?" I asked.

"Of course not. You think I'd be involved in a murder?"

"She's already involved in one."

"She knows she is."

"You shouldn't have told us what you just did."

"I don't care."

"Why did Jiyumi keep on seeing Uno?" I asked.

"You're blaming Jiyumi for her own murder?"

"I didn't mean it to come out that way. No. I just can't understand it."

"We all have our secrets," Detective Izuka said.

I turned and stared at him.

"Don't we," Ohashi said. He laid his left hand on the knee of his pinstriped trousers and glanced at his missing finger. It was a tactic that yakuza used to intimidate club owners and executives in companies, one he hadn't been able to break.

"Don't interfere with this investigation," I said. "If you learn something, call us."

He lit another cigarette. He had the look of retribution in his eyes. I knew he wasn't going to call if he found the killer. He'd kill him.

"If you go after Jiyumi's killer, we'll come after you," I said.

"In a way I'm responsible for her death, aren't I. Go ahead, do me a favor, arrest me."

What a revelation that was, coming from a former yakuza, now a slimy P.I., that he felt responsible for Tomomi's death. I couldn't quite come to terms with who Ohashi was, a slimy P.I., a man with a conscience, or a mixture of the two. Probably the latter.

"What's it like growing up in a dumpy town like

Kesennuma? The place must stink of fish," Detective Izuka then said, to catch him off guard.

"That's disrespectful, after all those people died in the tsunami."

Detective Izuka said, "Sorry. I didn't mean it that way."

He and I bowed, to apologize.

"There's honor among the police. I've never experienced that before."

"If you don't find Jiyumi's killer soon, I will," he said. "Justice must be served."

How ironic that was that a former yakuza thug, a man who now snooped around taking photos of couples entering love hotels, would speak of justice being served. He had the yakuza contacts to track down Tomomi's killer, too, contacts that we didn't have. I feared that he would get to Tomomi's killer before we did. I was the one who wanted to see that he was taken care of. Ohashi wasn't going to deny me that. I thought about arresting him right there, but knew I couldn't. He hadn't done anything. And it was even quite possible that we could use him, that he could lead us to Tomomi's killer.

"If you find who killed her, do yourself a favor and tell us," Detective Izuka said.

He drew on his cigarette and glared back at Detective Izuka. I decided to get at Ohashi another way and said,

"Maybe Uno talks in his sleep and your sister knows something. You wouldn't want her name in the tabloids now, would you?"

"She had nothing to do with the murder."

"She had plenty to do with it," Detective Izuka said. "She's the one who started it all off by having you hire Jiyumi to get some dirt on her husband."

"You know that she didn't kill Jiyumi."

"She might know what went on in that room," Detective Izuka said. "Some husbands talk."

"We're going to talk to her," I said, "to find out for ourselves what she knows. Don't warn her we're going to pay her a visit."

Ohashi said, "I won't. I'll give you some time with your investigation. Then I'll do things my way."

"You're a loser," Detective Izuka said. "You can't even shoot straight. How're you going to take care of Jiyumi's killer when all you've accomplished along those lines is shooting up some bottles of whiskey in an *izakaya*."

"I'll get whoever it was."

"Leave that to us," I said.

"Then find him and stop wasting your time questioning me and my sister. She knows nothing."

"We'll find out for ourselves what she knows," I said.

He nodded his head. "Okay. Talk to her."

"Don't warn her."

"I told you I won't. Are you deaf? Get on with this. Find Jiyumi's killer."

"We will."

"You better do it soon," he said.

"Stay out of police business," I said.

"It's my business. And my sister's."

"I've warned you," I said.

"Can you find your way out?"

Detective Izuka and I stood and left his office.

"Not exactly what I was expecting," Detective Izuka said, out by the elevator.

"He'll carry through on killing this man."

"A loser with a conscience."

"I'm going to give Junko Arata call," I said. "We need to

put some pressure on her."

I called her from the ground floor of the building.

"Mr. Ohashi knows about you," I told her. "You need to watch yourself."

"What? I need protection," she said. "Help me!"

"Call us if he comes near you. I'll see if I can have a court issue an injunction."

"You don't know who he is."

The strange thing is that I thought that the "he" she was referring to was Ohashi, but it wasn't. She was thinking that Ohashi would somehow get to Tomomi's meth dealer before us, and she had her reasons to fear him.

"Be careful," I said and ended the call. "That should do it," I told Detective Izuka.

"How many days will it be before she cracks?"

"Not many. She was about to piss."

CHAPTER TWELVE

We walked back to Kanda Station for the ride to Shinjuku. The crowd of commuters increased the closer we came to the station, becoming like the flow of a river widening as tributaries emptied into it.

We came to the station and went through the ticket reader and took the stairs up to the platform, which was three or four people deep. The Chou Line train arrived, packed, even if Kanda Station was the next station after Tokyo Station, where the line terminated. We got on the train and grabbed a strap and were at Shinjuku South Station about fifteen minutes later and went to the police building and wrote up our reports. By then it was after six.

Detective Izuka gave me his report and put on his jacket, heading for the door.

"Going home?" I asked.

"No. Not straight away."

I didn't want to know more about him and who he was seeing. I took our reports and went to Chief Inspector Saito's office and handed them to him. He'd been waiting for them.

"Just tell me what you learned," he said. "My eyes are old."

I told him about our visit with Ohashi.

"You're sure this girl Junko will talk?"

"She's guilt-ridden and afraid."

"But safe?"

"She's got nothing to fear," I said, which wasn't at all

true.

Chief Inspector Saito said, "The Chinese penetrated our territorial waters with a submarine. The Japanese era has come and gone. How long was it? Twenty years?"

"I suppose," I said.

"I get the feeling, Kawayama, that you don't fear them?"

"What can we do?" I said.

"I hope the Americans don't abandon us. We've got that crazy firing missiles into the Sea of Japan on one side and Chinese flying fighters into our airspace and hiding out in submarines in our territorial waters on the other. The Americans. . ." He sighed. "The way they pulled out of Afghanistan, and with a nut-job president who met with Kim, I get the feeling we're on our own sometimes."

"We've always been on our own," I said.

"Don't you think the Americans will look out for us?"

"I'm not a politician."

"Go home. I've got to go drinking with some higher-ups. I'm a politician. Unfortunately. I wish I were still on the street."

I bid him good night and left the building and returned to Shinjuku South Station and caught the Chuo Line to Yotsuya Station and walked home from there, only a fifteen minute walk or so along narrow streets that are dark and quiet and lined with homes.

On the drawn shoji screens of the traditional homes I saw the shadows of people having dinner. Mizuko was at the Keio Plaza on this night. I would have dinner alone. I couldn't be going to watch her play too often. She'd become suspicious, worried about the case I was working, and I didn't want her to be thinking about that. She might figure things out, and I wasn't prepared for it, for her to come to the realization that Tomomi was dead, murdered.

On the corner up the street from our house there's a Family Mart. I went into it and bought a bento, a prepared dinner, one of grilled salmon, rice, pickles, spaghetti noodles, some *shimeji* mushrooms, and a can of Funaguchi Nihonshu. The cashier was a young man, probably a university student, who I now and then talked to about novels or essays we'd read, but on this evening he sensed that I wasn't in the mood to talk. I think he got some thrill talking to a police detective.

Our house was dark and quiet and lonely. I turned on the light in the *genkan*, took off my shoes, put them away on a shelf there, and went to the kitchen and set the bento and my cup of Nihonshu on the table, then went upstairs and changed into a robe, before making my way back to the kitchen, where I put the bento in the microwave and heated it up. As the microwave was running, I popped open the can of Nihonshu, poured it into a glass, and sipped some of it. I wasn't in the habit of drinking Nihonshu, but from time to time I had a craving for it, and this was one of those days. Funaguchi isn't the best Nihonshu, by any means. A person would never find good Ninhonshu in a convenience store, but it was good enough for me. It went down like spring water. I didn't keep any bourbon in the house. I didn't want bourbon to become a habit.

The bento came with what we are called *warabashi*, the chopsticks that you pull apart. I ate while imagining that Mizuko was at the table with me and that we were having a boring conversation about the weather or a television show or something one of us had seen that day that had caught our attention—a car accident, two lovers quarreling, an old couple who looked happy together—but none of that kept away my loneliness and, worse, shame over Tomomi's death.

I couldn't get it out of my mind, as I chewed on that dry salmon and ate that crusty rice, that Tomomi had left us and ended up murdered. It had been my fault for not controlling my anger and striking her. I'd never even struck a suspect during an interrogation, which I was very proud of, unlike a few detectives who do resort to those means to extract a confession. I thought of what Mizuko had told me once about shame having a positive aspect, that we could learn from it and become better persons, but I was in a place that was far, far away from being an enlightened Buddhist. I wanted to believe in Buddhism, be a better person because of my beliefs, but it wasn't in me to feel that way. When I think about Buddhism, it just seems to be another set of religious ideals that attempts to make sense of an irrational, hostile world. And so I drank the Nihonshu and in that way I felt some release from the nihilistic world in which I lived my life.

After finishing off the bento, I went into the living room and turned on the television and began to watch the NNK news. There was a story about the Chinese submarine that Chief Inspector Saito had mentioned. The Japanese Navy, which we euphemistically called the Self Defense Force, had located it using American technology and our foreign minister had filed a protest with the Chinese ambassador, something that meant little. They'd do it again. I don't remember any of the other stories.

After the news, I watched a documentary on the Inca civilization of Machu Picchu, which I rather enjoyed, but all the time there was the *butsudan* off to my left, where Mizuko rang that brass bell every morning. The bell was next to the incense holder and a photograph of Tomomi in her high school uniform. The sound of the bell rang throughout that empty house, and it must have been the Nihonshu that released my subconscious just enough so that John Donne's famous line about the tolling of a bell came to mind.

Then my attention went back to the documentary about Machu Picchu. The Incas had had engineers who were skilled enough to build walls that didn't fall over during earthquakes and had terraces for maize. They were living a peaceful life. And then the Conquistadors came along. That wasn't so different from Japan, when it had been isolated during the Edo era; then it opened up to the West in the 1860s, which had led to two wars with China, one with Russia, and the last one with our now allies, the Americans. I had to admire the Americans for how they'd treated us after the war, unlike the Chinese and Russians, who would have occupied Japan, no doubt

I was on the sofa when Mizuko woke me.

"Time to go to sleep," she said.

I grunted.

"Nihonshu?"

"A little."

"Get upstairs and take a bath. I'm not sleeping with a man who smells like he pissed in his pants."

I got up off the sofa and we went upstairs. On the way, Mizuko said, "A man promised to marry me tonight, take me to Monte Carlo. He said he'd buy me champagne every night and let me play roulette as long as I liked."

"You had your chance," I said.

"I wouldn't have anyone to talk to," she said. "What would I have in common with a bunch of rich Europeans?"

"Does it matter if you're rich and drinking champagne who you talk to?"

"I'm not one of them. I'm Japanese. Keep moving up the stairs. You only have a few more steps."

She drew my bath, and while I was waiting for the tub to fill I washed myself and started to think about the case. What would Ayako Uno have to say? When would Junko Atada crack? Would Ohashi break his promise and seek revenge, killing Tomomi's killer? Would he kill Mr. Uno?

I got into the bath and not long after that Mizuko came into the bathroom and washed herself and got into the tub with me. "Do you mind?" she asked.

"It's been awhile," I said.

"I needed this bath. I'm getting old. My back aches from time to time."

"You could be flying to Monte Carlo right now," I said, "sipping champagne on a private jet. That would do your back good."

"I don't think so."

"You'd make friends. Find a place to play jazz piano."

"I don't think he'd let me. Rich husbands don't allow their wives to play the piano in a hotel bar." Her face turned red from the hot water. She had a Japanese round face, a bit freckled. Her eyes had a hint of gray in them. Above her left breast there was a mole. She now and then said that she wished it had been on her left or right cheek, so that she would look like a Japanese

Marilyn Monroe. "Have you given any more thought to retirement?" she asked.

I didn't say anything. I was thinking of the case again, how to proceed.

"You're ignoring me," she said.

"What did you say?"

She splashed water in my face. I splashed her back. We laughed. It was a brief solace. Her breasts, well, we were both aging. I had put on a few kilos. At home and at train stations the staircases were becoming steeper and longer and more exhausting to climb. I'd taken to riding the escalators from time to time.

"You need a hobby," Mizuko said. "All you've been is a detective. A year after your retirement, you'll be dead if you don't find another interest."

"Are we going to move to Shizuoka or Wakayama prefectures, where it's warm, like all the other old people?"

"We're staying right here," she said, very adamantly. "I love our house. This bath is ours." She dangled a leg over the edge.

"That's lewd," I said.

"We used to be that way," she said, "lewd." She grinned and wiggled her toes, smiled at me, then went on to say, "I saw a man's shell collection on Okinoerabu when I was a university student, long before my life turned a corner and I accepted an *omiai* to meet this fool English literature major. The man had categorized all different kinds of shells, by size and shape and put them into a case. The collection was quite beautiful. No telling how long it took him to collect all those shells. He was a retired principal at the primary school."

Okinoerabu was one of the islands between Kyushu

and Okinawa. The archipelago went as far south as Taiwan.

"Shells?" I said. "Are you mad, me collecting shells and sorting through them?"

"It isn't too far from what you do now, sorting things out. Is it?"

"I'll go on walks with my wife," I said. "I'd like to see Tokyo as a tourist, not a detective, for a change."

She smiled.

We got out of the bath and dried off and went to the futon and lay on it and my mind started to wander again. I thought of the case, uncertain about how it would proceed. And then Mizuko pushed herself up against me and I became a man.

CHAPTER THIRTEEN

The next morning I was at my desk going through the newspapers I always buy in the morning from a woman at a kiosk in the Shinjuku South Station, when I came across an article in the *Asahi Shimbun* about the intentional mislabeling of maguro in the sushi industry. The scam was relatively easy to carry out. Once the high grade tuna were caught, they could be mixed with tuna that were of a lower grade. Inspectors could be paid off. It was easy to switch around different grades of frozen maguro and sell the lower grade for one that was a premium grade.

The people eating maguro, they might think they were eating a premium grade of maguro when in fact they weren't, all because of the corrupt inspectors who graded the maguro and, more to my way of thinking, where these people were eating it, in high-end sushi joints where the reputation of the place affected their ability to taste the difference between two different grades. The atmosphere of a particular shop, that's what influenced people's tastes, not so much the actual taste. If a person had bought the highest grade tuna from a Family Mart, I am convinced they would have passed it off as inferior to the mislabeled maguro from a high end place that they raved about.

One of the sushi distributors listed in the *Asahi* story was Pacific Sushi. When I saw that name, I thought of Mr. Uno sitting in his office reading the same article, fearing that someone from the Ministry

of Fisheries would come and knock on his door, asking
him to produce the paperwork that proved the sushi
his company was distributing was indeed the premium
grade the company claimed it was.

Mislabeling of other meats is nothing new in Japan.
There had already been scandals involving the poultry,
pork, and beef industries. In Europe and China, a few
rogue McDonald's owners passed off horse meat as beef
in the burgers. So it was reasonable to think that those
in the sushi industry were not above doing the same.
The yakuza had to have their hands in the mislabeling
scandal, because a lot of money was involved. If the
yakuza could pressure someone in a company to play
their game, they would, and Mr. Uno, considering how
weak-willed he was and how much of a company man
he was, who placed appearance above honesty, would
be a primary target of theirs. Him going to a love hotel
and ending up in a room in which a young woman
had been strangled with a telephone charging cord,
that was something the yakuza could use to pressure
him into cooperating with them. But it didn't quite
explain who had murdered Tomomi. I just couldn't
believe that anyone in the yakuza would. They do have
their misplaced codes, and killing an innocent girl and
profiting from her murder, that was something they
were unlikely to do.

I called the *Asahi Shimbun* and got the reporter
who had written the story, a woman named Sayoko
Kumagai, and told her I wanted to talk to her. We
agreed to meet at the Blue Bean coffee shop near
Shinjuku South Station. I'd had a coffee there from time
to time after doing some shopping in Tokyu Hands,
a shop nearby that sells pens and mechanical pencils

and interesting electronical gadgets. It's a popular place with high school students and retirees with a hobby.

The Blue Bean is in East Shinjuku, near the busy Shinjuku Sanchome intersection. It's a spacious coffee shop on the second floor, above some exclusive clothing stores. It has a shiny blue counter that is up against a large window that wraps around the corner of the building. The window has a nice view of the main street, affording customers the pleasure of enjoying their coffees as they watch people and traffic pass by below. A few blocks away is the mesmerizing traffic of trains, coming and going from Shinjuku Station. Kabuki-cho is down a pedestrian mall that is across the street from the Blue Bean, and from the counter a customer can see the kitschy rooftop neon signs of some of the love hotels. The one that has prominence every night is one of a crescent moon that twinkles invitingly. A couple is sitting on the moon, the way they would a swing. The hotel is called Moonbeam.

I waited for Ms. Kumagai at the entrance. She didn't keep me waiting long. We introduced ourselves and exchanged *meishis* and went inside and got our coffees at the counter and found a table toward the rear up against a wall on which there were some monochrome arty photos of coffee beans and coffee workers carrying baskets of beans on their shoulders. They were all smiling, as if they were enjoying the back breaking, low paying job they were performing.

"You aren't my idea of a detective," she said, looking at my tie. I was wearing a green one with gold, red, and yellow maple leaf prints, in anticipation of *koyou*. Mizuko had bought it.

Ms. Kumagai was a small woman, perhaps one

hundred and fifty centimeters tall, and made no attempt to make herself appear taller. She was wearing brown leather pumps and boxy tweed trousers that made her look even shorter. Her shirt was plaid print, and over it she had on a green vest that was buttoned. Her hair was short. She wore tortoise shell glasses, the lenses making her eyes slightly bigger and bookishly attractive. If she was wearing makeup, I didn't notice it. The only jewelry she had on was a braided leather strap around her right wrist. She gave me the impression of being a very dogged, determined reporter. Small women, they seem to have something to prove.

"Thank you for meeting me," I said.

She sipped her black coffee and put the cup down. "It's a pleasure," she said. "I'm happy to know that someone other than a fisheries inspector has an interest in these mislabeling schemes. But why a police detective?"

I realized that during our conversation on the phone I hadn't told her I was a homicide detective. I told her.

She drew back, a look of horror registering on her cute little face just momentarily.

"A yakuza turf war murder?" she then asked, after regaining her composure. "I would've known about it. Who was murdered?"

"The investigation is ongoing," I said. "I can't tell you the details. But it might involve the yakuza and this company, Pacific Sushi, that you mentioned in your story."

"You've got to tell me," she demanded. "This is a real story!"

"You'll be the first reporter I leak the story to, if there is one," I said.

She smiled. Her cuteness was infectious. She sipped

her coffee. "I'll hold you to that," she said. "Can't you give me a tip, just a crumb to nibble on?"

"No."

"I had to ask, you understand."

"You're a reporter," I said, "for the *Asahi*, my favorite paper."

"Flattery will get you everywhere," she said and smiled again. I had the feeling that she was flirting with me, but that might have been just my imagination. I felt that there was an intimacy between us and couldn't stop myself from saying, "The murder is of a young woman."

"I know about her. What happened?"

I told her, and the distance between us closed a bit more, a dangerous thing when conducting an investigation and I'm searching for facts. But I couldn't help myself. She had a reporter's way of having people trust her and I'd been needing someone to talk to.

"This is off the record," I said and hesitated.

"Please," she said.

"The man who was with her is a *buchou* at Pacific Sushi," I said.

She drew back. "What a story!"

"I said it's off the record."

"But you'll tell me before the story breaks?"

"Yes. I promise you that. I'll give you the scoop."

She thanked me. I could see in those intelligent eyes of hers the look of someone craving recognition for her reporting. She might have been bucking up against an arrogant male editor whom she had to prove herself to.

"Is it Mr. Uno?" she asked.

Not much escaped her. I said nothing.

She continued on, "Maybe it was a renegade yakuza

looking to freelance."

"Don't stick your nose into this investigation. Understand me?"

"Of course I won't," she said. "I was just imagining a scenario."

"We have no solid evidence to back up that scenario."

"We both start with hunches," she said. "Sometimes they go nowhere; other times not."

"My hunches sometimes allowed my superiors to take credit for my arrests, when they could get publicity from them."

"At least I get a byline," she said. She laughed. "Excuse me. I shouldn't be laughing. A girl was murdered."

"Her parents would appreciate your respect for them."

"I usually don't meet with homicide detectives, just those in fraud."

"Your story might prove to be helpful. Any follow-ups planned? You owe me, too."

"I'm working on a series," she said. "People don't know what they're eating. They need to know. But murder. I couldn't ever have imagined that anything I do would be connected to such a murder. Yes, if I come across anything that I think might help you out I'll let you know."

"You wrote in your story how much money is involved. Money is often the handmaiden of murder," I said.

"Very poetic," she said.

I told her about myself. The stress and shame I'd been feeling drained away a little.

"The study of literature helps you understand people," she said.

"People aren't so difficult to understand," I said, "and

murder falls into a few categories. Money, jealousy, sex, and greed."

"I work with men who are jealous of my work, but I don't think they'd kill me."

I remembered Tomomi's sarcasm. Only intelligent people had the capacity to understand it.

"Do you have any hobbies?" she asked.

This was an odd question that had taken a turn toward uncomfortable familiarity.

"Collecting sea shells," I said.

"Interesting!"

"It's a bit like detective work." I went on, as if I knew what I was talking about, and said, "sorting through the shells, categorizing them by shape and color, it takes my mind off my work. I need to do something with my hands."

"I understand," she said. "Maybe we could talk about your hobby another day?" she said. "Could you show me some photos?"

"I don't have any." I was sure she didn't believe that. I drank some coffee. I knew where that invitation would lead and wasn't going there.

"My wife is the one who suggested I take up the hobby," I said. "She plays jazz piano at the Keio Plaza."

"I didn't mean to suggest . . ."

"It's quite all right," I said.

"It must be difficult, being married to a police detective, him always thinking about the cases he's working, not really being there sometimes," she said. "You aren't lonely, coming home to an empty home?"

"No," I said.

She smiled a coy smile. The promise of sex. That was a way to extract information from some men, and she seemed to have experience in that area.

"How did you ever end up as a homicide detective? Why aren't you a university professor? That's how you come across."

"Too many Dirty Hairy movies," I said.

She laughed. "He was a bit before my time, but I've seen a few of them on DVD. 'Now how many shots did I fire, was it five or six? In all the confusion, I can't remember.'"

"They were before my time, too. I saw them on DVD as well. Clint Eastwood was inspirational. What a fool I was to think I would be anything like him. I'm just a dull bureaucrat. My wife is the one with the career."

"I'll have to listen to her play one night. I like jazz."

"Please do," I said. I then told her I needed to get back to the police building.

"Hope we meet again," she said.

I wasn't sure if she meant this as a friendly or professional meeting.

We went down to the ground floor and walked along the street in the direction of Shinjuku South Station and through the station. The announcements for train departures and arrivals were going off every few seconds. I could feel the rumble of trains on the floor.

We talked about global warming, of all things, and how *koyou* might turn out this year. Sayoko, too, went to a mountain *onsen* to enjoy the turning of the leaves, a hot spring bath, and the specialty foods of the local area where the *onsen* was.

"But I've got no one to go with this year," she added.

"Not a girlfriend?"

"What a bore."

"There's plenty of men out there," I said.

"They're all bores." She smiled.

"Not all of them."

In the middle of the station, as people parted like water around us, she said, "There's some sadness in it, isn't there? the changing of seasons, the marching on of time."

"Inexorable time," I said.

"Dirty Harry never talked that way. You're no Dirty Harry."

What could I do but smile? I thought, *If I were younger and single.*

We passed the newsstand kiosks and bento stands and the lines of people standing before machines buying tickets, mostly out-of-towners, I reasoned, who didn't have a commuter or Tokyo day pass app.

Sayoko said, "It was a pleasure. You promised to give me that scoop."

"I will," I said.

She took a different exit and, as I walked back to the police building, my mind began to wander. I thought of leisurely walks with Mizuko through the older sections of Tokyo over by the Sumida River, or in Yanaka, where there are some old temples on a hill overlooking Asakusa, which the B-29 incendiaries had pretty much burned to the ground. A path leads through some cherry trees on the hill above Nippori Station near a temple, making it a very popular place during *hanami*, cherry blossom viewing season, when the karaoke machines crank up and drunks bellow out *enka*, Japan's country music.

All this revelry keeps Mizuko and I away. We prefer, if we venture out during *hanami*, to go to an isolated river in a city in the countryside that has levees along the banks of a river to prevent flooding, as so many rivers in Japan have. The levees often have a line of cherry trees along them. A river that flows naturally from its source to the sea, that's a rarity.

CHAPTER FOURTEEN

When I got back to my desk, I looked for Detective Izuka, but he'd checked out, and I had a feeling what that meant. He'd done this before. I asked Detectives Morita and Tsuchida if they knew where he was, and Detective Morita said, "I can make a guess."

That explained it. He was with a girl, probably that tea girl.

Detectives Morita, Tsuchida, and I went into a conference room, and I told them about my meeting with Ms. Kumagai and that I wanted them to once again go through the stack of CCTV disks they'd collected from shops near the Amour. "This time," I told them, "look for a yakuza entering the Amour."

"Boss," Detective Morita said, "we've found our man. I thought."

"I'm looking for a renegade yakuza," I said, "who might have killed Jiyumi and used the murder to blackmail Mr. Uno."

We left the conference room, and I returned to my desk and got to thinking about the history of the yakuza and the feudalistic Edo period. The yakuza got its name from a card game called *ochio-kabu,* which is similar to baccarat. The losing hand is eight (ya), nine (ku), and za (three). So yakuza take pride in being a band of losers. The Edo period was a time in which everyone had a designated place in society, the losers as well. Society was a stable pyramid. The emperor was at the top; merchants were at the bottom. The samurai and their *daimyos* were in the middle; farmers were just below them in status, because they grew the rice that everyone depended on to survive. It was a rigid system that held up for more than two hundred years, until Commodore Perry sailed into Tokyo Bay in 1853 with four steam-powered war ships, threatening to fire on Tokyo if he were not allowed to come ashore to deliver a letter, demanding that Japan open to foreign trade. The Treaty of Amity and Commerce followed, five years later, and Japan began to develop rapidly, becoming a modern country by the end of the nineteenth century.

The yakuza losers of the Edo period have, in modern Japan, turned corporate. The various gangs even have offices, in spite of the *Law to Prevent Unjust Acts by Organized Crime Group Members or Anti-Boryoku Dan Law* that the Diet passed in 1992, in an attempt to end organized crime. Where there's people, there's crime, and where there's crime, there's organized crime. As with any organization that seeks to survive in a highly regulated marketplace, many of today's yakuza changed. They are often graduates of prestigious universities who have weaseled their way into major banks or investment and insurance companies, where the big money is, to sniff out accounting cover ups and sex scandals involving executives. The yakuza soldiers —mostly poorly educated and from rural areas, men like Ohashi—never make it up the yakuza's corporate ladder.

Unlike in the West, where gangsters might make an attempt to blend in with others, yakuza soldiers do not. They want others to know who they are; and in a country where so many of us look and dress the same, it's not so difficult for them to achieve this by wearing flashy Italian suits that have jackets with peaked collars, tailored shirts, and silk ties. Their hair is slicked back, permed into curls, like Buddha's, or they have a brush cut. They may wear dark glasses. A boss might consider himself to be a modern *daimyo*—leader of a samurai clan—and is driven around in a black Mercedes Benz that is so polished that a drop of rain water beads up on the hood. There's irony there, that the yakuza, who believe they are the last holdout for Japanese traditions, drive a Mercedes Benz. Why? Because most Japanese drive a white Toyota.

Detective Izuka returned smelling of jasmine soap. I thought about asking him where he'd been but resisted. He was a good detective. I needed him to help me find Tomomi's killer. I just worried for him, that he might slip up and get fired. I didn't think that, even if the yakuza got some dirt on him, that he'd become an informant. Some police did, some with desks on floors above the floor my desk was on.

I told him about the mislabeling sushi scandal and my hunch that Mr. Uno was involved in it.

"Tsuchida and Morita are going through that CCTV footage again, to see if a yakuza entered the Amour," I said.

"How many yakuza were in bed with a girl in the Amour on that night? Maybe it would be better if we leaned on Uno, now that this sushi mislabeling scam broke in the *Asahi*—make him believe we're onto him."

"It's a risk."

"He's not a man who's experienced being questioned by the police. He's not Ohashi. Do you want Ohashi to question him? He will. And not in a polite way. He might even kill him."

He was right.

"Okay. We'll have a friendly chat with him," I said.

I thought it was better to catch Uno on his way to Seibu Station, rather than the American detective's way of barging into his office, flashing our badges, and humiliating him in front of those he managed. The gossip mill, which had already started to churn because of that *Asahi* story, would churn faster, and he might do something that these executives often do in circumstances like this, kill himself. He wouldn't be saying much then.

Mr. Uno, even in a flow of commuters heading for Shinjuku or Seibu stations, was easy enough to spot when he came out of the office tower Pacific Sushi was in. His complexion was a sickly white, like that of a grub worm found under a rotting log. His chin was round and without distinction. He walked with his head down, distraught; his dark blue tailored wool suit was wrinkled, his hair disheveled. The lenses of his glasses were smudged. A few specks of dandruff lay on the shoulders of his suit. This suit wasn't one he'd bought at the discount chain store Aoyama, where most of the police shopped. I wouldn't have been surprised if the men, and certainly the women, who saw him whispered about him behind his back, that he was hiding some personal troubles because of his appearance.

Mr. Uno didn't in any way present himself as a *buchou* in a major Japanese company, but with the exception of a Hermes attache case he was holding. Maybe Ayako or Uno's mother had picked it out for him. He probably hadn't done his own laundry or cooked a meal for himself his entire life. Maybe he couldn't even make himself a cup of green tea. I knew this kind of man. I'd been in classes with them in university. They were studious, outperformed me and everyone I knew on examinations, but they lacked the ability to connect with others, especially girls. They would become the man their mother wanted them to be, looking successful in their expensive suits and owning a modern house in the western suburbs; their children would get into prestigious private schools and wear the uniforms that identified them as successful.

I thought of Tomomi, what it must have been like for her to be with this man. He was exactly the kind of man she would mock. The lead singer of The Little Nipples would never bed down with such a man, I'd thought. Then I thought of her bank account. He must have paid her well. My daughter could be had by a man who had money, not a thought I wanted to admit to, but there had to be some truth to it. Ohashi had only paid Tomomi once for those photos.

I came up to Mr. Uno from behind him, on his left side, and Detective Izuka on his right, as he was walking along under the shade of a maple. I said, "Pardon me, are you Mr. Uno of Pacific Sushi?"

He stopped, like his feet had grown roots and were preventing him from taking another step. "Yes, I am," he answered. "What can I do for you?"

Detective Izuka and I both showed him our badges. He snapped up as straight as a bamboo pole used to hang futons over.

"What's this about?" he asked. "The inspectors for the Ministry of Fisheries have finished their work."

I hadn't heard about this and thought I'd made a mistake by not contacting them before deciding to question him. I said, "Oh, the inspectors. Yes. I heard something about them. But we're the police. We need to ask you some questions as well. Sorry we didn't call."

"I'm glad you didn't," he said. "My secretary would've taken the call."

"Wouldn't want word to get out," Detective Izuka said.

A tic started in the corner of his right eye, behind the smudged lens of his glasses. I knew what he was nervous about, of course, and it had nothing to do with maguro.

"Let's go over to a coffee shop and have a little talk," I said.

Detective Izuka added, "About a young girl."

The tic in his eye twitched more rapidly.

A coffee shop called the Treble Clef was in an office tower's basement level, on a concourse that led to Shinjuku Station. Along the concourse were expensive designer clothing stores and several restaurants, both Japanese and Western. Now and then Mizuko and I met at the Treble Clef and had a coffee. It was conveniently located between the police building and the Keio Plaza. The coffee shop had an area of cluttered little tables that had fake marble tops, resembling one of those Parisian sidewalk cafes. The chairs were made of flimsy wrought iron and wicker.

Mr. Uno, as the three of us made our way over to the Treble Clef, walked with his head down, as a man going to the gallows might. Soon after we'd sat down at a table in a corner we handed him our *meishis* and he said, "Homicide detectives? I have a train to catch."

I had underestimated him. I had to give him some credit for attempting to resist us with this weak excuse. He was showing a dash of courage.

I said, "We all have trains to catch."

"We're in Japan," Detective Izuka said, "not the Philippines. There's trains. Plenty."

"I don't have anything to say that I haven't said already," Mr. Uno said. "That article in the *Asahi*, it's all lies. I don't know anything about a homicide."

"Sure," Detective Izuka said.

Uno definitely had the look of a defeated man. That evening TV Asahi News aired a story on the maguro mislabeling scandal. Inspectors from the Ministry of Fisheries had showed up at the office of Pacific Sushi and carted off boxes of documents and several computers, putting them in waiting vans. The next day I got the lead inspector of the Ministry Fisheries on the phone and told him about the case I was working and that it might be connected in some way to this mislabeling scheme.

"How?" he asked.

"I don't really know," I said. "I'm just playing a hunch that there's a yakuza connection, that one of them had something on Mr. Uno. He was having an affair with a girl that was found dead in a Kabuki-cho love hotel."

"I read that story. Terrible. But Mr. Uno?" he said. "Are we talking about the same man? What kind of girl would be interested in him?" Then he caught himself and added, "He is pulling down a high salary. Girls nowadays. They can be had for a designer handbag or the latest iPhone. I have a daughter. If she . . ." And then he realized that the conversation might veer into one that was more personal.

"I have a daughter, too," I said.

"It's not easy being a father these days."

"If it ever was," I said.

He laughed. "We expect a yakuza connection as well," he said. "You'll be the first one I call if my team turns up some evidence to connect him to the yakuza. That girl deserves justice."

This inspector did contact me, but by that time the case had sorted itself out in ways that I couldn't have predicted and also in ways that I had to conceal.

A cute young waitress in a French maid's uniform that included a white pinafore trimmed with lace, the treble clef logo on the collar of the white blouse, came to our table. I ordered three coffees.

"*Kashikomarimashita*," she said and bowed. Loosely translated, this means, certainly, or, of course.

"Nice figure, that one," Detective Izuka said. He added, "There's probably plenty of her type in Pacific Sushi."

Mr. Uno stared back at him, looking a little puzzled. He might have been inexperienced with life, but he wasn't stupid.

"I'm a married man," he said.

The waitress brought us our coffees, all in little cups on saucers. The handles were so small that only a child could have gotten a finger through one. I sipped my coffee. The taste made me think of the coffee I'd had at the Blue Bean earlier that day and my conversation with Sayoko Kumagai, and I don't mean when we were talking about the mislabeling scam, but about me letting go a little about Tomomi's murder. Now I was regretting that I had. It was a private matter between Mizuko and I.

Mr. Uno looked at his coffee.

"Have some," Detective Izuka said to him.

"I don't have affairs," he said.

"If I were a big shot like you, the thought would cross

my mind," Detective Izuka said. "How could a real man not?"

Mr. Uno said incredulously, as a child might when learning that the Earth is round, "You're unfaithful?"

I said, "A young woman turned up dead in a Kabuki-cho love hotel."

The tic in the corner of his eye picked up.

"A charging cord was wrapped around her neck."

"Ever been to the Amour in Kabuki-cho?"

"No. Of course not. I don't know anything about that, that . . . What's this about, your reason for questioning me?"

"A murder investigation," I said. "We just thought you might know something about it."

Detective Izuka said, "The dead girl, her name is Jiyumi Harajuku. She was a hostess at a club called the Nankaitou near Tameike-sanno Station. Is that where you met her? Maybe you're a regular customer and have a bottle of whisky with your name on it there?"

"I didn't have anything to do with a murder," he said.

"We're going to find out if you did," I said.

"Ms. Nishikawa. She runs a place that is a refuge for girls who've made some wrong decisions."

"Wonderful woman."

"I don't know what you two are getting at," Mr. Uno said. He reached down to pick up his coffee cup, did, but his hand was trembling so badly that some of the coffee sloshed out of the cup onto the table. The waitress was right there to clean up the spill. She smiled at him, but he wasn't looking at her.

"Thank you," I told her.

She bowed.

"Very sweet," Detective Izuka said, "I wouldn't be able

to resist."

"I, I, I don't know this girl you're talking about, and I don't go to clubs unless I'm forced to."

I said, "You met this girl at the Nankaitou, and you began an affair with her, or, rather, you paid her to have an affair with you."

"We have a surveillance video of you with her," Detective Izuka said.

Mr. Uno looked at Detective Izuka. "We were, were, we were just friends. Only friends. We played video games together."

"Of course," Detective Izuka said, "the way I'd be a friend with that waitress there."

"Are the yakuza blackmailing you?" I asked.

"What?"

"Are they blackmailing you?"

"No. Why would they? How could they?"

"There was that article in the *Asahi*," Detective Izuka said.

"You. Girl. She was found dead in the Amour love hotel where the two of you went. There's a line of reasoning there," I said.

"We were only friends, I'm telling you."

"How much is the yakuza squeezing Pacific Sushi for?" Detective Izuka asked.

"You're wrong. You and those inspectors from the fisheries. That *Asahi* story. It's not true, not true, none of it. My company is honest. I'm faithful to my wife. That story is going to ruin me."

"'Honest' and 'company' shouldn't be used in the same sentence," I said. "As for a man saying he is faithful to his wife, only those who aren't say that."

"How's your wife?" Detective Izuka said.

"What? My wife? Why bring her into this?"

"You're the one who did."

"Maybe she'd like to know you had a lover?" I said.

"You don't know it all. You just don't. Who's the one blackmailing whom? I'd say it's the police who are intimidating an innocent man." He clutched the handle of that Hermes attache case. "I've got a train to catch," he said. "My wife will be worried if I don't return on time."

"Give her a call," I said. "How many times are you late returning from work? Weren't you late when you were sleeping with Jiyumi Harajuku? Go ahead, call your wife. Tell her to keep your curry rice and miso soup warm. *buchous* like you are often late. Ayako will understand."

"Sit back down," Detective Izuka said.

He sat. "You know my wife's name?"

"We know plenty," I said.

"What was Jiyumi's favorite video game?" Detective Izuka asked.

"What?"

"You said you only played video games with her. What was her favorite?"

"Final Fantasy," he said.

"Tell me about that one," I said.

"It's just a game, someone trying to rescue a friend from a castle plagued with rats, bats, spiders, things like that. If they go into the wrong room they meet up with a monster."

"You're a *buchou*?" Detective Izuka said.

"It relieves stress, playing those games."

"What about golf? That's what so many *buchous* do because they can afford to."

"There's no stress relief in that. I can't play that game. It just makes a fool of me."

"That little ball makes fools of many," I said.

"It seems you're forced to do a lot of things you'd rather not do—go to clubs, play golf. What else?"

"It's part of my job, socializing."

"I'm glad I'm just a police detective," I said. "No little white ball is going to make a fool of me."

"So what happens if a person rescues their friend in this rat-infested castle?" Detective Izuka asked.

"What?"

"The video game. Final Fantasy."

"She gives him a kiss."

"The friend is a girl?"

"Well, yes."

"How could a computer avatar give a man a kiss?" Detective Izuka said.

"The player has to use his imagination."

"I prefer the real thing." Detective Izuka looked in the direction of the waitress. "How could a video avatar satisfy a real man?"

"So maybe you didn't kill Jiyumi," I said, "but maybe you know who did?"

The corner of his eye had never stopped twitching, but now his right cheek started to tic.

"You know who did," Detective Izuka said.

"We're on your side," I said.

He hesitated before managing to get out, "No one is on my side. I'm a failure. I've shamed my mother and father and all my ancestors and family." He dropped his head, defeated, or like someone before a Shinto shrine praying. Then he lifted it again and said, "No one can help me."

"You should've thought of how you shamed your family before you went to the Amour with Jiyumi," I said.

"I really must be going," he said. "My wife will be worried."

"We're not stupid," Detective Izuka said, "so don't talk to us like we are. *buchous* often work late. Or they use that as an excuse."

"Go on, call Ayako," I said. "Tell her you have some work to do, and will be late for your curry rice."

"A *buchou* doesn't think of his wife," Detective Izuka said. "They think of their company. So what if you had a girl? You're a *buchou* at Pacific Sushi. Having a cutie on the side would give you prestige. Men would admire you."

Mr. Uno stared at Detective Izuka. I honestly think, as unbelievable as it seems, that he had never heard a man talk to him like that in his life. What easy prey he must have been for Tomomi, I thought, for her to seduce him and for her to fix it so that Ohashi got the photos his client needed.

"You've got it all wrong," he said, "both of you. I'm not that sort of man. I've told you. Believe me, won't you? I know other men do those sorts of things, but I don't. I have a son and daughter and wife, a nice house in Tachikawa."

"We know all that," I said.

"You know?"

"We're detectives," Detective Izuka said.

"Your wife's name is Ayako," I said.

"Have you told her?"

"We know plenty," Detective Izuka said.

"What else do you know?"

"We know that men should know what their wives are up to," I said.

"I do," he said.

"Sure you do," I said.

"What's my wife got to do with this girl?"

"Ask her," I said. "You can remember the girl's name, or should I write it down for you?" I wrote down *Jiyumi Harajuku* on a napkin and stuffed it into his shirt pocket. "Talk to Ayako about her."

"Call us," Detective Izuka said, "if she tells you something we could use to find her killer. You have our *meishis*."

"I must be going," he said.

"Don't want your curry rice to get cold," Detective Izuka said.

Just then a middle-aged man and a high school girl, still in her uniform, came into the coffee shop. Detective Izuka nodded toward them. "Nothing wrong with that," he said. "She's a pretty girl. What kind of man could say no to her?"

Mr. Uno studied the two, who had sat down at a table under a Picasso reproduction of Girl with a Mandolin. The girl was all giggles and smiles, not at all like sarcastic and ironic Tomomi, even when she was a high school student. Not even a middle school student.

"They look happy," Detective Izuka said.

"Don't they?" I added.

Mr. Uno was captivated.

I thought of Tomomi playing the role that this nitwit girl was playing, and how much it must have pained her to be with Mr. Uno. I thought of her *shabu* habit and how, in spite of it, she had money in her bank account. Yes, Mr. Uno must have paid her well.

Detective Izuka said, "I'd like to be a big shot company man with a girl like her."

"We were only friends."

"You paid her, didn't you?" I said.

"From time to time," he said. "She wanted to go traveling, to find herself, then return to Japan and reunite with her parents. She was a runaway, you know."

"We didn't know," Detective Izuka said.

"Did she tell you her real name?" I asked.

"No. And I didn't ask. We got along, as hard as it is for your two to believe. We had good talks."

"Sure," I said.

"We did. I've never been able to talk to anyone the way I could talk to her."

Detective Izuka said, "What's the best sushi joint in town?"

"What?" Mr. Uno said.

"I'd like to taste some of the genuine stuff."

Mr. Uno said, "The Bluefin near Shinagawa Station. My company supplies it. I can get you a discount. I know the master."

"That's bribery," I said.

"I didn't mean it that way."

"I didn't take it that way."

"Probably not the kind of place for police detectives," Detective Izuka said. "My budget fits Yadoya."

Yadoya is a cheap noodle and grilled fish shop where the customers, mostly men, sit at counters. The customers buy tickets at the door for the meals they want. They're all serious eaters who are in a hurry.

Detective Izuka looked back at the salaryman and his high school girl. He said, "She must be a real piece. A real piece. How was Jiyumi?"

"That's disrespectful," Mr. Uno said. "The girl is dead."

"Call us after you talk to your wife," I said, "and she tells you what you say you don't know about. We could've run you in to the police station, you know. We did you a favor, coming here."

He stared back at me the way an innocent child would. Then he said, "I have a train to catch." He rose up a little, and when it was clear that Detective Izuka wasn't going to force him to sit he said, "Excuse me."

"Thanks for the recommendation," Detective Izuka said.

"What?"

"About the Bluefin."

"You have our phone numbers," I said.

When Mr. Uno stood, I noticed that he had a wet spot on his crotch.

Detective Izuka and I watched him walk off. Now he walked with purpose, a man in a hurry to get home.

Detective Izuka said, "Did you see that piss spot in his pants?"

"Another happy marriage," I said.

"How did his wife put up with him for so many years?"

"Why don't you ask her?" I said.

"I plan on it," he said and let out a chuckle, then looked at the girl with the salaryman.

"They're your drug," I told him.

"Do you think he'll confess to his wife?"

"It's better to wait and see than arrest him now. Give him a break. He didn't kill her. We're sure of that," I said.

I paid the bill and we walked back to the police building and filed out our reports and checked out for the day.

From the police building I went over to the Keio Plaza. Chie was there. She asked me, "Bourbon?"

"Wild Turkey," I said.

She went to the bar. I watched Mizuko and thought about my marriage, wondering if Mizuko had ever entertained thoughts of leaving me. If she had, she had concealed them well. You live with a person for more than twenty years and you think you know them and something happens that changes all that and you realize you never knew them at all. So many couples live lives like that.

Chie set down my Wild Turkey and I sipped it. Its smokiness loosened the tightness in my neck and began to release me from the day's work.

Mizuko began to play "It Never Entered My Mind."

CHAPTER FIFTEEN

I woke with a throbbing headache, the kind a hard-boiled detective in pulp novels has but which I rarely do. I've submitted to being a mid-level bureaucrat.

At breakfast Mizuko asked me, "Why are you drinking so much?"

"Am I?"

She glared at me dismissively and said, "Is it a case?"

"No. I just want to go listen to you play, and I have to drink something. I can't just sit there, now and then talking to Chie."

Mizuko wasn't wearing her glasses. She rarely did in the mornings, unless she had something she wanted to read, maybe a text on her phone or to watch the NHK news. She rolled her eyes before saying, "You only come over when something isn't going right. Don't lie to me."

Her eyes were clear and sharp. I always found their alluring gray attractive. That morning, as is her habit, she had scrubbed her face before putting on the Shiseido lotion she favors. Her face glowed a fresh, youthful white. She'd also pulled her hair back and tied it off with a blue ribbon. I was struck by her beauty, a rare thing in a marriage that has lasted as long as ours. It was as if I was seeing her after we'd slept together for the first time, which had, well, been in the Cup of Tea love hotel in Shibuya. I thought back to that day and found great joy in the memory.

She was having her usual green tea and a few slices of that season's Fuji apples, a cup of unsweetened yogurt, and a slice of wheat toast. I was having a walnut scone that Mizuko had bought at a nearby bakery and a cup of yogurt mixed with granola. The coffee, which we make with a French press, tasted refreshingly strong, a welcome elixir for a hangover.

Mizuko finished a spoonful of yogurt and looked at me. "Is it the murder of that poor girl?" she asked. "I would understand if it is, considering... Do you want to tell me about her?"

I looked her straight in the eyes and said, "No."

Mizuko said nothing. I could see that she didn't want to push me about talking about that murder. It would be too difficult for either of us.

"There's some relief from it all when I pray," she said.

"You know that that sort of thing is not for me."

"You've been a detective for too long," she said. "It's made you more cynical than you were when I first met you." She grinned. "That was your charm, how you mistrusted everyone. People who study literature, they're that way, cynical." She smiled. "But I knew all along that your cynicism was just a shell. What's the name of that crab that doesn't have a shell of its own but uses another to move into to protect itself?"

"A hermit crab."

"That's who you are," she said, "a hermit crab. My little hermit crab."

"Knock it off with the sentimentality," I said. "I need to dress for work."

Unlike many Japanese wives, who lay out their husband's suit and shirt and tie for them, I insist on choosing what I'll wear.

"I'm going to the market today," Mizuko said. "Is there anything you want?"

I thought for a while. "Some Tongari," I said. Tongari, roasted corn in the shape of a bugle, was a favorite of mine when watching television and having a beer.

"And Asahi Black?"

"You didn't have to ask."

The market was five hundred or so meters away. Mizuko went there when the weather was fine by bicycle, and if it was raining, she walked, holding an umbrella. Her bicycle had a basket in front of the handlebars, as most Japanese bicycles do, to put the shopping bags in. We kept our Honda Fit under a plastic roof, where it collected dust. A bicycle, walking, or using the trains was so much more efficient and much less expensive.

"I've done some research about a good *onsen ryokan*," Mizuko said. "It will come earlier up in the mountains than down here, you know."

A *ryokan* is a traditional Japanese inn.

"There's several in Nagano prefecture that have a private bath."

"The kind of places lovers go to."

"Are we lovers?"

"That phase has passed," I said.

"Sorry to hear that."

"You know I didn't mean it. Just choose a *ryokan* that you think will do. I trust your judgment."

"We talk like an old couple, reading the other's thoughts."

"We've been married long enough."

"We're not old. But you soon will be if you keep on with your drinking. Are you coming by tonight?"

"You have a secret admirer you don't want me to know about?"

"One man in my life is enough."

"It's not like you, drinking the way you've been. And you stay the whole night."

"You're starting to get on my nerves, badgering me this way."

"Am I?" She laughed again. She often laughed at me, and I can't say that it annoyed me. It was her way of teasing me.

"I can't decide at breakfast what I'm going to do after work," I said.

I left the kitchen table and went upstairs and changed from my robe into a suit and headed for the *genkan*. I took my shoes from a shelf there and put them on and turned and saw Mizuko staring back at me. "*Itterasshai*," she said.

Itterasshai is a simple phrase, loosely translated as, please return after you go. There are so many set phrases and greetings in Japanese. Some are said because it's a custom to do so and therefore have no meaning, as this one does in many families. Mizuko didn't make a habit of saying it, because it brought on unhappy memories. She'd said it to Tomomi on the night she'd left and hadn't returned.

"*Ittekimasu*," I replied—I'll go and return. Tomomi had just walked out the door, saying nothing.

I left, knowing that Mizuko would go to the *butsudan* and light incense and ring that brass bell and look at Tomomi's photograph and pray for her return.

It was a crisp autumn day. The sky was blue, the kind of day that makes Tokyo a wonderful city to live in, unlike how it is during the dreadful days of summer, when temperatures sore and we all drip with sweat and there are only momentary air-conditioned respites from the heat in office and apartment buildings, coffee shops, and most homes. We don't have air-conditioning in our home. We'd made the decision long ago to go without one, to face the heat stoically, only relying on an electric fan. We sleep under a sheet in the summer, Japanese style, on the cool futon, our feet poking out from under it to stay as cool as we can as the breeze from the fan blows over us.

I came to Shinjuku-dori just as one of those right wing crazies in a sound truck drove past, blasting out a message about the Russians occupying the Kuril Islands north of Hokkaido that they'd taken from us late in the Pacific War. They remained a bitter source of contention between us and the Russians, whom few Japanese trust.

The Japanese flag was painted onto all the sides of the sound truck, and the two men inside were wearing *hachimakis*, headbands wrapped around their heads on which there was a red circle. They were the kind of young men who probably would have gone off to fight for the Emperor during the Pacific War, obeyed their officer when he'd issued a *banzai* charge, and been shot dead by American marines on some now forgotten south sea beach. They were misfits who couldn't fit in with Japanese society and needed a family, and these right wing crazies, who had yakuza connections and connections with right wing politicians, provided them with one. But these young men were harmless enough, only making a lot of noise, as did the *bosozoku* motorcycle gangs that cruise the streets late at night and early in the mornings. Young people. They can often be that way before they find themselves. If only Tomomi had found herself before she'd met up with Mr.

Uno, I thought.

I came to the entrance of Yotsuya Station and got caught up in the flow of commuters, which made me really feel like an anonymous bureaucrat. I was pushed along and came to the card reader and touched my telephone to it and went down the stairs to the Chuo Line platform. It was three-people or more deep with commuters waiting for the next train.

It came and I got on it. There were no seats to be had, a usual thing at this time of the morning. If there ever were seats, they were in the early morning hours when the train started, at around five, and late at night, before the trains stopped running and Korean pickpockets were active, sliding up to salarymen who had passed out from drink. I suspected that these Koreans were agents of the North, sending their booty back to Kim.

The train pulled into Shinjuku South Station. The flow of commuters took me up to the station level, where they headed for their respective exits. I stopped at the same kiosk where I bought my newspapers and said good morning to the woman who worked there and picked up the usual newspapers I read and continued on to the police building. I went up the front steps, passing the policeman in uniform holding a riot baton who was always on guard there, and climbed another flight of stairs up to the floor my desk was on and started to go through the papers. There was nothing that interested me. Or, I should say, nothing that was of any help in finding out who Tomomi's killer was. But there was front page news about China, how their air force and navy were penetrating Japanese air space and sea lanes. I wasn't sure how these intrusions would come to an end. Maybe the Americans would see to it that they did. We didn't have the will to do it ourselves and risk having one of their planes knock up against one of ours, as had happened with the Americans several years back, starting a confrontation between the two countries. I was sure that Chief Inspector Saito had read the stories. I did find myself hoping that I didn't have to listen to one of his rants about Chinese hegemony, even if the rant did have the ring of truth about it.

Soon after I had set the newspapers aside my phone rang. "Detective Kawayama," I said.

"This is Ayako Uno," a woman said. I was immediately taken aback. Why is she calling me? I wondered. Is it to ask me why Detective Izuka and I had questioned her husband? He had to have said something to her. Maybe he'd even confessed to her something that would help us solve the case.

"What can I do for you?" I asked.

"I wasn't expecting you to be a homicide detective," she said. "My husband said you were in the fraud division. Why would my husband have homicide detectives question him?"

"Murder," I said.

An eerie silence came between us. Unlike her brother, she had shaken off her rural Tohoku dialect and spoke eloquently, as if she had been born and raised in Hiroo, one of Tokyo's more affluent neighborhoods.

"Murder?" she said, "and not something about this mislabeling scandal?"

"The two could be related," I said.

"I knew about the girl," she said. "I know that my husband was seeing her. But he didn't kill her. He could never do such a thing."

"Then why did you call me?"

"Not on the phone," she said. "I'll come to the police station. You're in Shinjuku, right?"

I told her what exit to take.

She asked, "What's a convenient time for you?"

"As soon as you get here," I said.

"Yes. I see. There's some urgency."

"My partner and I will be waiting."

"I trust this meeting will be confidential?"

"You have something to hide?"

"No. It's not that."

"Then what is it?"

"I'm just not used to this sort of thing, talking to a homicide detective."

"Maybe you'd like us to visit you in your Tachikawa home?" I said.

"You know where I live?"

"We're detectives," I said.

"No. Please don't come here. Please. The neighbors, you understand."

"We'll be waiting for you," I said.

She arrived thirty-five minutes later, wearing a sunflower yellow skirt, a blue sweater, and a white lace blouse. Her shoulder length hair just brushed up against the blue wool of the sweater, underneath which there was a necklace of silver and turquoise. With her, to Detective Izuka's and my surprise, was her lover, Haruto Murata. The two made for a very dignified, matching couple. He had on a pair of khaki, UniQlo trousers, a pink broadcloth shirt with a button down collar, probably bought at UniQlo as well, and a navy blue blazer. He could pull off dressing youthfully, unlike other men who only bring attention to their sagging chins and large bellies.

We all bowed and exchanged greetings and *meishis* and then proceeded to go into the room that had the sofa and chairs and table for tea.

Ayako was a proud woman. I hadn't really been aware of this when I'd followed the two of them to the love hotel. I'd kept my distance. She'd just seemed like a wealthy housewife then who was carrying on an affair, as many were.

The girl who served tea entered the room and set the teacups down on the table. I noticed that she looked at Detective Izuka and blushed, which verified my suspicions about where he'd been the day before.

"Please," I started out. "I'm happy you braved coming to see us. What is it you want to tell us?"

Ayako looked at me confidently. Beneath her elegance was a determined woman who knew how to get what she wanted. Mr. Murata was sitting beside her on the sofa. "My husband is a weak man," she began. "He knows little of life, little of the life I knew growing up in a small town."

"You used him to escape that life," I said.

"Well, I, I have some regrets."

"Because you're involved in the murder of a young, innocent girl?" Detective Izuka said.

"What?"

"Your regrets."

"No. It's not that."

"Then what is it?" I asked, "that you have regrets about?"

Ayako stared at Detective Izuka, clearly annoyed by what he'd said. Women like her aren't used to men talking to her the way he had.

"You see," Mr. Murata added, "that girl who was

murdered, we're involved, but not directly, please understand. If we were, we would have come sooner."

"I don't understand," I said.

"Yes. Please explain," Detective Izuka said.

"We met one day at a PTA meeting," Ayako said, looking at me.

"I'm a widower," Mr. Murata said.

"I'm sorry," I said. "What's this have to do with this murder?"

"I'll explain," Ayako said. "We decided to have lunch together one afternoon."

"We don't need to know about your affair," Detective Izuka said.

"We already know about it," I said.

"What I want to say is that my brother, a private investigator, hired the girl. What was her name?"

"Yujimi Harajuku," I said.

"He hired her so that you'd have some photos of your husband going into a love hotel with her," Detective Izuka said.

"You know?" Mr. Murata said. He had his forearms on his knees. Ayako had remained straight-backed, sitting very properly on the edge of the sofa with her fingers knitted together. I imagined her working part time as a young girl in Pacific Sushi's Kesennuma office, and how she had managed to seduce Mr Uno. It couldn't have been that difficult for her.

"Then you must know why we asked Mr. Ohashi to do what he did," Mr. Murata said.

"We do," I answered.

What did it matter, her wanting a divorce? We wanted to know who had killed my daughter.

Detective Izuka said, "How did you manage it, being

married to him for so many years?"

"You have a very abrasive manner," Ayako said.

"Thank you."

"It wasn't meant as a compliment."

"I get what I want," he said.

"I saw the expression on that tea girl's face."

Detective Izuka smiled.

"We didn't have anything to do with the murder, you understand?" Mr. Murata said.

"We know," I said. I was becoming fed up with them telling us what we knew.

"The poor girl," Ayako said. "I can see myself in her. She was lonely and needed some companionship or only wanted to better herself the way I did. I believe that's all she was after. Don't you think so?" She was looking straight at me. I had become an etherized insect pinned to a cork board. I couldn't hold her stare and looked at the teacups on the table. Ayako had taken a sip of tea when the girl had served it, leaving a crescent red lipstick mark around the rim.

Detective Izuka reached for a teacup and sipped the tea and set the cup down and looked at me and then at Ayako. "You just came down here to assuage your guilt?" he asked.

"Of course not."

"Then tell us something we don't know."

"I will, if you allow me the time."

"We're listening," I said.

She sipped her tea again and set the cup down and then said, "Last night Yuji broke down and told me the story. He's ashamed of himself. He said he knew I was seeing someone and was going to file for a divorce. It's been building up for years, the division between us." She looked at Mr. Murata and said, "We just wanted to get married."

"You could've just asked for a divorce," I said.

"I did," Ayako said. "My husband refused, telling me how a divorce would affect his career. He suggested we could just go on the way we were."

"I doubt a woman like you would be satisfied with such an arrangement," Detective Izuka said.

She glared at him disdainfully.

"He didn't mention the mislabeling scam?" Detective Izuka said.

"I knew about it, of course. The Asahi News broadcast a story about it. It was in the paper. My neighbors all know about it. They must be whispering to each other about us. What shame my husband has brought on my family and his."

I thought she was just feeding us tripe. And she was.

"My husband," she said, "he doesn't tell me about his work. I didn't know anything about this mislabeling scandal until yesterday."

"When he also told you about him seeing a girl who was murdered," I said, "but you already knew about that."

"Now you're speaking for him?"

"He was afraid to tell you."

"You know."

"No. I don't."

"The reputation of Pacific Sushi would suffer," Mr. Murata said. "My company had some trouble with the Yamaguchi-gumi a few years ago, but we stood up to them. They tried to scare us by breaking some of our office windows and threatening our employees, but when we wouldn't play their game they left us alone."

"It's not like that with Pacific Sushi," Ayako said. "The president doesn't want any trouble."

"So he pays off the yakuza?"

"I don't know about that. My husband doesn't tell me those things."

"But you can imagine how Mr. Uno might react?" Mr. Murata said, "if he knew about those things."

"I certainly can," I said. "Pacific Sushi's reputation is more important than assisting the police in finding the killer of a young woman."

"That's not it," Ayako said. "That's cruel."

"He's a cruel man."

"Pacific Sushi is a very traditional company," Mr. Murata said.

"We know," I said. "A target for the yakuza."

"My husband can't help himself. It was the way he was raised."

Detective Izuka chuckled to himself.

"Why did you come to Shinjuku to tell us what we already know? We want to know what your husband knows about what happened in that hotel room," I said.

"She used *shabu*," Ayako said. "But I suppose you know that."

"We do. What's that got to do with who killed her?"

"She had a boyfriend who supplied her," Mr. Murata said.

"That's right," Ayako said, "a boyfriend."

"Your husband told you this last night?" I said.

"When he wasn't crying. You two frightened him."

"We're so sorry," Detective Izuka said. He had spoken ironically, and Ayako knew it.

"He didn't kill her," she said.

"Our job is to find who killed Jiyumi Harajuku," I said.

Ayako opened a Louis Vuitton purse and took from it a tissue that was in a stainless steel holder and blotted away some tears.

"What's this boyfriend's name?" Detective Izuka asked.

"He didn't say."

"He has something to do with Jiyumi's murder?"

"I don't know. He didn't say."

"Find out," I said.

"How?"

"You got where you are by seducing him," Detective Izuka said.

It had to be said, and I was glad he'd said it. I'd had enough of her whining about the murder of my daughter affecting her husband's company and her guilt.

"Can't you show my husband some respect?" Ayako said.

"A young woman was murdered," I said. "Finding her killer is more important than the reputation of Pacific Sushi or how her death upset your marriage plans, don't you think?"

A heavy silence filled the room. Ayako just sat there, looking at us. After a while, Mr. Murata said, "She'll try."

"Yes. I'll try," she said. She didn't seem too excited about doing so.

"You said you could see yourself in her," I said.

"Maybe under different circumstances you'd be the one with a charging cord wrapped around your throat," Detective Izuka said.

She looked at him, her face as hard as marble, before some life returned to her cheeks and she said, "I see."

Detective Izuka said, "You're an experienced woman. I

think you can get that name out of your husband."

"Maybe he doesn't know it," she said.

"I think he does," I said.

Ayako's face hardened a bit. Then she pinched and twisted her dress with her fingers, the first sign she'd made of being nervous. She turned and looked at Mr. Murata.

"You've got to do it," he told her.

She reached for her cup of tea and sipped it. Setting the cup down, she looked at it in a disdainful way. It was a simple cup, white, no decoration, the cup a policeman would use, not a cup she would have had in her home. It was too ordinary. She had probably seen such cups in her family home, when she'd been growing up in Kesennuma and they reminded her of the life she had wanted to escape.

"I'll do it," she said. "Excuse us."

The two rose from the sofa. Mr. Murata nodded at us. And then Ayako did, but a bit reluctantly.

I went to the door and opened it, and they nodded their heads again as they passed me, entering an office of detectives at their desks. "May I have someone show you the way out?" I said.

"We can manage," Ayako said.

As they walked past the line of detectives' desks, many of them stopped to watch her.

After they'd gotten in an elevator, Detective Izuka said, "She's a real woman."

I went to my desk, wondering who this boyfriend of Tomomi's was.

CHAPTER SIXTEEN

I was on a Chuo Line train, coming to work the next morning, when I felt my phone vibrate in the breast pocket of my jacket. I didn't answer the call. I saw that the number wasn't in my contacts and put my phone back in my coat pocket.

When the train arrived at Shinjuku South Station, I went up the stairs to the station level and found a corner out of the way of the crowd of commuters and called the number.

"This is Detective Kawayama," I said.

I recognized her voice instantly. Ayako said, "Good morning, Detective Kawayama." Her polite, obligatory greeting was followed by a brief silence, before she added, "The boyfriend goes by the name 'Pirate.'"

"'Pirate'?" I said. "Your husband doesn't know his real name?"

"No."

"Find out this man's real name."

"Do you want me to interrogate my husband?"

"You're his wife," I said. "You can be persuasive. Isn't that how you got him to marry you?"

"I can't believe what you say, sometimes."

"I'm just speaking the truth. Find out his real name."

"Jiyumi did tell my husband that he took his name from some stupid American movie about pirates."

I knew the movies, those *Pirates of the Caribbean* ones that were more cartoon than drama.

An anxious silence settled between us. Then she said,

"My husband is a weak man, Detective Kawayama. I fear he could break any day now."

"Tell him he means something to you," I said.

She hesitated before saying, of all things, something that took me by surprise, "He does mean something to me."

Marriage, I thought, is that way, complicated. She's in love with one man and still cares about her husband.

"I've been his supportive wife for so many years, raising our children too," she said.

"Find out who this Pirate character is, his real name. Help us find out who killed Jiyumi Harajuku," I said.

"I'll do my best," she said. She then said, "*Shitsure itashimasu*," an honorific way of speaking that both showed respect and resentment and ended the phone call.

Shabu dealers often take Western monikers as their street names. Even if Ayako didn't get Pirate's real name out of her husband, I knew I could rely on some detectives in the narcotics division who could. I just thought that it would be faster if she did it.

I went on through the station to the newsstand kiosk and bought my daily supply of newspapers and from there went to the exit. A few minutes later I was at my desk, looking at the photo of Tomomi and Junko and this man they went to Tokyo Disneyland with. I had a feeling that I was looking at my daughter's killer and that Junko knew who he was. If she didn't crack soon, I'd get some narcotics detectives to work on her.

A few minutes later Chief Inspector Saito called me into his office.

"Any progress with the investigation?" he asked. His meaty forearms, the shirtsleeves rolled back, were resting on his desk, on which there were piles of papers.

I told him everything I knew, including the conversation I'd just had with Ayako.

"'Pirate,'" he said. "Kids nowadays. What's gone wrong with this country?"

He had spoken rhetorically. I stayed there, standing before his desk, like an Imperial Army soldier at attention.

"Any idea where he came up with that name?" he asked.

"Those American movies," I said, "the ones about pirates."

"My daughter went to see all those. They romanticize being robbed. Those people who faced pirates in the Malacca Strait a few years ago would have a different take on pirates. Romanticizing crime. Why not romanticize police work?"

"Some movies do," I said. "Remember Dirt Harry?"

"Wouldn't it be nice if we could take the law in our hands and do what has to be done."

"I think that's called fascism," I said.

"I didn't work out too well for us, did it, fascism?"

"We're a democracy now," I said.

"Damn Americans." He smiled. He was being ironic.

"You're going to check with narcotics, see if someone there knows who this Pirate character is?"

"Yes, sir," I said. "I might even have a photograph of him." I showed him the photograph on my phone of Tomomi and Junko and who I thought was him at Disneyland.

"You do good work, Kawayama, always have."

"Thank you, sir. Is that all?"

"That damn lunatic Kim Jong Un. You know, Tokyo is

in range of those ballistic missiles he's firing off."

He was just talking. He knew that if the American's did that it would be the end of East Asia, if not the world. There was a method in Kim's madness. I hoped.

Chief Inspector Saito's phone rang, and he waved his hand dismissively, to signal that our meeting was over. As I was returning to my desk, I heard him say, "Yes, sir. Kawayama is on the case, doing an outstanding job. He has a lead. I expect an arrest within the week."

I knew what that meant. If I didn't close the case soon someone above Chief Inspector Saito would order the case closed and filed as a cold case. That girl who was murdered wasn't important. No one even knew who she was. Why waste money on investigating the murder of a girl who was a *shabu* addict and might possibly have been a prostitute? That was the thinking of higher-ups. There was no political capital for them in having me solve this murder. I had to solve it soon. Or Ohashi would. By killing the man I wanted to see hang.

Back at my desk I called Detective Enomoto, a detective in the narcotics division I'd talked to before.

"How have you been keeping?" he asked.

"Looking forward to retirement."

"You retire? Hard to imagine. The years creep up on us, don't they? Do you have a hobby?"

"You sound like my wife."

"A very wise woman."

"I won't argue with that. She suggests a hobby."

"Tai chi," he said.

"What?"

"You heard me right. I do it every morning in the park outside my place. I get some stares from time to time, but it relaxes me."

"I'll consider it," I said, just to shorten the conversation.

"What can I do for you?" he said.

"I'm looking for a dealer who goes by the name 'Pirate,'" I said. "He might have something to do with a case I'm working."

"That murder in the love hotel one?"

"Right." I didn't want to explain, again, how Tomomi's dealer had decided on that name, but felt obligated to do so, to aid him in finding out what Pirate's real name was. "I might have a photo of him," I said. "I'll send it over."

I thanked him and put the phone back in its cradle. I had trouble picturing Detective Enomoto, a hefty man with short limbs, doing tai chi in a park. Detectives in the narcotics division, they're an eccentric bunch.

The next person I called was Ohashi. Private investigators, they always have their ear to the ground and can do things that police, by law, are prevented from doing. It annoyed me a bit that I had to rely on him, but I wanted to know who had killed my daughter and had some doubts that the police could find out, privacy laws being what they were, preventing even the police from finding out the identities of some people, if they wanted to disappear, become one of the evaporated.

"Pirate?" he said. "How did he come up with that name?"

I told him.

"Whatever happened to the Japanese movie industry?" he lamented. "And now, these sappy Korean dramas are dominating—"

"You'll ask around?"

"I'll do whatever is necessary to find this punk. If I get

my hands on him . . ."

"I'll pretend I didn't hear that," I said.

"It doesn't matter to me if you don't forget."

I pictured him in his office, sitting in that big chair of his, smoking a cigarette, wanting to come across as the powerful boss he had maybe aspired to become but whose career had come to an end when he botched a hit.

I started to go through the newspapers and came across another story by Sayako about the mislabeling scandal. I just couldn't get it out of my head that Tomomi's murder didn't have something to do with this, considering she'd gone to a love hotel with Mr. Uno, a *buchou* at Pacific Sushi. If the yakuza knew about the two of them and got some photographs of him with her, he would buckle under their pressure and pay them off.

After talking with Ohashi, I got the idea for Detective Izuka and I to go back to Tomomi's room again and go through her things. Maybe we'd pick up a clue about who this man Pirate was that we'd missed before. This time, because there was no direct train line to her room, we took an unmarked police car, to avoid time consuming connections.

Tomomi's room had remained cordoned off by police tape. The manager of the building met us in the front of the building and gave the key to her room to me.

"Some tenants are so frightened," she said.

"They're moving out?" I asked.

"I didn't mean it that way."

"Yes, you did," I said. It wasn't such and uncommon occurrence, that tenants moved out of a building if someone who'd had a room there was murdered or committed suicide.

I had gotten the key to the apartment from the evidence room and opened the door. I was immediately struck by the musty smell of a sealed off room. It was similar to the smell of one that a real estate agent is showing that hasn't had the windows opened for a while. But in this case, when we entered the room, the feeling of invading someone's privacy prevailed.

"The man's name is probably in her telephone," Detective Izuka said. "Girls these days, they don't write things down, you know. But where is it?"

"I'd like to know," I said. But if it was an iPhone, we'd have a lot of difficulty getting it unlocked.

Detective Izuka and I hadn't spoken much on the ride over to Tomomi's room. He'd seemed troubled by something, and I believed I knew what it was, what it usually was with him: a woman. That, the "woman problem," as he now and then admitted it was, was of his own doing, so I had little sympathy for him, but plenty for his wife and children. Having passed a park on the way to Tomomi's room, in which there were stands of maples, I had mentioned *koyou*, saying,

"My wife and I go to an *onsen* every autumn. It helps to relieve the feeling of despair we feel from time to time as we get older."

"I've almost forgotten the pleasure of an *onsen*," he said.

"Try it," I said. "You've got some time off coming."

"With my wife?"

"That's what I meant."

"I haven't considered that."

"Do."

I told him to go through Tomomi's desk and that I'd go through her chest of drawers. Perhaps there was a phone number we'd missed, though I doubted it. The truth was that I'd told him to go through Tomomi's desk because I didn't want him pawing through Tomomi's "intimate apparel" and playing, again, with her vibrator. But I wasn't too keen on moving her bras and panties around myself.

I slid open the drawers and used a pen to move around bras and panties and some other things I didn't know the names of, flimsy garments made of silk that had the texture of gossamer, and saw that pink vibrator, which I didn't touch. Then I emptied the contents of the drawers onto the tatami and looked under the drawers, thinking Tomomi might have taped an envelope there, but she hadn't. It would've been an obvious hiding place for money and papers. Ms. Nodoka would have told me if there 'd been something there.

It was when I was going through the bottom drawer, which was stuffed full of charging and extension cords, sockets and lights and torches, that I happened to see a corner of a tatami mat beside the chest of drawers that was suspiciously raised up a few millimeters from the others. Putting something away under a tatami mat was a dated way of hiding something, but traditions linger.

I went to the kitchen and got a knife and pried up the mat. Under it was a brown B-5 envelope. I resisted telling Detective Izuka that I might have discovered something of value, because I was a bit fearful of what might be in that envelope. Detective Izuka had moved from the desk to the closet and was sorting through Tomomi's clothes and bags. I slipped out the envelope. Tomomi hadn't sealed it. I slid it open with the tip of a pen and shook out several photographs, the dried petals of a cherry blossom, some crushed sea shells, and, of all things, some glistening white sand onto a handkerchief I'd laid down on the tatami. There was no sand that sparkled like that in the Japan that I knew of. I quickly sorted through the photographs. In one Tomomi and Junko were standing on either side of Mickey Mouse, smiling, the way high school or middle school girls do. The sky was a deep blue, and in the background were the spires of that famous Disney fairy tale castle. There were other photographs of Tomomi beside Daffy and Goofy and Snow White.

And then I came to a few photographs of Tomomi —and now and then Junko with this man in a park bursting with cherry blossoms. He was the same man that was in the photo Ms. Nishikawa had shown us. I didn't know what that coincidence meant, but it had to mean something. The three were sitting on a reed mat, and on the mat they had several *bentos,* a couple of bottles of Nihonshu, and a karaoke player. I reasoned that the park was in Tohoku. I say this because there was another photograph of them in Tokyo Station on the platform for the Tohoku Shinkansen that had the same time stamp on it as the photograph. Over Tomomi's shoulder I saw a timetable for the departing trains, one for Aomori, another for Akita.

There was another photograph of them on a beach. A large white hotel with a lot of windows facing the sea was in the background. I didn't recognize the hotel, but it would be easy enough to identify. On the beach were several blue umbrellas. Green breakers were falling on the white sand. The sand in the envelope had come from this beach. The people on the beach all looked to be Japanese.

JAMES ROTH

I studied the man, whom I assumed was Pirate. He was splayed out on a mat on the beach. His hair looked like he rarely combed it. He was wearing dark glasses. His smile was a sneer, his face thin and serpentine; his cheeks were drawn in. He was wearing a bathing suit, which gave away his caved-in chest. In the other photographs he was wearing jeans and a T-shirt, over which there was a black leather biker jacket that had silver studs.

I went through more of the photographs and came to some of Tomomi, Mizuko, Satoshi, and I at Tokyo's Meiji Shrine during a New Year's holiday. She was a middle school student wearing her school uniform. We were all eating *mochi*. At another we were at Tokyo Dome watching a Yomiuri Giants' baseball game. She was then wearing her high school uniform. She was smiling and waving a Hanshin Tigers pennant, her team. The Tigers were from Osaka and were the main rival of Japan's most popular team, the Yomiuri Giants. She didn't care much for baseball, only to be anti whatever other Japanese were for, in this case the Yomiuri Giants. I recalled that the Tigers had defeated the Giants that night, which had thrilled her so much that she couldn't stop talking about the game for days. In another photograph Tomomi, Mizuko, and I were at Tokyo Tower. That one had been taken when she was in primary school. She would've never gone there after primary school. Tokyo Tower has become a place that only lovers and tourists visit, and she didn't want to be around either. The tower used to have a magnificent view of the city, but the surrounding office towers have grown up around it and put an end to that. Now there's the Skytree Tower in Sumida, near the river of the same name, which a person can see long from a train on one of the northern lines long before it has entered Tokyo. At over four hundred meters high, it is the highest freestanding tower in the world. I wouldn't want to be on the observation deck, taking in the city and Tokyo Bay when a major earthquake struck. That would be an experience visitors would survive but never forget. Their videos would soon go viral. They'd probably be thrown up against the windows, as the tower whipped back and forth.

When I heard Detective Izuka's footsteps coming up from behind me, I tucked the photographs of Tomomi and Satoshi and Mizuko and me into a coat pocket. I didn't know what, exactly, I was going to do with them, but I couldn't have Detective Izuka see them. I hoped to give them to Mizuko one day, once Tomomi's killer had been found and locked up.

"Find something?" he asked.

I said, "I believe this is Pirate."

"He's the same man that was in the photo Ms. Nishikawa has," he said. He studied the photographs.

"It looks like Junko didn't tell us everything she knew."

"Girls," he said. "They learn to lie from a young age. What's that?" He was asking about the broken up shells and sand that I had spilled out of the envelope onto my handkerchief.

"It was in the envelope," I said.

I pointed at the photo of the three of them on the beach, the hotel in the background, and he said, "I know that hotel. It's the Hyatt Regency in Saipan."

He hadn't been to Saipan with his wife. I was sure of that.

"It's first rate," he added.

It had been so long since our honeymoon to Saipan that I couldn't remember it, if it had even been there way back then. We'd spent our honeymoon in the Himawari, which was across the street from the beach, we were so poor then.

I placed the photos on the tatami and took photos of them with my camera and then put them in a plastic bag, along with the sand and seashells. I told Detective Izuka that it had been worthwhile, coming to Jiyumi's room again, and he agreed.

We returned to the 7-Eleven that we'd been to earlier, hoping that the same woman we'd questioned before was there, and, as luck would have it, she was. She was working the cash register.

"Nice to see you again," she said and nodded.

"How's the *oden* here?" Detective Izuka asked. It was nearing lunchtime. *Oden* is a kind of Japanese stew, in which a person chooses what they want in it, kelp, boiled eggs, Japanese radish. Almost all of these convenience stores have it. The smell of it fills the place. The *oden* is right there next to the cash register, each selection divided off from the other.

"It's fresh," she said.

He had her mix him an *oden*.

"And you?" she asked me.

"Maybe an egg sandwich and iced coffee," I told her. "Can you get someone to take over for you while we talk?"

She had a young man come to the cash register.

"We'll only be a few minutes," I told him.

I showed her a photograph of Tomomi and Junko and Pirate together on that mat, celebrating *hanami*.

She squinted at the photograph before taking a pair of reading glasses from a pocket on her apron and putting them on. "That man," she said, "yes. He's the type a woman doesn't forget. I always wondered what that cute girl saw in him. They never seemed happy together. It was embarrassing, the two of them arguing in public the way they did."

"We want to talk with him," Detective Izuka said between slurps of the *oden*. "Have you seen him recently?"

"Not in several days."

"Know anything about him?"

"Would I want to?"

She had a point. I told her to call us if she saw him. Detective Izuka and I thanked her and turned to leave when she said, "What about that egg sandwich and coffee, Detective Kawayama?"

I added a bag of Tongari corn chips and paid for them and the sandwich and can of Georgia Coffee.

Detective Izuka and I then went through the automatic doors back out onto the sidewalk, walking to the police car.

Once we were back in the police building, I scanned the photographs and emailed them to Detective Enomoto. He called me back within thirty minutes. "He has a name that is familiar to you—Tazu Uehara," he said.

"Ever see him with the girls?" I said, not even thinking of the name.

"He sees lots of girls. He gets them hooked, takes payments from them in a hotel room."

"Why not arrest him?"

"Think about that name again," he said. "Uehara."

The name came down on me like the blow of a hammer to the head. After gathering myself, I said, "The son of the Watanabe-gumi's boss, Taro Uehara?" The Watanabe-gumi was the same gang Ohashi had belonged to.

"Yes. But he and his father aren't close. The old man disowned him because he struck out on his own with his *shabu* dealing and womanizing."

"Then who is Pirate getting his supply from?" I asked, "if he and his father are on the outs?"

"Probably from someone in the gang, we figure, who wants to make a bit more on the side."

"A dangerous thing," I said.

I recalled corpses washing ashore in fishing villages on the Sea of Japan coast. The *shabu* was transferred from North Korean ships—it was often made in North Korea—to smaller, faster boats, and these boats ran the supply ashore on beaches near fishing villages where the median age of the residents was over sixty and they were often in bed by nine.

"Where is Pirate now?" I asked.

"I had my men ask around. None of them knows," he said.

"I know someone who might," I said. I told Detective Enomoto where to find Junko, and an hour later she was in an interrogation room, one that was not so friendly. Detective Izuka and I watched as Detective Enomoto and his partner, who was about ten years younger and wore a flannel shirt and jeans, looking like he worked undercover, interrogated her through a two-way mirror.

Detective Enomoto knew how to get what he wanted

out of Junko. It was by not asking her straight off about Tomomi's murder, which I'd briefed him about before the interrogation began. He laid the photos I'd sent him on the table and pointed at Tomomi and asked, in a stern but caring way, "Do you know her?"

"We worked together at the same club," she said, "until . . ."

"She was murdered," Detective Enomoto's partner said.

"What do you know about her murder?" Detective Enomoto asked.

"Nothing. I've talked to two other detectives about it. What do you want from me? I don't know anything."

Detective Enomoto's partner said, "Why are you two with Tazu Uehara at Disneyland, of all places. I don't think he went there to see Mickey Mouse?"

"Who?"

Detective Enomoto's partner jabbed his index finger down hard on the photo. "Him!"

"He's a *shabu* dealer," Detective Enomoto said. "Is he your supplier?"

Junko started to tremble. She snatched some tissues from a box on the table.

"Help yourself," Detective Enomoto said.

"We're not interested in you," his partner said. "If you want to destroy yourself by doing *shabu* and bringing shame to your family, that's your business, but when a girl ends up dead in a love hotel, that's our business, and if our business leads to you, that makes your business our business."

"I had nothing to do with Jiyumi's murder. Nothing."

"But you know who killed her, don't you? I asked you. Is he your supplier?"

"Yes. I mean, no."

"What?"

"Yes. He's my supplier. No. I don't know who killed Jiyumi. I was just doing her a favor." She looked at the mirror, as if she knew that I was Tomomi's father standing behind it and she was asking for forgiveness. She went on without Detective Enomoto having to prompt her, the burden of guilt was so heavy on her. She said, "I got a call from a friend, this P.I. named Mr. Ohashi, and he asked me if I knew a girl who needed some extra money. I told him about Jiyumi. She was always looking to pick up some extra money to save up to go traveling, she said."

"Why didn't you take the job?"

"Ohashi said I wasn't his type."

"That must've hurt."

"I could've used the money, sure. We all need money."

Detective Enomoto said, "You were jealous of her. Weren't you?"

She said nothing, which was an answer.

"'His type'? Who was this man? Did Ohashi say?"

"No."

"How did you come to know this P.I., Ohashi?" Detective Enomoto asked.

Junko glanced at him and his partner. "I met him when I was an actress," she said.

"A real actress?" Detective Enomoto's partner asked.

She didn't answer him, and so he said, "We don't care about your past."

"Ohashi helped me get out of the business. He knows people. He introduced me to Ms. Nishikawa."

"And that's where you meet Jiyumi Harajuku, at her club?"

"No. I met her in front of Shibuya Station one day, when I was waiting for someone."

"Who?"

"He'll kill me."

"We'll protect you."

"Really? Those other detectives, they lied. They said they'd protect me but they didn't mean it."

"Were you waiting for Tazu Uehara?"

She went all quivery. Detective Enomoto and his partner were on to something.

"Yes. Him," she said. "Pirate. I call him Pirate."

"And along comes Jiyumi Harajuku. Is that right?"

"Yes. She was there at the station. She looked lost, the way a lot of girls there do. Tazu asked me to go over to her and ask her if she needed some help. He said, 'She looks like she could use a friend. Go talk to her.' So I did what he told me to do. If I didn't, he'd, well, I don't know. I don't want to think about it."

"Some friend you turned out to be," Detective Enomoto's partner said.

"I did want to be her friend, but it wasn't easy. She never told me much about herself. I suppose she had her reasons. We all hide things, don't we?"

"What are you hiding from us now?" Detective Enomoto said.

"Let me finish, please."

"Go ahead."

"Jiyumi did tell me that she'd come to Tokyo from Kitakyushu. She'd had some romantic troubles there that she was running away from, she said. Her parents kicked her out of the house because of those troubles. Some parents, they're like that, you know, not caring about their daughter if she gets into those kinds of troubles."

I couldn't believe she'd said that. Tomomi hadn't told her any such thing. Junko had been in Fukuoka. I wanted to burst into the interrogation room and slap Junko until she told the truth. But I was a police detective, always under control. I just stood there, taking it, but then I knew things would not end well for her. I had to be satisfied with that.

"So you hooked Jiyumi Harajuku up with Uehara?"

"Okay. Yes. I did."

"And he got her hooked on *shabu*?"

"It was her choice, wasn't it? She needed something to get her through the day. Being a hostess is a tough job. Don't think it isn't. I was doing her a favor."

"Of course, a favor. You did her quite a few favors. Now she's dead because of one of your favors."

"How could I know this would happen? How?"

"What kind of work did Ohashi want from her?"

"I don't know."

"Try again."

She plucked some tissues from the box, blotted her tears, then said, "He needed her for some photos."

"Those photos he wanted ended up getting her killed, you know? Ever think about that?"

"I can't sleep. I know. I'm to blame. Yes."

"You're lucky you weren't this man's type. You might have ended up dead."

"I wish I had been. That's what I think. I wouldn't have all these problems now if I'd been his type. I'd be sleeping now."

"Don't blame yourself," Detective Enomoto said. "You meant well."

She nodded her head feebly. "Thank you," she said.

"But I do blame myself."

"Who killed Jiyumi Harajuku? Not Mr. Uno," his partner asked.

"Was it Mr. Uno, that salaryman?" Detective Enomoto asked.

"I don't know. Really. Maybe Pirate. I think him. But I don't know. I haven't heard from him recently. But he might still be around. I'm scared of him. He might kill me. I know he will if he's in Tokyo."

"Jiyumi told you nothing about Mr. Uno? That's hard to believe. You were working together and probably going out drinking from time to time. We're not stupid."

"Okay. Okay. Once when Jiyumi had too much to drink she said she was continuing to see that salaryman that Ohashi had paid her to see. He was working at a big sushi company."

"You told Uehara that because you were jealous of Jiyumi making some extra money."

She sniffled, took some tissues and wiped her nose. "I don't know," she mumbled.

Detective Enomoto said, "Just tell us what you know again, please."

"I guess I told Pirate. Yes."

"It got her killed, your telling him that."

She began to sob and sob. Detective Enomoto and his partner let her sob, believing that at the end of her sobbing she'd be more forthcoming. When she'd gotten over her sobbing, as tears slid down her cheeks onto the table and Detective Enomoto wiped them away with tissues, she babbled, "How could I have known what would happen, me telling Pirate about Jiyumi seeing that salaryman? She kept on seeing him because they got on well together is what she told me. I couldn't imagine her getting along for very long with any man. I was happy for her."

"No you weren't. You were jealous of the money she was making off him," Detective Enomoto's partner said.

"No. You're wrong. She told me that he really wanted to help her out. She was even thinking about going back to her parents after she went traveling to clear up her mind."

Another blow to my head. I didn't know how much longer I could take it, keep standing there. I had to put my hands out, to brace myself against the wall. Detective Izuka asked me if I wanted some water and I told him I was fine, I had to hear what Junk was saying.

"The poor, mixed up girl," Detective Enomoto said.

"She was a prostitute," Detective Enomoto's partner said. "She wasn't planning on traveling. She conned you and Uno."

"No! Jiyumi wasn't that kind of girl. Never. Never. She would never do that."

"So they just met in a hotel room to talk but he paid her for their talks?" Detective Enomoto said.

"A lot of men could use a cute girl to talk to. In a love hotel room."

"Maybe they didn't just talk. Is there something wrong with that? You're not just thinking about talking when you meet a cute girl, are you? I know about men after being a hostess. I know plenty."

"Did Uehara kill her?"

"I don't know. Maybe. He told me if I breathed a word about what I'd told him about the salaryman and Jiyumi he'd kill me. So what do you think?"

"He killed Jiyumi Harajuku," Detective Enomoto said.

"Yes. I guess. Yes. You've got to help me," Junko

whimpered. "Please. You don't know what kind of person he is."

"We know."

"We'll help you," Detective Enomoto said.

"How? I haven't slept in days. I don't even go to my room but to a capsule hotel over by Ueno Station. Help me!"

She looked at Detective Enomoto, then his partner, then at her fingers and knitted them together on the table. She then began to pick at the pink polish of one nail the way she had when Detective Izuka and I had questioned her in Ms. Nishikawa's club.

"Knock it off," Detective Enomoto's partner said. "This isn't a nail salon."

Detective Enomoto said, "We want to help you."

"How are you going to do that?"

"Trust us."

"Uehara won't be able to get to you," Detective Enomoto's partner said.

"Why do you say that?"

"Do you want us to help you?"

"Yes."

"You'll be safe with us."

"A lot of people saw us bring you here," Detective Enomoto said. "Word gets out."

"You'll be fed and be able to get some sleep. You do look tired."

"Do you have family?" Detective Enomoto asked.

"No. They won't have anything to do with me anymore, ever since I . . . "

"You became an actress."

"We'll protect you. We'll be your family. Trust us."

"Thank you."

"You're welcome."

She said, "I think Pirate had something on this Mr. Uno, but I don't know what. He told me once that he was worth a lot of money."

It was all becoming so clear to me now.

Detective Enomoto asked, "Where does Uehara live?"

"I don't know."

"You know. You were sleeping with him, weren't you, for your supply?"

"No."

"We're not stupid. Tell us."

"Do you want us to help you?" Detective Enomoto asked.

"Please. Yes. Please."

"Where does he live? What's his phone number?"

"We're not here to judge," Detective Enomoto said. "We want to help you. Just tell us where Uehara lives. We want to protect you from him. We'll arrest him."

"You promise I'll be safe?"

"He won't come near you."

"All right then, because you promised. He has a room in an old building over by Aoyama Icho-me Station. It stinks of instant ramen."

"You spent time there, then?"

"Well . . ."

"His telephone number?"

She gave Detective Enomoto that, too, but about all we could do with it was track down where he'd made calls from, which wouldn't have been helpful. He'd probably picked up a phone from a convenience store after Jiyumi's murder.

Tears started to run down Junko's cheeks and dripped off her chin, making water blots on the table. Detective

Enomoto took some tissues and wiped them away and tossed the tissues into the bin. He held the box for her. "Take as many as you need," he told her.

She said, "I didn't do anything wrong! Please understand! I didn't. I wanted to help Jiyumi."

"Sure. We know you did," Detective Enomoto said. "You'll be safe with us. Have a peaceful night's sleep."

Junko started to weep, a weep that turned into a sorrowful howl.

Detective Enomoto summoned two police women who'd been standing by the door.

They came in and handcuffed Junko. One gently covered her mouth with a handkerchief to muffle the howl and said, "Madam, you're disturbing others. Please come with us."

CHAPTER SEVENTEEN

Tazu Uehara had an eight-mat room in a dumpy building, just as Junko had said, not far from a prestigious girls' school, Aoyama Gakuin, which made for a profitable location for a *shabu* dealer. Students hung out in coffee shops and frequented designer clothing stores there.

I called a *kouban*, police box, a block away from where Tazu lived, and had one of the officers there go to Tazu's room, to see if he was home, and when the officer called back ten or so minutes later and said—not to my surprise—that Tazu wasn't. I then did an internet search and made a few calls and got the name of the manager of the building. His name was Riku Budo.

"You're the manager of the building that Tazu Uehara lives in?" I asked.

"Yes. Is he a friend of yours? I have an extensive listing. Are you interested in a room?"

I was immediately struck by his rural dialect, from up north somewhere, maybe Aomori prefecture.

"I'm a homicide detective," I said. "And I have a look in Mr. Uehara's room"

This alarmed him. His voice became tight and squeaky, which matched the kind of person, in appearance, that he turned out to be, a man who was small and nervous. His skin had the look of someone who has smoked for most of his life, gray and flaky and streaked with a network of pink capillaries, evidence of a heavy drinker, which he probably was as well.

"You have a search warrant, of course?" he then asked. I lied. "Yes," I said.

"What does he have to do with a homicide case, if you don't mind me asking?"

"The case is under investigation," I said. "Meet us at Mr. Uehara's building in fifteen minutes," I said.

We took a police car to Tazu's place. I had the feeling that whatever we found there—or didn't find—might lead us somewhere else. Taking a train and having to make connections, that would be a waste of time.

Mr. Budo was waiting for us in his late model black Mercedes in front of Tazu's building. He hadn't come up with the money to buy that car by managing dumpy apartment buildings.

I reasoned that he was connected to the Yamaguchi-gumi.

A Yamaha V-cylinder knock-off of a Harley with leather saddlebags was parked under a roof eave of the building. I guessed, and was right, that it was Tazu's. It looked like the kind of bike a *shabu* dealer would own, to maintain his image, one that would attract the kind of girl who found dangerous men attractive.

The building was two-stories, made of flimsy press-board siding, and had supporting cables connected to the corners that were anchored in concrete to maintain the building's rectangular shape. Otherwise, if a strong wind or an earthquake had shaken it, the place would have collapsed like a cardboard box.

Across from this dump was a modern building, maybe twenty stories, made of steel girders and white tile. It had balconies, from which some futons were hanging over the railings. The residents of that building must have been hoping that a real estate developer would buy up the dump across from them and put in a building that didn't blight their view of Aoyama Park's cherry trees.

Detective Izuka and I got out of the police car and met Mr. Budo. He bowed. We didn't. I had in my hand an envelope with some A4 copy paper in it, to bluff him that I did, indeed, have a search warrant.

"Which cave does Tazu live in?" Detective Izuka asked.

"If you don't mind," he said, "the search warrant."

I held out the envelope, and he reached for it, and as he did the sleeve of his coat and shirt slipped back, exposing a tattoo, which explained, very well, where he'd come up with the money for the Mercedes. The Yamaguchi-gumi owned dumps like this all over the country, as well as a few office towers and even exclusive apartment buildings, many in Minato-ku, where the Emperor's grounds are.

When Mr. Nanzai saw that Detective Izuka and I had taken notice of his tattoo, he drew his arm back. "Oh, well," he said, "I'm sure all the papers are in order."

"If you can't trust the police, who can you trust?" Detective Izuka said.

Mr. Budo said, "This way, please."

We followed him to Tazu's room. He was so short that I could see the top of his head. He had recently had a hair transplant. His head was a garden of little plugs of hair. Detective Izuka, who had also taken notice of the plugs, nudged me in the ribs with an elbow and pointed his chin at the hair transplants. Why he wasn't wearing a hat, I don't know.

We came to a rusty flight of metal stairs, over which there was a corrugated plastic roof, and climbed up to the second floor and went down a landing to Tazu's room, which was the last one.

Mr. Budo took a ring of keys from a pocket and sorted through them. As he was doing this, I looked away, toward the modern building that was casting a shadow onto this one, and saw another black Mercedes parked on a street beside it. It was odd that only one man was inside. The yakuza, being Japanese, are not solitary wolves but work in packs. Mr. Budo must have tipped off this person, whoever he was. Maybe he was a spy for the Yamaguchi-gumi. Or, more likely, he was Tazu's *shabu* supplier.

"You have a lot of keys," Detective Izuka said, losing patience with Mr. Budo fumbling through the ring of keys.

"I manage many properties," he replied.

"I'm sure you do," I said, "and they're all upscale places, like this one, for families. Your boss would only allow a responsible man like you to manage his buildings."

"I don't know what you're talking about," he said.

"Who's the man in the Mercedes there?" I nodded in the direction of the Mercedes across the street.

He said, "Why don't you go ask him for his ID if you're so curious about who he is?"

"Because you know who he is," I said.

"I have no idea."

"Just find the key," Detective Izuka said.

He did and opened the door.

The stench of instant ramen hit us. The time Junko had spent there hadn't been time spent eating ramen. Only women with a habit would spend time in this place.

Even so, we removed our shoes, put on some white

cotton gloves, and stepped up onto the tatami. Detective Izuka took his telephone from a jacket pocket and began to take photos. Mr. Budo had wanted to follow us inside, but I had told him, "Wait on the landing."

I closed the front door. The stench was suffocating.

The room was a garbage dump of Asahi Dry beer cans, cup-of-sake glasses, instant ramen noodle cups, and piles of dirty jeans and T-shirts. On a counter there was a rice maker that had moldy rice in it. On the tatami up against one wall was a futon that smelled of urine, and next to it an opened package of Okamoto condoms. The wastebasket in a corner was filled with tissues, and when Detective Izuka poked around in it with a chopstick he had taken from one of the plastic instant noodle bowls he registered his disgust.

We looked for *shabu* but didn't find any. He had probably taken it with him, wherever he had gone, or handed it to someone he could trust with it. Possibly the man in the Mercedes who'd been watching us. The *junk* was too valuable to leave behind or flush down a toilet.

What we did find were old shirts and coats, a bag of dirty laundry, a stack of porn manga, a PC, stereo equipment, an ashtray overflowing with cigarette butts, unwashed pots and bowls, and, most important of all, syringes, both new and used, in a kitchen drawer. He had spoons and a butane lighter, to prepare the junk. But what he didn't have with him was his passport. The fool had probably been in too much of a hurry and hyped up to remember to take it along with him. It was at the bottom of a drawer of filthy T-shirts and socks.

"I don't think he'll be going far," I said, holding up the passport.

"What an idiot," Detective Izuka said. "He must've

been cranked up on his own junk."

I put the passport away in a coat pocket.

We went back outside onto the landing.

"Find what you were looking for?" Mr. Budo asked.

"Lock the place up," I said to him.

He did, and I took some police tape and sealed the door. "If you let anyone in this rat hole, you'll be covering up your tattoos with a blue jumpsuit. Understand?"

"*Wakarimashita*," he said, and snapped over, bowing, as if I were his boss.

He went to his Mercedes and got in, and we went along the building, knocking on doors, hoping to question anyone who might have taken notice of Tazu. The only person who was home was an elderly woman in a robe tied off around her waist with a sash who lived on the first floor, directly under Tazu's room. The other occupants, we reasoned, must have been young men who worked at companies and wouldn't be home until that evening, if at all. This old woman's hair was short and had long since turned gray. Her face still had an angularity to it. She had, in spite of a stooped back, remained attractive. Her back was in the shape of an "L," all too common among elderly women, especially those who have worked in rice fields for most of their lives and have spent too many hours sitting on tatami mats serving dinners and beers to a domineering husband. Her eyes, though, were good. And that was what mattered the most to us.

We showed her our badges. She introduced herself. Her name was Aki Ono. After studying our badges, she smiled and invited us into her room for tea. Her room was as clean as Tazu's was messy and smelly. In it there was a *butsudan*, shelf of books, television, and a Spartan kitchen, only a two burner gas range, a rice maker, and an electric hot water kettle. We sat at a Japanese table in the middle of the room on *zabuton* cushions. On it was a bottle of Kikkoman soy sauce, salt and pepper shakers, a small bottle of vinegar, and, of all things, the latest iPhone and pair of Bluetooth earbuds.

The television was on, tuned to some talk show for women. She turned the television off with a remote, saying, "It gets me through the day. It's difficult for me to go on walks these days. I used to go for walks."

"Do you know anything about the man who lived above you, Tazu Uehara?"

"I'm not surprised that the police showed up. What did he do?"

"We'd like to talk to him," Detective Izuka said. He showed her the photo of Tazu with Junko and Tomomi at Disneyland. "Is this him?"

"That's him, all right," she said.

She then poured us our *houjicha*.

"There was always a lot of noise coming from his room," she said.

"Music?" I asked.

"It wasn't always music," Ms. Ono said. "The girls showed up three or four times a week, often different ones, all hours of the day and night. Some had that orange hair that is in fashion or tinted even green. You'd think they would respect the people around them and would go to a hotel. There's plenty of hotels for what they were doing. Young Japanese, they have no shame. The constant thumping over my head. It kept me up at night. Some girls, you'd think they'd make an effort to be quieter about what they're up to."

Ms. Ono was clearly a woman with a history. "Was she one of the girls?" I asked.

She took the photo and put on a pair of reading glasses and studied it. "She looks familiar," she said, "but not a regular. Cute girl. She could've done better than that bum."

"He doesn't seem to have been in his room for a few days," Detective Izuka said.

She looked Detective Izuka in the eyes and said, "Does his room stink? I think he did all his shopping at that 7-Eleven on the corner."

"Nothing gets past you," Detective Izuka said. He sipped his tea.

She said, "Age allows a woman the freedom to say what's on her mind. Are you married?"

Detective Izuka said he was.

"Handsome men are all trouble, I can tell you that, from experience. My first husband. Do I have stories! I was too young. I should've never listened to my friend's advice and married him. I later heard he seduced my best friend. And she was married!" She laughed. "She's dead now." She pressed the palms of her hands together in a Buddhist prayer.

I thought that Ms. Ono didn't have the chance to talk to many people and was now taking advantage of the opportunity. "What about Tazu Uehara?" I asked. "Have you seen him lately?"

She set her tea cup down and said, "The last time I saw him was maybe a week ago. He looked really frightened. He'd always had a swagger, but not this time. He was in and out of his room in a few minutes. Do you think he was a drug dealer? I think that is why those girls were coming to his room."

"We can't say," I told her.

"Right. You're police detectives." She sipped her tea. "He left with a backpack over his shoulder," she said.

"What color was it? Do you remember?"

"Black. The Japanese battle flag was on the back of it." She was coddling her teacup.

"Is that his motorcycle?" I asked.

"It makes so much racket. You'd think he'd respect other tenants when he cranks it up, but, oh, no. He seems to want others to know about it. I've seen him take a few girls for rides on it. They're all smiles. What's gotten into girls nowadays?" Ms. Ono leaned forward and whispered, "Sometimes he had a visitor who wasn't a girl. He wore a suit and drove a big, black car and pushed out his chests when he walked. You know the kind of man I'm talking about. I think they were both drug dealers."

"You seem to know a lot about these things," I said. I set my tea cup down.

She nodded over to a stack of gossip magazines on the floor and added, "I watch the Yomiuri news too."

I thought of the man in the Mercedes who'd been watching us from across the street and had her stand up. We went to a window and I pulled back the shoji screen ever so slightly and pointed at the Mercedes.

"That's the car," she said.

We went back to the table and sat.

"How often did he come by?" Detective Izuka asked.

"Maybe once a week or so."

"Was he carrying anything?"

"A gun."

"You saw him with a gun?" I said.

"I assumed that that bulge under his jacket was one."

"Other than a gun," Detective Izuka said.

"A black bag, like one people use to go to health clubs. He always came with one. You wouldn't let it out that you learned all this from an old woman?" she said. "I've got grandchildren."

"You can trust us," Detective Izuka said.

"What does it matter?" she lamented. "I'm eighty-nine. I've got a granddaughter who wants me to come join her on Okinawa. My bones ache when it's cold. How much longer do I have?"

"Winter is coming," I said.

"There was a time when it snowed in Tokyo," she said

"I remember those days," I said.

"You've heard about this heat island of Tokyo?"

"Not much gets past you," Detective Izuka said. "Go live with your granddaughter. Okinawa is a fine place."

"I'm worried I'll be a bother. I don't want to be a bother."

"You won't be a bother," I told her.

"My old bones, how they ache." She was again coddling her teacup, as if for warmth.

"Go live with your daughter," I said.

"That thump, thump, thumping over my head. And some of those girls! You'd think they'd have some respect for their neighbors."

"Tazu is not returning," I said. "Give moving in with your daughter some serious thought."

We thanked her and were about to leave, when she said, "That photo you showed me, from time to time when he wore an eye-patch. The girls must have found it to be mysterious. He was only conning them. When he wasn't with a girl he wasn't wearing it."

"Thank you," I said. "That'll make it easier to track

him down. If he does happen to return, call us."

She grabbed her iPhone and held it up.

We thanked her for the tea and information and left her room.

"He was a drug dealer, wasn't he?" she asked.

"Call us if he shows up," Detective Izuka said.

"Some girls might show up, looking for him."

"I think they might call first," I told her.

"If you see something that you think might be of interest to us, maybe you could take a photo of it with that iPhone," Detective Izuka said.

"I will," she said. "My daughter, we talk every night. She checks up on me. She's the one who bought it for me."

"Go live with her," I said.

Detective Izuka and I thanked her for the tea.

We put on our shoes and left her place and made our way to the police car. As we were, Mr. Budo came out from his Mercedes and said, "You were in there a long time. What did the old woman have to say?"

"We were having tea," Detective Izuka said.

"If any harm comes to her," I told him, "I'll see that you lose more than a little finger. Understand? Just remember my promise, you hiding your tattoos with a blue jumpsuit up in Abashiri."

Abashiri was a notorious prison on Hokkaido's northern coast. The winters were bitterly cold. And long.

He bowed and scuttled off to his Mercedes.

Detective Izuka said, "I'd rather be an honest policeman who drives a Toyota than that guy."

I said, "Let's have a talk with him."

We took a few steps and he made a U-turn and sped

off. Detective Izuka, who was prepared for him doing just that, had his telephone ready and snapped a photo of the car.

I said, "Tazu's supplier."

"The old man will want more than a finger."

"Let's pay him a visit," I said.

Detective Izuka glared at me. It wasn't police protocol to visit a yakuza boss without getting approval from someone higher up the chain than Chief Inspector Saito, but I was in no mood to wait around for that, which could take days, if it ever came. Tazu might be out of the country by then, on a forged passport. He knew where to go to get one. I was sure of that.

"What's gotten into you with this case?" Detective Izuka asked. "You're risking your career, breaking protocol?"

"Are you with me?" I asked.

"It's just a career," Detective Izuka said.

We got in the police car. Detective Izuka drove. As he was making his way toward Nakano, where the Yamaguchi-gumi's office was, I called the station and told Tsuchida and Morita to look over the CCTV videos in Tokyo Station during the time that Ms. Ono had told us Tazu had left Tokyo.

"He'll have a black backpack with the Japanese battle flag on the back of it. He might be wearing an eye-patch," I told them.

"Eye-patch?" Tsuchida asked.

"Eye-patch. His image of himself as a pirate," I said. I ended the call.

Detective Izuka and I didn't talk much on the way to the Yamaguchi-gumi's office. I could see that he was a bit nervous about breaking protocol.

"You were following orders," I told him. "You had no choice. I'll take full responsibility."

He said nothing.

CHAPTER EIGHTEEN

Taro Uehara lived in a large house near Nakano Shiki no Mori Park. The home was hidden behind a thicket of pines. The roof was tarnished copper and looked like Buddhist temples' the way its peak poked up over the pines.

On the street, a hundred meters or so from the massive wooden gate to the home, was an unmarked police car. It was always a presence at yakuza offices throughout the country. Police protocol was that we always kept the yakuza under surveillance, and we wanted them to know that we did. Two broad-shouldered yakuza with brush cuts wearing dark glasses were standing on either side of a massive gate, through which all visitors had to pass. Around the house there was a stone wall, high enough so that it was impossible for anyone to see over it into the garden. The two yakuza were meant to be intimidating, but they hardly were.

As Detective Izuka and I were about to get out of the police car, a couple of women on e-bicycles passed before them, carrying their children. The children were in navy blue pre-school uniforms, wearing sailor's caps. One of the kids dipped a stick into some soapy water and held the stick out, leaving in the wake of the bicycle a trail of soap bubbles. One of the yakuza, when a bubble approached him, stuck out a finger and popped it. He and his fellow laughed. But their laughter was short-lived. They returned to their stony selves when they saw us walking toward them.

They closed ranks, coming shoulder to shoulder, preventing us from reaching the button to an intercom. We showed them our badges, and I said, "We have something to discuss with Mr. Uehara. Get out of the way."

One of them grunted disrespectfully. The other said, "Wait." He took a telephone from his coat pocket, walked a few steps away from us, and whispered something into the phone. He grunted in reply to whomever he was listening to and put the phone away and joined the other yakuza but said nothing. A minute or so later a man in a double-breasted suit came and opened the gate. I knew who he was, Uehara's lieutenant, Hiro Toda. He was a graduate of Waseda University, lean and elegant. He had played on the university's tennis team. He now played squash and golf, which fit into his specialization—becoming chummy with company men so that he could get some dirt on them in the form of a sex scandal—sleeping with an actress—or learning about an accounting irregularity—hiding debt, usually—then he would threaten to embarrass the company if the man didn't siphon off company profits to the Yamaguchi-gumi. His cover was that of a stock wealth management advisor. He had an office in Minato-ku, near the Emperor's palace. He said, "It's a pleasure, officers," and bowed. "Follow me."

The two guards stepped aside, and we followed Toda into the garden along some flagstones that led to the entrance of the home. In the middle of the garden there was a pond choked with lily pads and around the pond manicured pines, several *sakura*, some maples, and, in a corner, on display among white stones raked into spirals, several pine bonsai on stands, bent over, as if they were braced up against a prevailing wind.

We came to the entrance, two traditional sliding Japanese doors that had slats of fir before panes of smoked glass. Toda slid one of the doors back, and we all went inside. The *genkan* was about the size of Tazu's room. In it there was a holder for umbrellas, lockers for shoes, and a shelf of leather sandals. It was like entering a company headquarters, and, I suppose, that was what it was, in a way, this home, a headquarters for the Yamaguchi-gumi.

We took off our shoes and put on some of those expensive leather slippers.

"I'll return shortly," he said.

Detective Izuka said of the slippers, "I wonder if I can take a pair of these back home. Mine are cotton, about to wear out."

"I don't think it would be a good idea," I said, "having a pair of Yamaguchi-gumi slippers in your house. How would you explain them to your wife?"

"Oh, her?" he said.

Toda returned. "President Uehara will see you."

We followed him through a cavernous space that did indeed remind me of a Buddhist temple. The floor was hardwood and lacquered and was so polished it shone like a mirror. Against one wall there was a *tokonoma*, in which there was a scroll and a flower arrangement of chrysanthemums and cherry tree stems. In a corner of the room was a suit of armor from the Edo period and not far from that a display of samurai swords, which kept up the image the yakuza had of themselves as warriors.

We came to a room toward the rear of the home. It was partitioned off by a series of *fusuma* sliding doors, on which were painted, on one side, a pair of Japanese cranes in courtship, and, on the other, Mount Fuji. Toda slid back the *fusuma*, and there, sitting in a very thick leather chair, with two bodyguards standing on either side of him, was Tazu's father, Taro Uehara, the boss of the Yamaguchi-gumi. He was wearing a blue business suit, white shirt, and yellow tie. In one hand he held a cigarette that was in an ivory holder and in the other a staff made of Japanese cedar. He was in his sixties but looked much older. I had heard he was suffering from stomach cancer and emphysema, and his shrunken in jowls and wizened face, his gray complexion and skeletal frame, were all evidence that this rumor had some merit. The cedar staff that he held confirmed the rumor that he had, a few years back, suffered a stroke.

Across from him were two chairs, also leather, but not as large as the one he was in. Uehara's chair was on a dais, which allowed him to look down on any supplicants, the way a *daimyo*, a feudal lord of the Edo period, would.

He let the staff lean up against an armrest and made a feeble, palsy-ridden gesture with a hand for us to sit, which we did.

"What is it you want?" Toda, who was now standing beside the old man, asked.

"Where is your son?" I asked the old man, not bothering to look at Toda.

The old man smoked on his cigarette before having Toda bend over, so that he could whisper something in his ear. Toda said, "You're mistaken. President Uehara doesn't have a son."

"This son that he doesn't have murdered a girl," I said. I handed the photo of Tazu with Tomomi and Junko at Disneyland to Toda, who studied it momentarily before handing it to the old man.

Their code of not killing innocent civilians now became visible. The old man's cheeks quivered. Once again, he bent over to whisper something in Toda's ear. Toda said, "You're mistaken. This isn't his son."

"No, we're not mistaken," I said. "That's his son and that girl on the right is the girl he murdered."

"You're mistaken," the old man squeaked. He had a raspy voice, eaten up by too much smoking. He reached for the mask of an oxygen bottle that I now saw was resting beside his chair and put it over his nose and mouth and took some deep breaths. He stared back at us as he sucked in oxygen.

"We just visited his rat hole," Detective Izuka then said. "He skipped town. Call him, see where he is. We tried. He won't answer a call from us." Detective Izuka looked around the room and added, "The suit of armor is a nice touch. It makes a person think the Yamaguchi-gumi has bushido. Where's the porn screening room?"

Toda said, "I allow you into President Uehara's home, and you insult him?"

"We know who the Yamaguchi-gumi is," I said.

I threw the photo of Tomomi, dead, lying on the floor of the Amour, at the old man's feet.

The old man and Toda looked at the photo but didn't pick it up. The old man turned his head and slurred, "My son didn't do this."

"So you do have a son?" I said.

Toda said, "President Uehara's son couldn't possibly have committed this heinous act."

"His son is a *shabu* dealer and killer. His name is Tazu. He gets young women hooked on the junk." Detective Izuka then showed Toda the photo he had taken of the Mercedes outside Tazu's building. "He's your son's supplier. He's stealing the junk from you and selling it to your own son. Did you know that?"

Wada studied the photo, obviously committing the license plate number to memory. He then said, "We don't know this car."

"Right," Detective Izuka said.

The old man and Wada looked at each other. We knew what was going to come of the man driving that Mercedes. If he were lucky, he'd only lose a digit of his little finger. If he weren't, his corpse would wash up on the beach of some fishing village on the Sea of Japan coast.

The old man took the oxygen mask from his face and put the cigarette to his mouth and drew on it. I feared we might all be blown up.

"We are honorable and don't engage in these acts of violence against women," Toda said. He took the old man's cigarette from him and tapped off some ash in a crystal ashtray and let it lay there as the man sucked on oxygen.

"You just force girls into doing porn," Detective Izuka said. "Very honorable."

"They come to us," Toda said. "We pay them well."

"And to get their pay they have to fuck the director and you and whoever you tell them to fuck. Very honorable."

"Shut up!"

We stared at each other and, as we did, the sound of a Japanese harp, a koto, filtered into the room from somewhere above us. It was an arresting sound, momentarily taking me far, far away from where I was and why I was there. I had heard something about the old man's daughter, who was in her early twenties, being a koto sensei, a teacher.

"We respect women," Toda then said. "They bring us joy." He looked up, to hint that he meant the sound of the koto.

"You're a filthy bunch," Detective Izuka said, "who cover your dealings by wearing tailored-made suits and driving Mercedes Benzs."

"Your son is a *shabu* dealer and killer," I said to the old man, looking him straight in the eyes.

He sucked deeply on the oxygen.

"*Shabu* is a dirty business," Detective Izuka said. "You're paying that loony Kim Jong Un to supply you with the junk, not very Japanese, I'd say, dealing with North Koreans. It's all about money. You have no code other than money."

The old man removed the oxygen mask and wheezed, "You insult me in my home."

"What did he say?" Detective Izuka asked Toda.

Detective Izuka and I stared at the old man as the sound of the koto filled the home. We knew we'd rattled him. In a concert hall or temple, the sound of the koto might have been pleasant, but here, where plans were made to bilk companies, distribute *shabu*, and traffic young women, the tune now reminded me of how the yakuza front themselves as upholders of Japanese traditions. What a lie that was. They were nothing more than parasites who preyed on weak men like Mr. Uno.

"Will there be anything else you'd like to discuss?" Toda asked.

I looked at the photo of Tomomi lying on the floor at the old man's feet and said, "Keep it, as a reminder of who you really are."

The old man had put the oxygen mask back on. His face had turned a deathly white, but some pallor was returning to it, as he sucked on the oxygen. He then motioned for Toda to hand him his cigarette. He removed the mask and I feared we'd be blown up again. He drew on the cigarette several times, until it was down to the tobacco-stained ivory holder, and then said in a whisper, "My son. He's not a member of my family."

"So you won't mind when I track him down and see that he's put away in prison for life, maybe even hanged?"

He had Toda crush out his cigarette and light him another. He then raised a hand and motioned for us to leave his home.

"You won't touch him," Toda said, "no matter what he's done, and you know you won't."

"Keep thinking that way," I said.

Detective Izuka and I stood.

"I'll show you out," Toda said.

We followed him back through the house to the *genkan* and put on our shoes and left the house.

Passing through the garden, I said, "Does the sight of such a beautiful place make you feel better about yourselves?"

Toda's face showed no reaction.

I looked over my shoulder, up to the second floor, where I saw the old man's daughter, dressed in a kimono, her hair in a comb, looking down at us. I waved to her, and she snapped the shoji screen closed.

We stepped through the gate. Toda said, "Good day,

officers." He locked the door of the gate.

We stood there for a moment, in front of the two guards, and then I said while facing the two guards, "We're lucky to get out of there with our lives, him sucking on oxygen while smoking. What an idiot."

Detective Izuka and I laughed.

The two guards said nothing, just remained there like mute gargoyles.

We walked up the street. More mothers riding bicycles, their children in seats behind them, were taking their children home from school. It had to bother them to live in the neighborhood of the Yamaguchi-gumi's office, but there wasn't much they could do about it. I wouldn't have been surprised if the old man, through a back channel, contributed to the upkeep of playgrounds and the budget of private schools in the area, to placate the people there. That's Japan. Harmony, even between gangsters and ordinary Japanese; that's what's important.

We got in the police car and returned to Shinjuku.

###

No sooner had we entered the office than Chief Inspector Saito barked, "Izuka and Kawayama! In my office. Now!"

We both went inside knowing what was going to happen next.

"Close the door," he said.

Detective Izuka did.

Chief Inspector Saito, by shouting at us, had threatened other detectives in the room who were considering breaking with police protocol. He sat, staring at us over his desk. We had remained standing before him, the way soldiers do before a commanding officer. We hadn't dared to take a seat.

"What's this all about?" I asked.

"Don't get smart with me, Kawayama."

"You went along with him, you fool," he said to Detective Izuka.

"Right, sir. I'm a fool." Detective Izuka said, I knew from working with him that he wasn't showing regret. He was, in his way, mocking Chief Inspector Saito, but the Chief wasn't aware of his irony.

"See these lumps on my head," the Chief said. He tilted his head forward. He was, of course, speaking figuratively. "They're from someone upstairs beating on it with a hammer." He looked at me, then Detective Izuka. "Why didn't you get approval for this visit?" he snapped.

"We're investigating the murder of a young woman," I said. "I didn't want to waste time."

"A prostitute!" he said. "Have you gone weak, Kawayama?"

It was all I could do to control my rage, but I did. I wanted Tazu Uehara too badly not to control my rage. I had worked out a plan to put him away. For good. I said, "I suppose the closer I am to retirement, the less I feel an obligation to protocol, sir."

"That's not like you Kawayama. Not like you at all. You've always played it by the book, but this case, it's gotten to you. Care to explain?"

"She was an innocent girl," I said.

"Aren't they all," he said.

"Uehara's son killed her," Detective Izuka said.

"I heard that that's what you believe. And that you

think he was dealing *shabu*."

"We know he was," I said.

Detective Izuka took his phone from his pocket.

"I don't want to see any photos," he said. "I want discipline."

"Politics, sir, isn't that it?" I said.

"Watch yourself, Kawayama."

"Who is it that Uehara has in his pocket?" I said.

"How many more years before you retire?"

"I'm not counting," I said.

"You need to because you might not make it that far. Think of your wife. Your children. You've got two, right."

He was sounding like a yakuza boss, the way he was threatening me. Maybe I should have begged for forgiveness by offering to cut off my little finger right there on his desk.

"And for you," he said to Detective Izuka, "you've got a lot to make up for. You're not so near retirement. Maybe you should consider keeping your penis sheathed for a while. I can't go on ignoring your behavior."

"Yes, sir," Detective Izuka said.

"Get out of here!" he barked, "both of you."

We left his office. Detective Izuka said. "I'm not keeping my penis sheathed."

"It wouldn't be you to keep it sheathed," I said. He asked me if we were going to press on with the case, and I said we would, that with any luck Morita and Tsuchida would see Tazu on CCTV footage boarding a train in Tokyo Station. It would be easy for them to spot someone with a backpack that had the Japanese battle flag on it. What an idiot Tazu Uehara was.

"How's your wife?" Detective Izuka then asked, which

came very much as a surprise. He usually never asked about her or my children.

"Fine," I said.

He shook his head. "I wish I could be a better husband and father," he said.

"You're not the only man who has a shaky marriage," I said.

"How have you remained loyal to the same woman for so many years?"

"We grew together," I said, "the way vines cling to each other for support in a jungle."

He looked at me with a puzzled expression on his face. I don't think he'd ever thought of a woman that way.

CHAPTER NINETEEN

That evening Mizuko and I went out to dinner. I wanted to get away from the case, if only for a few hours. Mizuko put on a lavender UniQlo fleece jacket, jeans, and leather walking shoes. I changed into jeans, too, and a flannel shirt and a blue North Face hiking jacket. It felt good to get out of a suit and not be a police detective, to just walk along beside Mizuko. I felt as if I had entered another world, the one of marriage and trust among two people who share a life together, one in which the other can finish the other's thoughts.

We went to a tempura chain restaurant called Tenya. A person can have a nice dinner there for less than fifteen hundred yen, or about twelve U.S. dollars. A Tenya was a ten minute walk from our home, near a busy corner, so that the shop could attract people headed from a nearby subway station.

It was pleasant to walk along that busy street, among others, on our way to the restaurant. We passed shop windows that had on display women's clothes, telephones, and TVs. We walked past an *izakaya* from which came the arresting aroma of fish grilling over charcoal and continued on under a canopy of ginkgo trees. Streetlights cast the shadows from the leaves onto the sidewalk. A breeze came up, rattling the trees. The breeze made me think that winter wasn't far off. It was time for us to take our yearly trip to a mountain *onsen*.

We came to a park and walked past it. Lovers sat on benches in the shadows of pine boughs. Seeing them,

I was reminded that Mizuko and I had secreted away on occasion to a park to have some time to ourselves. I wondered if Tomomi had done the same. She probably had. I knew she had. I hoped she had found some solace in these meetings. She had discovered some of life's pleasures at an early age. Maybe too early. And it had made life difficult for her, perhaps. No boy her age could meet her expectations. Maybe she had been happy with Junichi Wada. The two had to have had a few happy moments together before the car accident that had forced her to find her way in the world.

Tenya's facade is made to look like an old, traditional *izakaya* that has wooden supporting beams—fake, in this case—as part of the exterior wall. The color scheme is an attractive blue and yellow.

We went inside. There was an immediate welcome, "*Irasshaimase!*" that all the workers chimed.

We found an open booth and took it. Like most Japanese shops, there's also a counter. The ones in Tenya are made of Japanese fir, and along the counter there are bottles of soy sauce, salt and pepper, pickled ginger, and tempura sauce. The place settings have a hot towel the customers use to wipe their faces to clean their hands and wipe their faces. On the table at the booth there was an electrical device, a button that rang a bell, which got the attention of the waitress, usually a university student, now and then a housewife.

Mizuko, looking at the menu, said, "The autumn dishes are already out."

Tenya, like other Japanese shops—and breweries—comes out with seasonal foods. The menu on this day had shiitake mushrooms, slices of pumpkin, bell peppers, and sweet potatoes. Then there was the shrimp, Hiroshima oysters, and fried whiting. All of the orders came with rice and miso soup.

A girl came to our table. Her apron was smeared with oil, and she looked a bit haggard and tired. But, nonetheless, she did her best to put on a face and smile."I'll have the oyster dinner," Mizuko told her. The girl punched in the order on an electrical device she was holding.

"The fall assortment for me," I said.

The girl turned and trotted off back around the counter. Some tempura restaurants cook the orders right there in front of the customer and place it on their plates, straight from the oil, before the vegetables or shrimp get a touch soggy from the oil, but Tenya isn't so high class. It profits from turnover.

Mizuko said, "I've got a bit of good news."

"Am I supposed to guess?" I asked.

"That would be fun."

"That's too much like work," I said. "I do that on most days, questioning people. Out with it."

"I've been offered a contract with a production company."

"That's wonderful," I said. "You deserve it. If I'd known I would've taken you to some other place, not here." I shouted to the counterman, "And we'll do with a large bottle of Kirin lager!"

"*Kashikomairmashita*," he said. He was wearing a white paper cap and was a few years older than the girl who'd waited on us.

Mizuko's face had flushed red. "What?" I asked.

"You didn't have to order a beer," she said.

"Let's celebrate. Stop being a Japanese woman from the last century who walks a few steps behind her husband."

"Have I ever been that way?"

The shop had suddenly filled up, leaving only a few seats at the counter. Most of the customers were salarymen talking about work, another Japanese tradition, colleagues drinking together.

Mizuko told me about her contract. The hotel had set it up to both promote her and the hotel. Online. The production company, Jazz Holiday, was going to make a live recording.

"I don't think I'll make much money out of it," she said. "But it could help us with our retirement."

The girl brought the beer, and I took the bottle from her and poured some into Mizuko's glass. She poured some into mine. We touched glasses. "*Kanpai*," we said. I couldn't recall the last time we had celebrated anything together.

"Have you told anyone else?" I asked.

"I was waiting to surprise you," she said.

"You need to call Satoshi."

"Don't get all excited," she said. "It's a small thing."

We clinked glasses again and drank.

"I hope he knows what he's doing, marrying that girl," I said. We hadn't talked much about him and his fiancee since our visit to Sendai.

"Don't start with her," she said.

"All she knows is dogs."

"It's Satoshi's decision," she said.

I drank some beer. She was right about that. Tomomi had made some decisions too that she had come to regret. I didn't want Satoshi to regret any of his decisions, particularly when it came to his marriage, but that was beyond my control, I had come to realize.

"Anything new with that case you're working?"

"I'm here to forget about that," I said.

"Sorry."

"No. Nothing wrong with asking."

Her face had started to flush a rosy glow from the beer. If I'd told her so, it would have embarrassed her. She thought that the glow made her look like a drunk.

"Don't tell me," she said, reading my mind. "And I've only had half a glass."

"Relax," I said. "You're with a police detective. He's not going to arrest you if you get drunk."

She laughed. "You've always been the funny one. You charmed me."

"I made no attempt to."

"It comes naturally, and that's why you're so attractive."

"Knock it off."

The girl brought us our orders.

The tempura was still sizzling. It was served on squares of paper, arranged very artfully. The rice was served in bowls made of china and the soup in lacquerware ones, the traditional way to serve it.

"*Itadakimasu*," Mizuko said.

"*Dozo.*"

Just then I got a call from Detective Morita. "What is it?" I asked. I didn't want to answer the phone but felt an obligation to when I saw that the call was from him.

"That punk Tazu. He boarded the 10:07 Nozomi for Osaka the day Jiyumi Harajuku was murdered."

"Good work," I said. I put my phone away in a coat pocket.

"What is it?" Mizuko said.

"Nothing," I said.

"You're a terrible liar," she said.

"Just work," I said.

We continued to eat, but my mind had gone elsewhere. I'd already come up with a plan to deal with Tazu Uehara, and it had nothing to do with following police protocol.

"What about another bottle?" I said.

"That phone call must've been good news."

"You don't know how good."

"One day you'll tell me?"

"I promised that I will," I said.

CHAPTER TWENTY

The next morning I was so eager to put my plan into action that I called Ohashi from Yotsuya Station before going to the platform.

"Good morning," I said.

He groaned. I had woken him. "What is it?" he asked.

"How would you like to get some payback?" I said.

He, of course, had no idea what I was talking about and said as much. And then I heard a girl's voice, "Who is it?" she asked.

"Hush," he told her. "Didn't we have a good time?"

"We had a great time. Thanks for dinner, too. But . . ."

"What is it?"

"I could use five thousand yen. Please."

Ohashi said, "Get it out of my wallet, over there on the dresser top." He spoke to her in a very kind, understanding way.

I heard the creaking of a bed as she apparently rolled off it. He wasn't as much of a Japanese traditionalist as he made himself out to be, sleeping on a bed.

"Your little finger," I said. "Pay back. And for Jiyumi."

"How?"

"I know who killed Jiyumi—Tazu Uehara."

There was a momentary silence.

"You're sure?"

"I want to question him first. Then I'll know."

"You know who he is?"

"Yes."

"I was loyal to his father for years, and where did it get

me? I lost a piece of my finger, marking me for life. How can I help?"

"Tazu skipped town, boarded a train for Osaka the day of the murder. You must have some contacts with the Omi-gumi." The Omi-gumi was an Osaka yakuza gang that was the rival of the Yamaguchi-gumi. Now and then one of them would shoot a member of the other, if he was found in their territory.

The girl interrupted us, saying, "See you this evening. Thanks for the five thousand. You're a darling."

I heard a door open and close. I could understand how Tomomi had ended up working for Ohashi, even had some grudging respect for him.

"I've got contacts," he said.

"Find Tazu Uehara," I said. "He forgot his passport."

"The idiot. The police aren't looking for him?"

"You know how slow the police are, and him killing Jiyumi Harajuku, that isn't a murder that's high on the police's list of crimes to solve."

"I'll find him."

I had the idea that Tazu was hiding out in a neighborhood of Osaka called Kamagasaki in Nishinari-ku, where many fugitives go. In the back alleys, there are printers who forge documents, even passports, that make it possible for them to escape to the Philippines or Thailand. No, I wasn't going to rely on the Osaka police to find my daughter's killer.

Kamagasaki is populated with flophouses that offer cheap, three-mat rooms with shared toilets, sinks, and baths. The Omi-gumi skims the profits off the owners of these flophouses, if they don't own them outright. The managers of the flophouses keep an eye out for the Omi-gumi, who want to know who is hiding out from the law.

The flophouses have many of Japanese society's rejects, but they're treated well there; they've found a home and don't usually cause trouble. The management has even connected the TVs in the rooms to stream porn, to keep the men from turning on each other. The girls who work in the traditional red light district nearby are inexpensive but too pricey for these men who line up on a street near the Haginochaya Station on the Nankai Line every morning, hoping someone will come by and offer them a job at a construction site for the day. The best these men had it was back in 1992, after the Great Hanshin Earthquake, which destroyed many old buildings in Kobe, less than an hour away, killing over five-thousand people. They cleaned up the rubble of the homes and buildings. Often it was the Omi-gumi that loaded them up in trucks and took them to Kobe, to the gratefulness of those whose homes had been destroyed. The yakuza, they're clever that way, responding to disasters faster than the Japanese government can, at times.

The men living in the Kamagasaki flophouses aren't all fugitives from the law though. Some suffer from mental illnesses or alcoholism or they are homosexuals who have been outed by someone in their company and disowned by their family. When there are no jobs and these men run out of money, they sleep in the doorways of shuttered shops. The owners of the shops don't mind, unless the men get into fights over a particularly sought after space on the sidewalk.

Westerners tend to believe that there are few homeless in Japan. There are plenty. They live in cardboard boxes covered with blue tarps in Osaka,

Nagoya, and Tokyo, and they prefer that life to the one they have left behind in a company or as a husband or father. They form their own groups and governments, mirroring the very groups that they have rejected.

Running through Kamagasaki is a covered shopping arcade, to protect those who venture into the area from the rains when they come in June and the typhoons in August. Along this arcade are liquor stores, pachinko parlors, restaurants, and *shogi* and *go* gambling dens, thick with smoke from cigarettes. The Omi-gumi also leans on the owners of these places for protection money.

After ending the call with Ohashi, I went to the platform and got on the next train and bought the same newspapers that I always do when passing through Shinjuku North Station. When I got to my desk I started to go through them, starting with the *Asahi*. The front page had the usual international and domestic stories—Kim Jong Un firing off another missile into the Sea of Japan; politicians debating whether Japan's constitution should be changed, allowing for a build-up in the military; a Chinese submarine entering Japan's territorial waters; and predictions about climate change. Then I came to a headline in the metro section that made the back of my neck tighten. I stooped over my desk, staring down at the story, putting my elbows on the newspaper, my hands against the sides of my head, as if in the pose of that stricken man by a jolt of anxiety in Edvard Munch's "The Scream." I read:

Pacific Sushi Executive Found Dead

Uno Yuji (48), a buchou responsible for the purchasing of high grade sushi, was found dead in a hotel room in Shinjuku. Mr. Uno, who was from Nara prefecture, was a graduate of Kyoto University and had been with Pacific Sushi since his graduation. He was married and had two children. A company spokesman issued a statement, saying that it was with great sorrow that the company had lost one of its own. The company had extended its condolences to Mr. Uno's family.

Pacific Sushi is under investigation by the Department of Agriculture, Forestry and Fisheries for mislabeling maguro.

There was no byline, but I had the feeling that Sayako Kumagai had written the story. It was like her to end it with a line about the sushi mislabeling scandal. People would want answers, and the *Asahi* editors would turn to her for those answers.

Yutaka Hamasaki, a detective I knew well, was investigating Mr. Uno's suicide. There was an entire department that investigated suicides, which occurred much more frequently than murders. One of the most popular means of killing oneself had been to jump in front of an approaching train, but the train companies had taken to billing the family for the loss in revenue, which had cut down on those suicides. Now men hung themselves. Women took sleeping pills.

Detective Hamasaki had a desk one floor above mine.

"What about the death of that sushi executive? Did he leave a note?" I asked.

"He did. He mentioned something about that girl's murder and the shame he'd brought his family and company."

"So it was suicide?"

"Without a doubt."

"He named Tazu Uehara as the killer of Jiyumi Uehara. We're keeping that out of the papers. I was just about to call you."

"No details about the murder?"

"None."

"You need to know about Uno's wife," I said.

"We've talked to her."

"I'm certain that she didn't tell you what I'm about to. She used her brother, a P.I., to hire Jiyumi to seduce Ono to get some photos of him with her, so that she could divorce him. It goes way back with her and her brother."

"Complicated."

"I've unraveled it all. But yes, complicated."

"You've always been a good detective."

"I just do my job."

"My marriage almost unraveled a few years back."

"What saved it?"

"Shame," he said. "Neither of us wanted to face our relatives if we divorced. Now we wear two faces and live two lives under one roof. How are you getting along?"

"Counting down my days to retirement," I said.

"It'll kill you, sitting at home watching TV all day."

"I'm going to take up a hobby—collecting seashells."

"You? Unbelievable. But it will give you an excuse to go to the beach. I heard you paid old man Uehara a visit? It's a wonder he's still alive."

"News spreads quickly."

"He disowned his son because of him striking out on his own, selling *shabu* and getting young girls hooked. The old man has contacts, you know, who can see that his son doesn't spend much time in prison, if any at all.

She was just a prostitute and no one has even showed up to identify her body."

How it hurt to hear that and not be able to set people straight. "She had a family," I said.

"What are you holding back from me?"

"You don't want to know."

He then abruptly changed the topic, saying, "My son's a Shibuya slacker, picking up girls. I wouldn't be surprised if he's a porn scout."

"Are you going to disown him?" I asked.

"He's no longer welcome at our home. If he cleans himself up and gets a real job, I'll do what I can for him. You won't tell anyone about him, will you?"

"Of course not."

"You could blackmail me with that information." He laughed.

"Your confession is safe with me," I said. "My wife and I are going to get away from all this and go to an *onsen* up in the mountains for *koyou*."

"That's what my wife and I need to do to put some hope back in our marriage," he said. "I'll suggest it. You and Mizuko. You've always been a pair. How're your children?"

What could I say? "Satoshi is getting married."

"You'll be a grandfather."

"Don't make me feel older than I am."

"And your daughter?"

"She's a singer in a punk band."

"And you approve?"

"She has her own life. What can I do to stop her?"

"That's being understanding. I wish I could be that way with my son."

"In time, maybe," I said. "How did Uno's wife take the

news?"

"She put on an act, now that you told me she was about to divorce him."

"She's probably relieved that she doesn't have to go through with the divorce now."

"Cold."

"This job has made me into a misanthrope," I said.

"Maybe that *onsen* trip into the mountains will restore your faith in mankind."

"It's nice to think so."

"We must go out for a drink. The only time we meet is for the year end party. What about at the bar where Mizuko plays?"

"She signed a contract for an album," I said.

"Congratulate her for me," he said.

"Sure," I said. "We'll go out and have a drink one night after I've closed this murder case."

"I'll hold you to it. Give Mizuko my best and congratulate her."

We both hung up. It then suddenly struck me that the photograph I had left with old man Uehara might have contributed to Mr. Uno's suicide. Maybe he had used it in an attempt to blackmail Uno. Or had I? No. Uno had nothing to do with that photo. It was his son and Tomomi's murder and that sushi scandal that had convinced Uno that it was best for him to take an early exit. Tomomi had taken an early exit by becoming one of the evaporated, a form of suicide.

I called Sayako Kumagai to find out what she knew about Mr. Uno's suicide. If anyone knew more about it than Detective Hamasaki did, it would be her.

"I thought I might hear from you," she said.

"Mr. Uno's suicide," I said. "What do you know about

it?"

"It was predictable, now that I think about it. But how could I or anyone have prevented it?"

"Was the Yamaguchi-gumi squeezing him?"

"He'd be a good target, but I don't know if they were. Do you know his wife? I tried to reach her but she won't answer her phone."

"She doesn't know anything," I said.

"You talked to her?"

"She doesn't know anything. That's all I'm telling you now. Please leave her alone."

"Why? What are you hiding from me?"

"I'll clue you in at the appropriate time, as I promised. You'll be the first to know."

"Fine. The sushi business is dirty. I go to the market, pick out my own fish. I don't trust those labels anymore."

She had a point. I could've been eating horse if I went to some places for a burger. MOS Burger, a Japanese chain, I trusted.

"If you have some free time, perhaps we could meet up for coffee again?" she said.

I thought of Mizuko. It wouldn't be right to have coffee with Sayako and make her think I was interested in having an affair with her, if she was thinking along those lines. Or I was just flattering myself. I was too old for her. As a reporter, she was probably only interested in developing a police contact. That was fine with me. We'd use each other.

"I'll call you," I said.

"I'm waiting," she said.

I ended the call and then, using my private phone, called Ayako. The phone rang several times, but she didn't answer. I began to wonder about how long it would take for Ohashi to track down Tazu Uehara. I needed to get to him before he got out of the country on a false passport. And then I thought of myself with Mizuko far away from the realities of life, up in the mountains of Nagano prefecture enjoying an *onsen* bath and the chef's specialties. That day wasn't too far off. Maybe I'd break the news to Mizuko then about Tomomi. She was going to find out one day, and it would be better if I were the one who told her. Secrets, they cause rifts in a marriage.

Ayako answered the phone. She didn't speak with the elegant voice I remembered. She had trouble getting the words out. Her tears had been real, not staged, as Detective Hamasaki had thought.

"How are you holding up?" I asked.

"He was a weak man, but he didn't deserve this," she said. "You did this to him."

She kept on blaming me for her husband's death, but as she was talking I found it difficult to listen to her. Rather, I was thinking of the reality of the situation, that it was her desire for a divorce that had set these tragic events in motion, including the murder of my daughter.

After a while a silence settled on the line and before she said, "I just wanted a divorce."

"I want to meet with you," I said, "when you can make the time."

"Have you no respect for what I'm going through? Why?"

"You know. About the murder your husband was involved in. What did you learn before he . . ."

"Does it matter, now that my husband is dead?"

"You learned something before then?"

"I'll meet you."

"What about tomorrow?" I said.

She hesitated before saying, "I'll call you," she said. "Maybe I can get away from these reporters who've been hounding me all day. I suppose you need to know." She then ended the call.

CHAPTER TWENTY-ONE

Ayako called me the next morning when I was having breakfast with Mizuko.

"I can get away for a few hours," she said. "I have something important to tell you."

"Tell me now."

"No. I need to talk to you in person. I would feel better about it if I did."

"Where can we meet?"

"Not Shinjuku."

She didn't have to explain. I knew that, because Pacific Sushi's headquarters was in western Shinjuku, she risked being seen by someone who knew her and that, if that happened, she would be furnishing the tabloids with more salacious copy about her. The tabloids had already started to churn out stories about her husband, which included photos of him and Ayako, even their home out in Tachikawa. Mr. Uno was too far up the corporate ladder for the editors of the tabloids to ignore. A few photos of Mr. Uno going into a love hotel with a young girl, those were worth a good chunk of money, but Ohashi had resisted the temptation, out of respect for both his sister and Tomomi.

I said, "What about somewhere near Ikebukuro Station?"

"There's a coffee shop in Minami Ikebukuro Park," she said, "right off the Seibu line. Is that convenient for you?"

"It's fine," I said.

"Can you be there in an hour?"

"Yes."

Ayako was, indeed, in so many ways, a very determined woman. Growing up in a Kesennuma, and having a father who'd shoveled fish guts into barrels and a mother who tolerated his drunkenness and abuse, I suspected, had probably formed her early, filling her with a desire for a better life.

"Thank you," she said.

She ended the call, and Mizuko, looking at me, said, "You're arranging a tryst?"

"Work," I said.

"How is that case going?"

"Another time," I said. "Detective Hamasaki sends his congratulations on your recording contract."

"You told him? Why?"

"Publicity."

"It's nothing special. Anyone with a digital recorder can produce an album and advertise it on YouTube these days. Really, it's nothing, the album."

"Don't sell yourself short."

"How is Detective Hamasaki?"

"Determined to make his way up the bureaucratic ladder," I said.

"I'm glad you gave up on that. It would've just worn you down to a nub, all the politics."

I hadn't told her about Chief Inspector Saito threatening Detective Izuka and I the day before. It would only make her worry for me. I told her, "I need to get to work."

"To meet your lover?"

"In the morning? For coffee? We could do better, meeting in the afternoon. Find an *onsen* for us. Will you?"

"I'm doing some research," she said.

I left home and walked to the station and took a train to Shinjuku South Station, where I changed to the circle Yamanote Line, and rode it up to Ikebukuro Station, another major station serving both JR East and two private lines, Seibu and Tobu.

Going up to Ikebukuro Station on the Yamanote Line, I looked out the window, seeing the gray office buildings and the signboard advertisements flash by. An advertisement for a clinic that treated venereal diseases always caught my eye when I ventured north on the Yamanote Line. It was on the side of a hill, under some cherry trees, past the Takadanobaba Station. I had to wonder—were there so many people living with an STD that an advertisement was justified? I wondered, too, about the men—and women—who visited the clinic, their heads tucked down, their face covered by the brim of a hat. And then I couldn't stop myself from thinking of Tomomi, if she had ever been in need of a doctor who provided such a service. Tomomi's lifestyle made me rethink how she had lived and the lives of other young women like her who had fallen victim to men. In some ways, Detective Izuka was such a man. His libertine ways were not as amusing to me now as they had been before Tomomi's murder. Other men might have envied his good looks and confidence with women, but I no longer did. When he mentioned a "woman problem" he had gotten himself involved in, it had never occurred to him that he had brought such a problem on himself. I had to think that one day his wife would have enough of him and file for divorce and that that would cause him to reflect on who he was, no longer a *kendo* expert who others admired. I found it hard to believe that Ms. Nodoka of the forensics unit had gotten involved with him, but, well, romantic relationships, they defy logic. Tomomi was a perfect example of that. Why had she married a music producer who was on the verge of bankruptcy? She was lucky she had survived that car accident, but then, her luck ran out when she went to work for Ohashi, but he was suffering from her killing as a father would.

The train came to Ikebukuro Station. I got out of the car and followed the crowd along the platform and up an escalator and found my way through the cavernous station to the east exit and came out onto the street, where there was an old man picking up litter with a pair of bamboo tongs. He was wearing a yellow vest that had a patch on it, indicating that he was a member of a neighborhood volunteer group that cleaned up litter and collected aluminum and plastic bottles for recycling. Mizuko and I, and almost all Japanese, were on a neighborhood committee whose members cleaned up their neighborhood and tidied up the area where the garbage and recycling baskets were kept. It was part of being Japanese, tending to one's neighborhood.

I came to the park. It took up one block and had an office building at one end that was twelve or fifteen stories high. A coffee shop was in the center of the park that had some tables outside under the covering of maple tree boughs. This was a bit unusual for Japan, drinking coffee outside in the fresh air of a park, but we were catching on to a continental atmosphere. Coffee shops such as these were becoming more popular with the younger generation, who had their feet planted in both worlds, Japan's and the West's.

I took a seat at one of the cedar tables and waited for Ayako. She arrived dressed as I had expected, in a black wool skirt cut well below her knees, shiny black shoes that had a bit of a heel to them, a tartan Burberry coat with a fleece collar, and a pair of sunglasses set in a gold wire frame. I guessed that there wasn't one woman in Kesennuma who looked anything like her.

I stood when she approached my table.

"Good morning," I said.

She looked up at the sky, as if she hadn't noticed it until then. The sky was a deep, autumnal blue. The clouds were cotton white.

"I suppose it is," she said and sat.

She put her handbag, an expensive leather one, hand-tooled, on the seat of the chair between us. Her initials were etched into the burnished steel buckle.

"Thank you for coming," I said. "Coffee?"

"Taszo chai, please," she said.

This coffee shop didn't have a waiter, but a counter that customers went to to order. The girl poured my coffee and Ayako's chai into paper cups and snapped on the lids.

I set her chai down on the table. She popped off the lid and said, "I detest drinking something through a hole. It makes me feel like a suckling baby."

I had to laugh. I could never imagine her as a suckling baby.

"How much time do you have?" I asked.

"A half hour or so before I have to get back. There are so many arrangements to make. And the reporters . . . I never knew."

She took her sunglasses off and put them away in a case in her handbag. "Maybe my marriage wasn't a happy one, and maybe I was about to file for divorce, but I never expected..."

She reached for the chai and raised the cup to her mouth and sipped it and set the cup back on the table. A trace of lipstick remained on the rim of the cup. "I shouldn't have accused you," she said, "for what happened. I have myself to blame. Forgive me."

"You had your reasons to accuse the police," I said.

"Maybe my husband and I could've worked out a divorce. I should've never asked my brother to..."

"Your husband didn't kill himself because of a divorce," I said.

"I know," she said. "But I feel responsible, still."

"I understand. But don't be. Did he tell you anything about this mislabeling scandal, if it was connected to Jiyumi Harajuku's murder?"

"I feel so filthy telling you this. He confided it with me, the way a husband should confide secrets to his wife."

"You know what happened in that hotel room?"

"I know."

"What?" I said.

"He told me before he . . ." She took some time to compose herself and before saying, "She was murdered right in front of my husband."

"What? Tell me what happened."

"That man named Pirate, he found out about my husband and Jiyumi and the scandal and got into the room. My husband even opened the door for him, thinking the person was a maid. Then he burst inside. He and Jiyumi had a horrible argument. He lost his temper, and . . . they got into a fight . . ."

"He killed her?"

"Yes."

269

"Your husband just watched, did nothing?"

She glared at me, keeping her anger in check. The expression on her face was stony. I suppose she thought that I'd asked a question that was insulting to her, but how could I not ask such a question? Was her husband such a coward that he couldn't protect Jiyumi, a girl he'd been seeing for some time? Her anger at me had been boiling away in her, as mine had in me, at her and her husband and Tomomi's killer. Then the stoniness in her face eased. She had the capacity to wear so many masks.

"You interrupted me," she said.

I told her to go on with what she had to say.

"My husband tried to help her. He did. Honestly. That's what he told me."

I thought, he didn't try too hard, or maybe he would've ended up dead rather than my daughter. She could have run out of that room when he fought Uehara. That's what most men would've done, I like to think. I would not have hesitated to sacrifice myself for Mizuko.

"He was afraid," she said. "That man, he said he'd kill my husband if he interfered."

"So he just watched as Uehara killed Tomomi . . . Jiyumi Harajuku? What kind of man were you married to?"

"Tomomi?"

"I was thinking of someone else."

"He was weak. Very weak. I've told you that many times. All he'd known all his life was studying and work. How do you think I got him to marry me?"

She'd blurted that out without thinking, which had never happened with her before, as it did with so many others I'd questioned. She'd always been in control. Now

270

I knew the truth about her, what I'd suspected all along. She had seduced Uno and become pregnant by him, just to get out of Kesennuma. She had used sex, her brother had joined the Yakuza, both of them to seek better lives. I had to think that there had been opportunities available to them. She was intelligent. She could've gone to a university or technical school and graduated with a degree and found a job and met a loving, but maybe not so wealthy, husband. Ohashi could've gone to a trade school, learned a skill and worked in a factory or machine shop. But no, they'd chosen what they'd thought was an easier route, and that route had led to my daughter's murder.

"So now you know," she said.

"I'm not interested in what you did to get out of Kesennuma," I said.

"How could I have known this would happen? Isn't that punishment enough? Guilt. And my husband killing himself? He told me that he'd wanted to do something to break up the fight, but when he saw the man take that cord and . . . he just couldn't. He became paralyzed, he told me. He admitted that he wished that man had killed him too. He was crazed. His eyes were like that of an animal's, my husband said, who has no soul. It was after he killed that poor girl that he suddenly realized what he'd done and ran off. My husband went over to the girl, to see if she was alive, but she wasn't. He panicked. Who wouldn't? He ran out of the hotel and came home. I remember that night. He was so shaken he couldn't eat. He had some whiskey, which he rarely does, and passed out. I just thought it all had something to do with work. The next morning, he went to work, as usual."

"He could've called the police," I said. "It would've been easier on him."

"Would it? He would've lost his job. Who would hire him?"

She did have a point. His career would be finished.

She looked at me. Her anger had drained away, as if she had confessed some dark secret to a lover. Then I realized that I had a dark secret of my own that I had to confess to someone to relieve the burden of guilt I felt. In that way, I understood her. I felt both pity and sorry for what she'd gone through, and would continue to go through, what with her husband's suicide and the stories the tabloids were after about Uno being involved in a sushi scandal. It didn't seem that they would find out that he was having an affair with my daughter. Her name, her alias, anyway, wouldn't make it into the stories. He'd saved her of that, by not mentioning her in his suicide note. It wasn't much, but in the end he'd done something for Tomomi. He was a coward who had ended his life in a cowardly way.

"He paid for what happened," Ayako said. "I want to do something for her, but what? I can't do anything to make things right, can I?"

"No," I said flatly.

"You're so cold sometimes."

"No," I said, "I'm honest."

"Why are you so emotional about this case? You mustn't be this way with other cases."

"I have a daughter," I said.

She didn't say anything for quite a while. We just looked the other in the eyes, as if we were lovers who'd had a lull in an argument. We were both old enough to know that in situations like this there were no words to express what we were thinking. Speaking might even led us somewhere we didn't want to go. She then said, "I understand." She sipped her chai, set the paper cup down, and, again, looked me straight in the eyes, the way a lover would, and said, "Do you think she loved my husband?"

What a surprise that question was, her talking of love. "I wouldn't know," I said. "I'm a police detective." The truth was I had asked myself the same question.

"She was a strong girl with principles. That could've been the attraction. She had what he didn't. Love works that way sometimes."

"I wouldn't know," I said. But what I was thinking was, yes, Tomomi did have some principles; they just didn't always fit in with what was acceptable in Japanese society. If she had just gone along with Uehara's plan to blackmail Uno, she'd be alive but she couldn't, because of who she was. Did she love him? I would never know. Possibly. They were both, in their very different ways, outsiders in a society where everyone is supposed to fit in. Maybe that was it, that was what had held them together, their alienation from Japanese society.

I wanted to know more about what Uno had said about my daughter and asked, "What did your husband tell you about Jiyumi Harajuku?"

"Only that he was happy with her. That's all I know, because they continued to see each other long after my brother had taken the photos I'd asked him for. How odd it is that my husband would find companionship with a young woman he must not have had much in common with."

"They must've had something in common," I said.

"He said they could talk. They had good conversations. We never did. He paid her a little. She said she had a dream of leaving Japan one day and traveling. She was a runaway. She wanted to return to her mother and father but pride prevented her from going through with it. She thought that if she traveled for a few months she'd find who she was. If only . . . I don't know. There's a lot of 'if onlys' in life, isn't there?"

What she'd said was like a dagger in my side.

"I think she showed my husband a good time," Ayako continued. "He deserved as much. I never did much for him."

"Jiyumi," I said. "Her name is Jiyumi Harajuku."

"What a lovely name, beautiful freedom. It wasn't her real name, was it?"

"I can't say."

"It doesn't matter. I wish I'd met her. I think that in another life we would've gotten on well. It's not easy for a woman to find women friends. Most are conniving rivals. Does your wife have friends?"

I had never thought about that until then. Mizuko didn't have many close friends outside of her jazz music circle. It wasn't quite like that with me. If I'd wanted to talk to one of the other detectives about anything, I felt I was free to do so. There was that police officer brotherhood that bound us, sometimes, I can honestly say, for the worse. When evidence is concealed or confessions are forced, we cover for each other.

"My husband knew I was going to divorce him," she said. "I suppose he sensed it. Or maybe he even hired a private detective too. I don't know. He spotted my brother near a Family Mart, a camera around his neck. And yet he still went through with going into that hotel with her. That's what I don't understand. Why?"

"You wanted your brother to find the right girl for him," I said. "He couldn't help himself. He wanted what he'd never had before."

"True. So true. I was a liar from the day we met."

"Are you going to get over all this?" I asked.

"What a strange question for a police detective to ask. I thought police detectives were only interested in solving crimes."

I said, "You only did what you thought was required to better your life."

"That's what Haruto tells me."

"How is he?"

"We get along. We can talk. That's all new to me. We don't have any secrets between us."

"I'm sure the two of you will be happy together. I recognized that right off, when I saw the two of you for the first time."

"He's there for me, a rare thing in a man." She offered a smile. "You're there for your wife. I can see that you are."

I didn't want to talk about my marriage.

She quoted a famous haiku from Kobayashi Issa: "'Everything I touch/with tenderness, alas,/pricks like a bramble.'"

She sipped her chai, looked up at the sky, watched some maple leaves flutter in a passing breeze, then turned and looked back at me. The poem had made me think of Tomomi, lying there on that love hotel floor, dead. Ayako was right about some of us touching feeling like the prick of a bramble when we touched things. She continued on, "The day before my husband . . . " She stopped to gather herself. "I got him to talk the way a seductress can, by first getting him a little drunk before . . . I purred like a kitten and whispered in his ear, 'Tell me what happened in that room.'" She looked at me and smiled a smile of contempt and guile. And then she said, "I hate myself for doing that, but it had to be done. How confounding."

"I'm glad you did. Don't be hard on yourself."

"Thank you. What an evil man, Jiyumi's boyfriend. Pure evil. I never knew until now how evil a person can be."

"There's a lot of evil people—both men and women," I said.

"You would know. That woman poisoning her neighbors with arsenic-laced curry. How could she?"

This crime, which had happened back in 1998 in the city of Wakayama, was one that was so reprehensible it had become etched into the psyche of all Japanese. Masumi Hayashi, the wife of an insect exterminator, had killed two adults and two children, a girl and a boy, when she had served curry rice laced with arsenic at a neighborhood summer festival as retribution for feeling shunned by her neighbors. She was later executed by hanging, very rare, the execution of a woman.

"Find this man," she said, "and see that he meets the same fate as Mayumi Hayashi."

"I promise you I will."

"As I said, under different circumstances, it could've been me in that hotel room. This poor girl, how she ended up being killed by her boyfriend for defending my husband. I will never forget her. Ever. I wish I knew her name, her family. I'd pay them my respects. I hope I've been of some value to you."

I just sat there for a minute or two, a bit numbed

by what she'd said, having to keep my secret my secret until the time came and I told Mizuko. The feeling was unbearable.

"Are you all right?" she asked.

"It was a tragedy," I said, "for the both of them."

Ayako looked away, at the swaying bough of a maple. "It's been a long time since I've enjoyed *koyou*," she said. "In Kesennuma, it was so beautiful. And then along came those awful winters." She looked back at me and sipped her chai.

I said, "My wife and I always take a trip up into the mountains this time of year."

"My husband and I never went anywhere together."

"The tabloids," I said. "It's a good idea for you and Mr. Murata to avoid each other for a while."

"It's difficult, but I know it's the right thing to do. What's your wife like? Tell me about your daughter."

"She's fine," I said.

"You don't want to talk about her?"

"No."

"It doesn't seem fair that you used me the way you did but that I know so little about you and your wife."

"We get along," I said.

"I'm happy for you." She looked at the maple again and said, "I never thought I'd miss Kesennuma, but the tsunami changed all that. A lot of people I grew up with died."

"Your parents?"

"My father was fortunate enough to pass on before the tsunami. My mother is now living with a sister in Sendai. Haruto and I plan to take a trip to Sendai to visit her."

"Give yourself time. Don't let the tabloids get wind of

your trip."

"Waiting. That's torture."

"I'll see that Jiyumi's killer is taken care of," I said. "That's something you don't need to wait too long for."

"But don't do it for me," she said. "Do it for her parents. I can't imagine one of my children dying that way. How awful, when she had her life before her."She stared at me and said something that took me by surprise, "My brother. I don't want him to go to prison."

"What are you talking about?"

"He called me last night and said he's looking forward to seeing that this man is taken care of."

I wasn't sure what that meant, if he was going to do the deed or was going to trust me to.

"He feels so guilty and responsible for what happened," she said.

"Your brother isn't going to prison," I said.

"He has a weakness for protecting girls who've lost their way."

I said, "He's not the man I first thought he was."

"Maybe you could lock him up for a while, for his own good, before he does something he might regret?"

"We can do that," I said. "We'll just keep an eye on him."

"Thank you. My brother and I are close. I don't want any harm to come to him."

Considering how the end to all this would come, what she'd said was all the more poignant.

She looked across the park at a Family Mart. They really did seem to be on every corner of the city. A young couple, perhaps university students, was about to go inside. They were holding hands. It was such an ordinary act, but there was something romantic in it, the two of them being together, perhaps buying a piece of cake, some canned coffee, who knows what. It didn't matter. They were doing it together.

Ayako said, "I was never young the way they are. My youth passed me by."

We looked at each other. "Thank you," I said, "for telling me."

She smiled a smile that showed anything but happiness. It was a smile of despair. "Excuse me," she said. "I should be getting back home. I need to look after my children."

She took those sunglasses from their case and put them on and stood. I stood. She walked off. I sat back down, watching her until she turned a corner and vanished, heading toward the station. And then I saw the two youngsters come out of the Family Mart. The girl was holding a shopping bag. She had the most youthful, full of promise smile, which both made me feel happy for her and filled me with sorrow.

My phone vibrated in my coat pocket. I took it out and looked at the screen. The call was from Ohashi.

"My associates have Tazu Uehara," he said.

CHAPTER TWENTY-TWO

"I want to see him," I told Ohashi

"Where is he?" I asked.

"Call me before you arrive at Shin-Osaka Station," he said. "I'll arrange for my associates to meet you."

I agreed to his terms and called Detective Izuka. "We're going to Osaka," I said. "Meet me at JR Central Ticket station in Tokyo Station in thirty minutes. This is just between the two of us."

"I sensed as much."

"You don't have to get involved, if you don't want to."

"I owe it to her. I have a daughter."

"You're sure?"

"Yes."

I went back to Ikebukuro Station and took the Yamanote Line around to Tokyo Station, which is exactly a seventeen minute ride, and went to the Central Ticket station. Detective Izuka showed up a few minutes later.

We bought our tickets from a vending machine and went to the Tokaido Shinkansen platform and caught the Hikari for Shin-Osaka Station. The Hikari is the fastest train to Osaka. The trip is about two and a half hours. It would arrive at Shin-Osaka Station at 13:37. We'd be back in Tokyo by late that afternoon.

Soon after we'd found our seats—all reserved—I said to Detective Izuka, "Don't expect to be reimbursed for this trip."

He glanced at me wryly. "I wasn't expecting to," he said.

Twenty-seven minutes later the train pulled into Shin-Yokohama Station to pick up more passengers. It was there for two minutes. The next station was Nagoya, then Kyoto, and finally Shin-Osaka. The "shin" refers to the "shin" in Shinkansen. Those stations serve the shinkansen and a few other lines.

Businessmen in dark suits and women in equally dark dresses or, now, slacks, filled the car at Shin-Yokohama Station. Some of these people would be back home that evening as well. They were going to the Kansai region for a business trip.

It wasn't long after the train had departed Shin-Yokohama Station that the girl who sells coffee and tea and *ekibens*, box lunches, came along, pushing her trolley down the aisle. All of these girls are in their twenties. They are all chosen for their smiles, the warmth of their greetings, and the youthful glow of their faces. Tomomi had often made jokes about these girls, that, with their starched uniforms and aprons and their hair held in a bun under a hairnet, that they were all wind up dolls. She, of course, wasn't at all right about that. They had their lives outside of work. As did I.

"I'll have a coffee," I told the girl.

"I'll have one, too," Detective Izuka said. He smiled at her, and she blushed. "Don't you get tired, walking back and forth between Tokyo and Osaka every day?" he asked.

She held a hand over her mouth, to conceal a smile, and then when she'd gotten control of herself, said, "I'm proud to be on this train; not so many girls are so fortunate."

"Admirable," Detective Izuka said. He had reached into a pocket on his coat and removed his *meishi*.

She took it politely with both hands and offered a humble nod. She looked at his *meishi* and said, "A real detective?"

"That's me," he said. "We're going to Osaka to question a killer."

"Really?"

"Really."

"Don't listen to him," I said. "We're just bureaucrats."

She looked at his *meishi* again. "But it says right here that you're detectives."

"We're just bureaucrats," I said.

She nodded and smiled.

"I'd like some coffee," a man said from somewhere behind us.

"Excuse me," she said. She pushed the cart down the aisle.

"She's cute," Detective Izuka said.

"Soon they'll be half your age," I said.

He looked out the window at the flickering of buildings and bridges. Now and then an eastbound train swept past, making the coffee on my tray ripple. Then we came to a stretch of the line that faced a mountain on which there were tea trees.

He mumbled, "My wife is leaving me."

This was hardly a surprise. I'd been expecting it for years. What was a surprise was that he'd let me in on the news.

"Sorry to hear that," I said.

"I can't help myself," he said.

"You can't continue on this way."

"When a pretty girl crosses my path, it's like I'm struck by a bracing spring breeze."

"I think some famous Japanese writer said that before you, but I can't recall off hand who. Probably one who killed himself."

"That doesn't narrow down the field," he said. "Do you have any idea what we're going to do when these yakuza thugs meet us at the station?"

"Take us to see Uehara," I said.

"How did you connect with them?"

I just looked at him. He nodded, saying nothing.

"Ohashi isn't the loser I thought he was. He has a conscience. We need to get to Uehara before he leaves the country on a fake passport or the Chief forces us to close this case. You know he will. A girl with no past who was one of the evaporated, it's not one of high priority."

"Us working with Omi-gumi thugs. It galls me. Why not let his old man deal with his son?"

"He's not going to execute him."

He looked at me and, though he said nothing, knew what I had planned.

"You can get off the train at Nagoya," I said.

He thought for a moment. "No," he said, "I'm with you."

"You could be risking your career."

"I'm with you. I don't want this punk to get off for what he did, but it's not going to look good, two Tokyo detectives walking off through the station escorted by yakuza thugs. We'll be on CCTV."

"I know. You can get off at Nagoya."

"What is it with this case? It's not like you, breaking with protocol?"

"I have a daughter."

It took a while for Detective Izuka to say something. "How is she?" he asked. "Shouldn't she be in a university now?"

"Something like that," I said.

We'd worked together long enough for him to read my mind and know when he should not ask what he was thinking. I said, "My wife has a contract for a jazz CD."

"Great!" he said.

"You should come by and listen to her play. She plays jazz standards." And then I thought of him meeting Chie and regretted that I'd extended the invitation, not that I thought Chie would submit to him. She was her own woman. He was charming and handsome. Then I thought, so what if she finds him attractive? She was a modern Japanese woman who could handle herself.

"I'll take Nao," he said.

"Who?"

"Ms. Nodoka?"

I wasn't used to anyone referring to her by her first name. It was a modern one. I'd known plenty of Naokos but no Naos. The loss of the *ko* (子), meaning child, had become a popular way of naming daughters. The *mi* (美), meaning beautiful, was also becoming less popular.

"So why did you give your *meishi* to that coffee girl if you've got Ms. Nodoka?" I asked.

"Habit."

"A bad one. You're a drunk," I said.

"My wife is taking the children, moving in with her parents."

"Are you going to kick in some money, to help her out until she finds a job?"

"I'm bad, but not irresponsibly bad," he said. "I never thought I'd be missing the kids. Her? Not so much. We've grown apart. Maybe it's been the job. But my children. I've got to see them."

"Maybe you two can work something out. That's how it's done these days, when it comes to custody of the children."

"I hope so," he said. "She's better off without me, I know, but it still hurts. I feel that I've failed somehow as a man."

That was quite the confession. I'd never expected him to admit to that. And he was right. "Maybe things will work out with you and Ms. Nodoka," I said.

"She's too good for me," he said.

"Don't lose her," I said.

"I'm doing my best. Honestly."

I wanted to believe him, but addicts don't give up their drug so easily. Ms. Nodoka, however, was tough. If any woman could straighten Detective Izuka out, she could.

After the train had departed Shin-Kyoto Station, I left my seat and went to a section of the car set aside for people to make telephone calls and called Ohashi.

"We just passed through Shin-Kyoto Station," I told him.

"They'll be waiting for you at the West Gate," he said.

"That's all, 'waiting for you?'"

"They've got it all arranged."

I had a feeling what that meant and returned to my seat. "We'll soon pass the point of no return," I said. "In the West, they say 'crossing the Rubicon.'" I then explained to him how Caesar had crossed the River

Rubicon and entered Rome, becoming emperor.

"He was assassinated. I hope things turn out differently for us," he said.

"I don't know how you ended up as a police detective," he said.

"Sometimes I wonder myself."

"Too many television dramas and movies. That's my excuse."

"Same here."

"I would've thought that you'd have had more sense than to buy into that romanticism."

"I guess not," I said.

The train pulled into Shin-Osaka Station, and we got out and went down the platform, passing through the ticket readers, and continued on past shops and lockers and ticket offices until we came to the escalator for the West Gate. We took it down to the street and standing there at the curb were two men, one with curly hair, the other's head shaved, both wearing dark glasses, dark suits, double-breasted coats with peaked collars, white shirts, and fine, Italian silk ties.

The smaller one had a yellow handkerchief stuffed into the pocket of his jacket. The other was broad-shouldered and had a menacing look, as if he took pleasure in shaking down those club owners who didn't pay protection money. I doubted that he had graduated from high school, but even so, as an enforcer, he had become somebody.

They both bowed. Neither Detective Izuka nor I bowed in return.

"Detective Kawayama," the smaller one said, "it's a pleasure." He was holding a plastic shopping bag. He took from it two cans of black Boss coffee. He handed one of the cans to me, the other to Detective Izuka, and said, "I heard you like black coffee." He had a rough, urban Osaka accent.

"Please," he said, gesturing to a black, very polished Toyota GranAce minivan that was parked at the curb, the kind of minivan to ferry people to and from airports.

The larger yakuza slid open the door.

"Please," he said again, making a hand gesture, as if we were passengers of importance, and I suppose we were.

Detective Izuka and I got in the minivan and sat in two separate seats, like those you would find on an airplane with armrests.

"The police department should up-grade to something like this," Detective Izuka said.

We weren't getting this treatment for free. The yakuza never did anything for free. They'd come to me one day, asking for a favor, as Ohashi would, but I was willing to accept that price in return for what they'd promised.

Detective Izuka opened his coffee and drank some. "Still hot," he said. "Good service, these two."

The bigger yakuza got behind the wheel. The smaller one sat beside him. He turned, facing us, and said, "Excuse me, but I need to put up a shade."

He pressed a button and a pane of tinted glass that was so dark we couldn't see through it rose up, preventing us from seeing outside.

I looked at my watch. It was 2:37. The GranAce started off and picked up speed. The larger yakuza turned left and right, as if going around the station, to confuse us, maybe, before I felt the minivan go up a ramp onto an expressway. It stayed on the expressway for five or six minutes and then it exited it and the big yakuza made more turns to keep on confusing us. I had been trying to memorize the turns, but it was an impossibility. I did, however, start to hear the sound of jets taking off and landing, which meant we were somewhere near Osaka's Itami airport, which serves mostly domestic flights.

I continued to look at my watch. After seventeen minutes, the GranAce went up an incline, into what turned out to be a warehouse, and I heard the sound of a metal door rattle shut behind us.

The tinted glass came down, and the smaller yakuza said, "We've arrived. I hope the ride wasn't too uncomfortable. Forgive us for having to put the shade up."

He got out and came around to the sliding door and opened it, and Detective Izuka and I got out. We were in some kind of abandoned warehouse, which had once, it seemed, been a factory, but which now served as sound stages. Around the cavernous space were bedrooms and kitchens and offices, schoolrooms lined with desks, a doctor's office, a hospital room—including a bed—and even the fuselage of an airplane. Over in one corner there was some lighting equipment, piles of electrical cords, and dressing rooms made of cheap press-boards.

"I recognize that bedroom," Detective Izuka said. "What was her name?"

The smaller one smiled. "You must be referring to Aoi Miura," he said. "She was a star."

"What ever happened to her?"

"She retired. She now runs a club here in town. Interested in paying her a visit?"

"Not today," I said.

"Yes, indeed," the smaller yakuza said. "Today is only

business, but next time the visit will be on us."

"The supply of actresses is thinning out," the larger yakuza said.

"The aging population doesn't help," the smaller one then said.

"And taxes," the larger one said and sighed. "They keep going up. It's not right. The politicians, they're only out for themselves."

"Her club must be a popular one," Detective Izuka said.

I stared at him.

"Just making conversation," he said.

The place smelled of burned out electrical lamps and dust.

A freight elevator was on the opposite side of the room from the film sets. We followed the smaller yakuza to the elevator. His larger companion trudged on behind us. I could hear the soles of his shoes crunching on the concrete. At the elevator, the smaller yakuza pushed a button and the door opened and he said, again, "Please," and made that offensive obsequious hand gesture, as if he were a doorman at the Keio Plaza Hotel, when all he was was a thug in an expensive Italian suit.

We got in the elevator and took it up to the sixth floor. The doors opened onto another space that was void of anything but walls and I-beam support columns. Across one wall there was a line of grimy gray windows that let in some yellow light. A jet came over the building, rattling the panes of glass in the windows, making me wonder, of all things, how the filming was done when there was air traffic noise. Junko Atada was probably familiar with places like this in Tokyo.

"Follow me," the smaller one said.

We did and came to him, yes, *him*, Tazu Uehara, who was in a corner of the room. I had expected a rage to build up in me at the sight of him, that I might not even be able to control myself and pop him one in the jaw, but all I could do was just stare at the loser. What came to mind was his father and the understanding why he had disowned his son. Tazu was a pathetic little runt, withered up by *shabu*, his hair grimy and oily, as if he hadn't washed in the past few days. He made no attempt to show any of the faux-dignity—the face the Yamaguchi-gumi wore—that his father had certainly raised him to be proud of. Families. They all have their problems, each one unique, as Tolstoy had written.

Tazu was tied to an office chair that had casters on the legs and a padded back. The chair was in a shaft of yellow light coming through a window. The light must have made it difficult for him to make out who we were, because he squinted.

Standing next to him was a third yakuza, also with curly hair and broad shoulders and dark glasses, but wearing a blood-spattered white jumpsuit, like those inspectors wear who venture into the Fukushima nuclear plant. He was expressionless, like a slab of marble. He'd wrapped a length of galvanized chain around one of his fists. Tazu, I now saw, after my eyes had adjusted to the light, had a black eye and battered jaw and nose. A couple of his *shabu*-decayed teeth were lying on the concrete floor. Blood had flowed from his nose over his lips onto his chin and dripped onto his jeans and a Harley-Davidson T-shirt.

The smaller yakuza took a rag from the one who'd

beaten Tazu and wiped Tazu's face with it, but not very well. He only managed to smear the blood around. He then tossed the rag onto the floor and said, "Mr. Uehara, I'd like you to meet two Tokyo homicide detectives."

Tazu looked up at us, but I don't think he saw us clearly, his eyes were so swollen. Tazu's arms showed evidence of *shabu* use. Lines of syringe marks lined them, up to the ragged sleeves of the T-shirt. He wasn't Japanese. He was some kind of foreign trash, marked by that Harley-Davidson T-shirt. It disgusted me that he had used Tomomi's addiction to have his way with her, as he had so many other young girls. With that thought, it was all I could do to stop myself from knocking out a few more of what teeth he had remaining in his head. But I stayed under control.

A tic started on Tazu's right cheek. He said, "Do you know who my father is?"

"Shut up, you piece of shit," the yakuza who'd beaten him said.

I suddenly felt a kinship with this thug. That's not how it's supposed to be, I know, a policeman having any connection with a yakuza, but that's how I felt. I even wanted, for just a few minutes, to trade places with him, to wrap that chain around my fist and be left alone with Tomomi's killer.

Detective Izuka said, "You're going to hang."

"My father has contacts."

I said, "We had a talk with your father. What a disappointment you turned out to be."

"He's still my father," he said. "We're family. Tight."

"Tell me about Jiyumi Harajuku," I said.

"Who's she?"

The yakuza standing behind him gave him a good

JAMES ROTH

punch in his ribs. It took a while before Tazu could get his breath back.

"These gentlemen asked you a question," the little yakuza said. "Tell him what you told us."

"That wise-ass girl?"

"Your scheme didn't quite turn out the way you planned, did it?" I said.

"What scheme?"

"You know very well what scheme," Detective Izuka said. "Your scheme to blackmail Yuji Ono."

"You got me mixed up with someone else. That's what I keep telling these goons."

The yakuza standing beside him punched him a good one in the ribs again and he doubled over, gasping.

"I don't think so," I said. "You killed her."

Tazu spit blood at my feet.

The yakuza punched him again. "Apologize!" he said.

The smaller yakuza said, "These gentlemen came all the way from Tokyo to pay you a visit. Show some respect."

Tazu by now had caught his breath and said, "They can go back to Tokyo."

Detective Izuka said, "You killed her!"

"So what if I did?" he said. "We could've made a lot of money off that man, but she wanted to protect him. She was trouble for me from the beginning. Always trouble. I should've never had Junko ask her if she needed help. I never met a girl like her. Only trouble. I did want to help her, you know. I could have."

"That's rich," Detective Izuka said.

"You know what I should've done? Gotten another girl to fuck Uno. I should've known that Jiyumi wasn't going to work with me. There's plenty of other girls to

292

be had. Plenty. I had a feeling about her not telling me about Uno."

"You won't be getting any more girls," the smaller yakuza said. Don't you have shame?"

"They'll be a war if something happens to me."

The three yakuza all laughed.

"Something to look forward to," the smaller one said.

"We're ready for those Yamaguchi-gumi losers. They know better than to come to Osaka, a real city."

"I don't think they'll be a war," I said. "You're a disgrace to your family and to all Japanese."

"What year are you living in?" Tazu said.

The yakuza standing beside Tazu popped him in the mouth. "We're Japanese," he said, "not trash, like you and your father's gang. It doesn't matter what year it is, we're Japanese, and that'll never change."

Tazu spat out some more blood. "I'm an entrepreneur," he said. "That's how business is done nowadays, not the old way."

"We have honor," the smaller yakuza said.

"What's that?"

The little yakuza nodded his head, and the bigger yakuza knocked out what few teeth were remaining in Tazu's head. "We've managed to keep our teeth," he then said, "by playing by the rules."

"The only rule is making money. You need to modernize. That Japan you're living in is finished. All she had to do was play along with me and she'd be alive."

The little yakuza spat in Tazu's face.

"I wouldn't have even had to go to that room if she'd been another girl. We could've planned it all out. But not Jiyumi Harajuku. She always went her own way. Damn her."

There he was, showing no remorse, blaming Tomomi for her own death. He was a psychopath. The country was better off without people like him.

The yakuza who'd been punching Tazu in the ribs and mouth was about to punch him with one of his fists wrapped up with the chain when the smaller one said, "No! If he's beat up too badly the police might not buy it." He looked at me. I didn't think it mattered. Tazu's face was already bruised, bloodied, and battered. The Osaka police would pass off his beating as gang related and not bother to investigate it. Higher-ups would see no point in it.

"Where's the telephone?" I asked.

The little yakuza reached into his coat pocket and took from it two telephones. He handed them to me.

"The yellow one is hers."

Holding Tomomi's phone, I felt strangely close to her. I slipped the phone into my pocket. I wasn't sure what I was going to do with it, but I had time to think about that.

"This one is his." He handed me Tazu's iPhone.

Tazu looked up at me. His pupils were the size of .5 millimeter dots from a pen.

The smaller yakuza said, "Anything more you need?"

"Nothing," I said.

"We've got a room for him in Kamagasaki that will work," he said. He took a plastic bag from his pocket. It contained a syringe, a spoon, a butane lighter, and some *shabu*.

Tazu popped upright; I think he had finally come to the realization that his father could do nothing for him now.

I bowed. Detective Izuka bowed.

The three yakuza all bowed deeply in return.

"Shall we escort you two gentlemen back to the station?" the smaller yakuza asked.

I got home at my usual time, around six. Mizuko was at the Keio Plaza bar. Stepping into the house, I felt as if I were entering a sepulcher, it was so dark and empty. I'd never felt that way before when coming home. My trip to Osaka had changed me in a way that I didn't quite understand. There wasn't this closure that Americans are so fond of talking about. Tomomi was dead and embracing this closure that Americans talk about wasn't going to bring her back. All that remained as a means to feel release from what had imprisoned Mizuko and I was knowing that Tazu was going to come to his end.

I came to the *butsudan*; on it were the incense Mizuko had lit that morning, now burned out, the brass bell, and the photo of Tomomi in her high school uniform. I put my hand in my coat pocket, feeling Tomomi's telephone, then brought it out and stared at it, thinking of all the stories that it contained, wanting and not wanting to know what they were. I kept on looking at the phone, knowing it had to go there on that *butsudan*, but this was not the time to put it there. I had to tell Mizuko what I knew first, and I wasn't prepared for that quite yet. I wasn't sure when I'd tell her, but not on this night. Then there was the matter of seeing that Tomomi was properly sent off and having Mizuko and Satoshi and I together when she was. I had that to think over as well.

After a while some kind of spiritual need came over me and I put my hands together and bowed my head and remained there, praying for Tomomi's spirit. As I did, I recalled the good times we'd had together, a family trip to a beach in Shizuoka, when she was thirteen, her going swimming in the Pacific and riding the waves onto the beach. I recalled her girlish laughter and the sheer wonder that was on her face that day. I thought of other ordinary times as well, a trip to the Ueno Zoo, making faces at the orangutans, and later eating ice-cream in the Ueno Park. I recalled her learning to ride a bicycle, me holding the handlebars steadily, then pushing her along, and her falling over and skinning a knee and bursting into tears and me feeling guilty about pushing her too hard. I recalled those times when she'd been the lead singer in that punk girl band and me tolerating it. That had brought her joy, being in that band, if only temporarily. I resisted feeling guilty about her running away. I told myself that it was just in her to be that way, independent and rebellious, and that those qualities weren't such a bad thing. She'd even tried to fight off Uehara and died because of it.

I stayed there before that *butsudan* for I don't know how long, my hands clasped together, feeling her in me. It wasn't any religious feeling. I don't believe in that rubbish. I'm no Buddhist. Buddhism, that's too often a con run by corrupt priests who profit from the sale of family tombs and funerals in their temples. Those priests are in their way like the yakuza, passing down from one son to the next and the next their tradition of profiting off others. What I've come to believe as I've told this story is that all a person can do is live their life as best they can, not causing trouble for others, while attempting to preserve the social harmony of Japan.

CHAPTER TWENTY-THREE

It wasn't long after I sat down at my desk the next morning that Chief Inspector Saito called me into his office, saying he wanted to have a word with me. He was intimidatingly polite. I was certain that it had something to do with the trip to Osaka, but so what if it did? He wasn't going to fire me. He couldn't fire me. Review boards went on interminably. I was a bureaucrat who'd spent too many years on the police force to face one. What concerned me were two things. The first was that the Omi-gumi would ask me for a favor one day, as I knew they would, and that Detective Izuka might be facing some kind of disciplinary board because of me.

I knocked on the wall outside Chief Inspector Saito's office, and he said, pleasantly, "Come in, Kawayama."

I did, and rather than him having me stand there before his desk, as his meaty arms and pig knuckle fingers resting on his desk, he said, "Have a seat."

He had rarely been that chummy toward the detectives he managed—except when he'd had too much to drink—and when he wasn't drunk this kind of talk was usually a prelude to very bad news, usually a transfer to a small town in Tohoku. I am suspicious of a politician's kindness, and Chief Inspector Saito had become more of a politician than a police detective. Whatever it was that he was going to tell me, I was up for it. I decided to catch him off guard by saying,

"The Chinese are at it again." I had read an article about Japanese F-15s intercepting a flight of Chinese fighters in that morning's *Asahi*.

"What's that?" he said. His lack of awareness of that morning's news was a tip-off that he had something on his mind that troubled him.

"The Chinese," I said, "invaded Japanese airspace between Ishigaki and Okinawa." Ishigaki was the southernmost island of the Ryukyu Islands, the Okinawa archipelago that extends from Kyushu all the way south to just east of Taiwan.

"Have they now?" he said.

"It was in the *Asahi*," I said, "and on this morning's NHK news."

"I missed it. We have to keep an eye out for them."

He turned to look out the window at the maples and firs and pines in the park. "It won't be long until *koyou*," he said. He looked back at me and said, "Where are you and your wife going this year?"

"I leave the planning up to my wife," I said.

He asked, "How is that case progressing, the one involving the prostitute?"

"You mean the young woman in the love hotel?"

"That's the one, the prostitute and the man. . . what's his name? Who hung himself?"

"Mr. Uno, a *buchou* at Pacific Sushi."

"Yes, him. He should've come to us, not let the yakuza push him over the edge. When will Japanese regain the courage they once had?"

It was a rhetorical question. He went on, "She couldn't have been bedding down with Uno because of his sex appeal, from what I've seen of him. How did he end up with a wife like that? I did see her on the news."

"It's a question we all ask," I said.

"She's from Kesennuma, from what I've heard. What do police do up there but arrest drunks and check if the Filipino bar girls have overstayed their visas?"

"Some marry," I said.

"So I've heard. I don't like it, the mixing of races. How did Uno end up with a wife like that?"

"I wouldn't know," I said.

"You questioned her."

"Not about how she ended up marrying Mr. Uno," I said.

"Fine. Don't tell me. You must have your reasons."

I had nothing to lose and said, "Why am I here?"

He raised an arm and put his big head in the cradle of a palm, looked at me, dropped his arm, and then said, "You've had a lot of experiences over the years, many different cases."

I agreed that I had.

"You're a valuable resource to the department," he said. He was setting me up for bad news. I also knew that whatever he was going to tell me hadn't been his decision, the way he was troubled by it. Someone above him who would remain a faceless bureaucrat had made the decision and he was responsible for carrying it out. He finally got it out, saying, "You'd serve this department well as a trainer."

Training was a demotion at the worst, a step to the side at best. It was as near to a firing as the police department could manage. It wasn't necessary to go through a review board, which might get into the newspapers and embarrass the department. Reporters like Sayoko Kumagai would ask questions.

"I don't want to train new detectives," I said.

He pushed himself back in his chair and said, "You have no choice, Kawayama. You should have never broken protocol, visiting Uehara and taking that trip to Osaka with Detective Izuka. Don't think I didn't hear about it. I got a call from a friend of mine in Osaka. Why did you meet those Omi-gumi goons?"

"I was following a lead."

"You should've told me first."

"Yes, sir."

He sighed. "Don't be insolent," he said. "Haven't I been a good chief?"

I admitted that he had.

"And that's how you pay me back? You deserve to be a trainer. Damn you!"

"I was doing my job. Sir. Sorry. You're right. I should've let you in on what I was doing."

"It's too late for that now." He then grunted something unintelligible. I could sense that he was on my side but that meant nothing.

"What's going to happen to Detective Izuka?" I asked.

"He went on your orders. Right?"

"Yes, sir. It's my fault that he went. My responsibility."

"I doubt that. I know who he is. Nothing will happen to him if he keeps his cock sheathed. I warned him."

I didn't dare tell him about Detective Izuka and Ms. Nodoka. I had no idea what might happen to them. It wasn't unusual for police to marry other police, but Detective Izuka and Ms. Nodoka would have to be the ones who went public with their romance, not me.

Chief Inspector Saito took a deep breath, exhaled, and said, "You've only got a few years before you retire, Kawayama. Why is it that this murder of a prostitute has gotten to you? None of the other cases you've worked has?"

How could I answer that? I couldn't. Or I didn't want to. Or I was a coward who wanted to protect my secret. It did anger me, what he'd said about Tomomi.

"No one cares about her," he went on. "Move on. Uno is dead. She's dead. The case is closed."

"Mr. Uno didn't kill her," I said.

"But it looks like he did. Make use of his suicide."

This upset me. So many people cared about Tomomi. Chief Inspector Saito probably cared. He just couldn't show it. He had to carry out what some faceless higher-up in a tailored suit had told him to do to close the case. But I knew who cared. Detective Izuka cared and so did Ms. Nishikawa and those other girls who worked in her club, especially Junko, who had, by telling Uehara about Tomomi and Mr. Uno, led to him killing my daughter; so many girls who'd gone to her band's concerts, they cared. Even those Omi-gumi goons had shown some caring for her. Then there were those old women in the Amour who cared, who had unknowingly allowed a killer into the hotel, love hotels being what they were, protectors of lovers' anonymity. The manager of the hotel, Mr. Tanaka, he cared. Sayoko Kumagai cared. All those anonymous people I didn't know who'd read about her murder in the *Asahi* and wondered who she was and what had happened in that hotel room, they cared. Ayako and her lover, Haruto Murata, who shared the guilt over her murder, they cared. Their lives had been unalterably changed by her murder. But who cared the most was Ohashi, and he'd just wanted to help Tomomi out by paying her to do one of his jobs, a job he'd certainly hired other girls to do for other clients over the years.

"Ever track down her parents?" he then asked.

"No."

"There you have it," he said. "She doesn't even have a family."

That hurt. It hurt a lot, because all I could do was sit there and take it. I thought then of other cases I had worked involving runaways whose parents I couldn't find—or who didn't want anything to do with their daughters or sons, because they had shamed them—and thought of how their ashes had ended up in anonymous Tokyo Metropolitan tombs. I wasn't going to have that. Tomomi deserved a proper send off. Her ashes were going in our family tomb.

"Help out these young detectives," Chief Inspector Saito then said, "so that they don't make the mistakes that so many do when they first start out. Or are nearing retirement."

"Help them track down the killer of young girls?" I said.

"I'm trying my best to be civil here, Kawayama."

We stared at each other, and as we did I recalled the first murder case I'd worked of a middle-aged actress who could no longer find work because of her age. The manager of her building in Setagaya had found her dead. Her death had been made to look like a suicide. A bottle of Nikka whisky and some sleeping pills were on the nightstand beside her bed, but her right hand fingers were crushed. She was right-handed. On the nightstand was a suicide note. A woman with broken fingers doesn't write a suicide note. The handwriting didn't even match hers. She had a boyfriend who was a fourth generation Japanese-Korean who had turned up dead in his place; the case was closed by another faceless higher-up, to the regret of the lead detective I was junior to. My senior told me,

"Kawayama, it's how things are. Forget this case. You have a long career ahead of you."

Their deaths were ruled a homicide-suicide after they'd had a lovers' quarrel. The man owned a chain of pachinko parlors, all connected to the yakuza, as most pachinko chains are. It was the belief of the led detective —and mine—that she was a double-agent, operating in Japan for the Naicho, Japan's intelligence service, gathering information on North Korean agents before Prime Minister Koizumi's historic trip to Pyongyang, to learn about the whereabouts of Japanese the North Koreans had abducted and brought to North Korea to teach North Korean spies Japanese. The faceless higher-up, when our investigation led us to the Naicho and the actresses' connection with the organization, shut the case down. All I could do was accept the order to close the case, bow, and say, "Yes, sir." The case still galls me, as do a few others.

"Is that all, Chief?" I asked.

"Yes," he said, "you'll be a valuable trainer."

"I'll do my best," I said.

"I knew I could count on you to do the right thing."

That evening I went to the Keio Plaza's bar. Chie met me. "How are you this evening, Detective Kawayama?" she asked.

"Very well," I said.

"You've been visiting us quite frequently," she said.

"I come here for the jazz."

"Tonight there's a recording session for your wife's album. The producer felt that it would be better to have the background sound of people talking, the tinkle of ice cubes, real applause, not those fake background sounds that are mixed in in a studio."

She showed me to my table, and I ordered a Wild Turkey. Yes, that was the drink to have with jazz, an American bourbon. The news that I was finished as a detective also gave me a taste for something strong, as did the joy that Tomomi's killer would be taken care of soon, if he hadn't already been. The manager of the flophouse he'd been hiding out in would find him on the tatami, a syringe and some cooked *shabu* at his side.

Some microphones had been set up around Mizuko, but they weren't very distracting, just little things on stands around her, and two facing the people in the bar, who were there after work, some, executives with their half-their-age lovers. They made me think of Tomomi and her marriage with Wada, if she'd been happy with him and later Uno, a man who'd never grown up. I had to believe that she must've found some happiness with him. Why would she have kept on seeing him?

Chie brought me my Wild Turkey and I sipped it. "The taste of jazz," I said to her.

She had some glitter on her face this evening, silvery flakes of something that made her look as if she were from another world. Women. The lord gives them one face and they make themselves another. But, well, I liked her new face, and she seemed to notice that I did, and so I said, "You sparkle in the lights."

She blushed, and that didn't happen much with a law school student at Tokyo University.

"How are your studies going?" I asked her.

"Fine," she said, "if not boring. I don't know if I'll be an attorney or not. I enjoy the law, but I might not enjoy the business of law."

"Any plans, then?"

"Backpacking in Southeast Asia with my boyfriend," she said. "You know, I've only been to Saipan and California, never Asia. That's a shame, being in Asia and not having seen any of it."

"A boyfriend?" I asked. "Lucky him."

She smiled proudly. "He's an English literature major," she said, "like you. He's going to be a teacher. That seems to be a more rewarding career than the business of being an attorney and putting personal stamps on documents. How did you end up as a police detective?"

I told her.

"Movies? How odd but a touch romantic. I like that."

A couple, the man Western, wearing Levi jeans and a green and red checkered shirt, entered the bar. The woman was African, as black as charcoal, tall, thin, and with an angular face. She was from some east African country, I thought. She was wearing an exotic yellow African dress with prints of a bird that had long red tail feathers; her hair was all braided together like a crown. All it needed was a ruby or sapphire in the center to make her appear as if a deity. Her neck was long and regal. She seemed to have the ancestry of royalty, that her image had been carved into the stone of a mountain high above the arid bush.

"Excuse me," Chie said and went over to their table.

The woman made me think of Africa. I almost never thought of Africa, except when there was a documentary about an African animal on NHK. I wondered if Mizuko and I would go on a safari one day, to Kenya or Tanzania or Zimbabwe, where we'd stand before Victoria Falls, its rising mist enveloping us in a bubble of euphoria. It was a nice thought. It took me away from my dull future as a trainer and an even duller retirement. I sipped some more Wild Turkey and cheered up a bit and thought of taking walking trips with Mizuko through parts of Tokyo we didn't know well, if at all; and there were trips to the Sea of Japan coast we could go on, where we hadn't spent much time. We'd walk the craggy shorelines and collect seashells and put them in a basket and sort through them later while sitting on a blanket on a patch of sand. I sipped some more Wild Turkey. We weren't going to wither away from age in our home.

Mizuko spotted me and smiled, ever so slightly. She was wearing a blue dress and pearls and playing a Bill Evan's piece, "Waltz for Debby." I liked how she played it, slowly, precisely, each note hanging in the air, mixing with the hushed conversations and tinkling of ice cubes. The producer had been right, jazz should be recorded before a live audience, in a small bar, where people speak to each other in whispers, polite applause, and the muted laughter of lovers.

She finished the piece. A kind, admiring applause followed. I saw that the man and the African woman, who had taken a table up near Mizuko, were smiling. The African woman knew she was beautiful and the center of attention and she seemed to revel in it. She was a deity among those who looked so much alike. I had never stood out physically in my life, only intellectually, if that, and I was lucky enough for Mizuko to have been taken in by my eccentricities. She could have married a company man. I wondered what her life would've been like if she had. That's that parallel universe some of us slip into, thinking: what if I had made that decision rather than another? And then we construct a life based on a decision that we didn't make, believing our lives would be better. It's all so ridiculous. We live the life we have. That parallel universe? It doesn't exist.

Mizuko started in with "It Never Entered My Mind." I hung on every note, now and then sipping my bourbon, dreaming of us and what *onsen* resort she would find for us for *koyou*, and even where we would vacation the following summer. Probably Hokkaido. We'd been there a few times to escape the broiling Tokyo heat, staying at a traditional Japanese inn, a *ryokan*. We'd be served dinner in our room and hear the waves of the dark Pacific crashing on rocks and eat freshly caught sea bream or crab and those large, famous Hokkaido scallops cooked in their shells over a hibachi. We'd drink beer and tease each other and laugh and later lay on the tatami and hold each other and go to sleep that way while listening to the waves of the Pacific crashing on distant rocks.

Mizuko and I took a taxi home. Soon after I'd told the driver where we wanted to go, I said, "You played beautifully. The background sound of people whispering, the music of ice cubes in glasses, it'll all fit in with the songs you played."

She lay her head on my shoulder. This was so unusual for a middle-aged Japanese woman to do that I wasn't sure what to do at first, and then I thought of Western movies I'd seen in which couples did this and I no longer resisted the intimacy brought on by it.

"Thank you," she whispered in my ear. Her breath was

warm and arousing. It took me back to the days after we'd first met and spirited off to love hotels. "You've been coming by a lot recently. Any reason for that?"

"I like the way you play."

"You've heard me play before. Many times. Is it that case you're working?"

I wanted to tell her that it was because of her playing, but she'd see right through that and know I was using flattery to hide something. And so I said nothing.

"It is," she said.

I wanted to tell her everything but was afraid to. Would she lay her head on my shoulder if I did? I didn't know.

We got out of the taxi in front of our home. We went through the gate and along the flagstones that led to the front door. I unlocked it, and we stepped into the *genkan* and went inside.

Mizuko had put a fresh flower arrangement of an orchid in a vase in the *tokonoma*, below the scroll. In a small cabinet were some family heirlooms: sake cups and rice bowls that had been handed down to us from our ancestors, antiques dating back to the Edo period.

We went into the kitchen. Mizuko opened the refrigerator and took out some hard boiled eggs and put them in a bowl and began to peel the shell off one. I turned on the electric kettle and made some instant miso soup and a pot of *oolong cha*.

We ate there at the kitchen table, and I wanted to tell her again about her playing that night, but I knew her well enough to realize that it would annoy her if I did, so we talked as couples often do, about nothing of importance, the weather, what we would do on the weekend, television programs, something we had read, just to listen to the other, the words meaning nothing but the feeling meaning had so much.

After a while she said, "I read about that man who killed himself. He was involved in some sushi mislabeling scam. Do you know anything about that?"

I said I did. That was all.

"I saw a photo of his wife in one of those tabloids."

"Everyone talks about his wife."

"You've seen her?"

"I've talked with her," I said.

"Did it enter your mind? It's a vulnerable time for her."

"No. The thought didn't enter my mind."

"I'm sure it did with other detectives."

"It's a natural thing with men."

Mizuko, holding a hard boiled egg, was staring at me with those penetrating, intelligent eyes of hers, made even more so by the frame of her glasses, which brought attention to those eyes.

"All the annoying gossip she must be having to deal with from neighbors," she said.

"It'll fade away when another scandal comes along."

"I read the statement issued by his company expressing its condolences to her and her family. The thing is, she'll have to move."

I sipped my tea.

"Can you imagine how she'll feel in the neighborhood with everyone knowing about her husband?"

I stirred my soup with my *warabashi*.

"I asked you a question," Mizuko said.

"Yes," I said.

"Did she tell you she was moving?"

"I wasn't interested in her personal life."

"Why would you be interested in her husband's suicide? It has something to do with that case you're working, doesn't it?"

"We had our reasons to question her."

"Don't tell me, then. What was he thinking? He should've been thinking of his wife and family."

"He was."

"Do you want to talk about this case that's been on your mind?"

"No."

"You will. One day."

She knew me well.

"You should've been an English professor, man of few words, Clint."

"And watch my students go to sleep in class when I'm lecturing them on some work of literature that moves me. No thanks. I'm happier as a bureaucrat."

"Homicide detective."

"Bureaucrat."

"You track down killers," she said.

"I've tracked down a few."

She ate a slice of yellow *tsukemono*, a Japanese pickle.

"Too many Dirty Harry movies prevented me from pursuing a position as a literature professor," I said.

Mizuko drank some tea. "You're not Clint Eastwood, nor were you meant to be."

"An educated woman."

"Professor Endo, my second year at Waseda. He was passionate about T.S. Eliot. I didn't fall asleep in his class. 'Prufrock' I understood, with his mentoring, but the others. 'The Wasteland,' the English was lost on me. The Japanese translation was stupid."

"Did you have a crush on him?"

"He was sixty-four, about to retire, and had children. But he was debonair and intelligent. Of course I did. When we spoke my heart fluttered. I was young."

"You could've been his second wife. He could've set you up for life, after he keeled over from a stroke or whatever."

"Right," she said. "What's it like to be a kept woman? I've always wondered. One of my friends had an affair with her history professor. He was married, with three kids. The stories she told!"

"She didn't demand that she marry him, the way young women do?"

"No. She was smart. She broke the affair off before she was expelled and he was fired."

"You were a good girl."

"I wish I'd had a fling or two. Maybe three. What a dull life I led."

"There's no turning back," I said.

"Professor Endo is surely in his family tomb by now."

"That African woman in the bar this evening was a poem," she said.

"Yes, she was."

"Ever fantasize about black women?"

"How am I supposed to answer that? If I say 'no,' you'll say I'm lying. If I say 'yes,' you'll be jealous."

"So you have.

"All men have. Yes. Jealous?"

"I'm past the age of being jealous."

We finished our meals and went upstairs and had our baths and then rolled out the futon and I lay there for the longest time staring up at the ceiling in the enveloping darkness, wondering how to tell Mizuko about my demotion and Tomomi's murder. Then I somehow managed to fall asleep.

CHAPTER TWENTY-FOUR

Mizuko booked two nights at the Kokuya Ryokan and *Onsen* in the small tourist town of Yudanaka in Nagano prefecture, only a few hours' train ride from our home, but a feeling that was far, far away.

The *onsen* was easy to get to. We took the Hokuriku Shinkansen to Shin-Nagano Station and changed to a private rail line, the Nagano Line, which took us along the Yomase River to the town of Yudanaka, at the foot of Japan's Northern Alps. The town was also the terminus of the line. The train ride from Tokyo Station to Shin-Nagano Station was only a couple of hours, and the ride on the Nagano Line another hour and ten minutes.

The Hokuriku Shinkansen is a line off the Joetsu Line, which goes to Niigata on the coast of the Sea of Japan. The train first stops in Omiya, just north of Tokyo, to allow for passengers to change lines.

A spine of mountains runs down most of the main island of Honshu, separating the two coasts, and it is because of these mountains that the Hokuriku Line has tunnel after tunnel, until it reaches the plains of Niigata or Toyama prefectures along the Sea of Japan. The air against the windows of the train compresses when a train enters a tunnel, and one's ears feel this, the way they do when in an airplane that is descending and the air pressure is increasing.

Not long after leaving Omiya Station the girl who

serves drinks came into our car and I got a coffee and Mizuko a tea.

When she had pushed her cart past, I said, "Detective Izuka's wife is leaving him."

"Didn't he have it coming, from what you've told me about him?" she said.

"He's taken up with the head of the forensics department, a tough woman."

"Maybe she'll straighten him out. What do you think about becoming a grandfather?"

"Satoshi's wife is pregnant?"

"She has a name. You need to prepare yourself."

The train entered a tunnel and my coffee shook.

"Are we that old?" I asked.

"We're not so old. Plenty of grandfathers get out and enjoy life."

"Collecting seashells."

"What else have you got to do? What progress are you making in the case of the girl who was murdered in the love hotel?"

Her question had taken me by surprise. I wasn't sure how to answer it. I certainly couldn't tell her everything I knew. That wouldn't do. And this train wasn't the place for me to tell her. I'd been hoping that I would pluck up the courage to tell her after we'd had an *onsen* bath and had a beer and the tension in my shoulders and neck had melted away.

"Chief Inspector Saito told me to shelve the case," I said.

"Why would he do that?"

"She wasn't his daughter," I said. "He's a bureaucrat who likes cases to be closed. He's bucking for a promotion."

"Then he'll become one of them."

"Yes. A faceless bureaucrat issuing orders to subordinates."

"It's time for you to retire. How investigations are run isn't going to change."

"I know. But it isn't right."

"There's a lot of not right in the world."

She didn't know how true that was.

The cars of the local train to Yudanaka were filled with old men and women who had come to Nagano for shopping and a few high school students in their uniforms.

At one station, the conductor, a young woman with a complexion as white as snow, noticed that an old man had gone to sleep. She woke him by shaking one of his shoulders. The man, in a tweed overcoat and wearing a knit hat with a bill, got to his feet, bowed to thank her, and stepped out of the car onto the platform; it was that kind of local train, in which the conductor probably knew most of the people who used the line. She had probably grown up in the area.

We arrived at Yudanaka Station at two-thirty-seven. We took a taxi to the *ryokan*. The driver, a warmhearted local man who had a sun-baked face and gray hair, said soon after we'd left the station, "I was born and raised here. It's a peaceful little town."

"How is your family?" Mizuko asked him.

I would've never asked him such a question. I might not have asked him any question at all, preferring, rather, to sit there, looking out the window at the scenery, the blue and red tile roofs of the homes, the river flowing through the town between two stone walls, there to protect the town from floods; and women and men, mostly older than me, students and children, on bicycles.

"I have three children, two daughters and a son," the driver said. "They're all working now. One is in Kobe, another in Tokyo, and the youngest in Kitakyushu. It's just my wife and I now. We're a bit lonely, but we try to fight off the loneliness by going on hikes up into the mountains and visiting friends. I go for a swim three times a week at the local health club. It's sad that young people have to leave their hometowns. But there aren't any jobs here that pay much. I was lucky. I got a job at a farmers' coop down in Nagano. It's only tourists that keep our economy going now. Thanks for visiting." He sighed.

Mizuko said, "We're a shrinking country. So many women want careers. All those government policies to increase the birthrate, they'll fail. Young women aren't stupid, you know. One day Japan will go the way of the dinosaurs. We need immigrants."

I doubted that this was ever going to happen, Japanese being Japanese, closed off to other races and cultures, for the most part, except for those few eccentrics who are friends with them, as a way of escaping their own cloistered culture.

"The dinosaurs went extinct because of an asteroid strike," I put in.

"I thought you'd gone to sleep," Mizuko said.

The driver said, "You're a spirited one. You and my wife would hit it off."

"We have a son whose wife is expecting a child," I said.

Mizuko glared at me.

"Congratulations," he said.

"It's our first grandson," I said.

"Grandchildren are a pleasure," he said. "I have three."

Mizuko continued to glare at me.

We came to the entrance of the *ryokan*. It was three-stories, made of cedar, river stones, and concrete, over which lay a soft, yellow decorative plaster. The driver opened the taxi door and got out and went around to the boot and picked up our bags and carried them over to the *genkan*. A *nori short curtain, on which was embroidered* Kokuya Ryokan and Onsen, was at the entrance. The sliding doors of the ryokan were open.

"Enjoy your stay," the driver said. "The food is delicious here. Local specialties."

"I'd expect as much," I said.

After the driver had returned to the taxi, Mizuko said, "That was a bit much, about us having a grandchild."

"I couldn't stop myself, this talk of Japan's demise."

"I've always suspected you of being a closet nationalist. I fully expect to see you with a *hachimaki* wrapped around your head, the rising sun on it, going around town in one of those sound trucks that your fellow loonies annoy others with, shouting about restoring the emperor to power. That'll be how you spend your retirement. Just don't wear that rag around your head when you're at home."

I smiled. "Thanks for the idea. Better than collecting seashells."

"I should have married a boring company man," she said, "not a sarcastic literature major."

A young woman wearing a red *yukata*, appropriate for the season, said, "*Irasshaimase.*" She bowed and, when she straightened up, gestured toward the front desk.

As we were taking off our shoes and putting on the slippers, a young man in blue trousers and matching vest, a white shirt and tie, took our bags and escorted us to the front desk, where another woman, this one middle-aged, dignified and poised, bowed and greeted us again, saying, "*Irasshaimase.*"

She, like the girl at the *genkan*, had a fair complexion. Her face was round and her cheeks had red crowns, which might have drawn a few stares in Tokyo, her unmistakable rural roots. She might, if working in certain companies, been the butt of jokes for those red farmer's cheeks, a sad thing, how Japanese treat others who don't fit into their group.

After I had filled out the check-in card, the young man carried our bags to our room. The room was on the first floor, at the end of a long corridor. He set our bags down in front of the door and slid it open, and we all went inside, leaving our sandals on a shelf by the door. He put away our bags in a closet and bowed and left. The room was eight-mats, had a Japanese table in the middle of it, and on each side of the table two chairs, Japanese style for sitting on tatami. The tatami was quite new, even had the smell of being new, but the green had faded from the straw.

At the opposite side of the room there was an *engawa*, or Japanese porch. On it were two Western-style chairs made of bamboo and a table between them. One step from the *engawa* was our private bath, what we call a rotenburo, because it is outside. The "ten" in *routenburo*, 天、 means sky, furo, 風呂, changed to buro here, means bath. Around the bath, which was deep enough for the water to rise to the middle of one's chest, were a few small pines, some decorative pebbles, and a row of ferns up against a reed screen that insured the bathers' privacy. Steam was rising off the surface of the water.

We sat down on the chairs in the engawa and said nothing, just enjoyed the sound of the water filling the bath from a spout of bamboo, and the water from the bath draining off across the pebbles and gurgling over a few rocks.

I don't know how much time passed before Mizuko said she wanted to go for a walk. It could've been thirty minutes or two hours. I suppose that's what comes from the intimacy of two people who have lived together for so long that they no longer feel the need to speak; time takes on a different meaning.

We changed into the ryokan's *yukatas* that had been laid out on the futon and went back out past the front desk. The woman there smiled and bowed again. The young woman who greeted guests at the genkan had remained there, as if a soldier who was on sentry duty. She took some *geta*, wooden clogs, from a locker, and put them down on the stone floor for us and we changed from our slippers into them and left the *ryokan* and found our way to a narrow lane lined with tourist shops that sold what are called *meibutsu*, local specialty items. In Yudanaka, these were almost all made of cedar —shoe horns, boxes for tissues, cosmetic cases, chairs and tables, and Go boards. A few shops sold polished stones or jewelry—bracelets and necklaces—made from white marble. Teahouses were there, too, and inside them people wearing *yukatas* were sitting at tables drinking tea and eating Japanese sweets made from beans.

The aroma of tea leaves being roasted drew us to a shop up the lane. It was an old teahouse made of wood, and in a window were packages of various teas that were roasted there. A vent blew the scent of the tea leaves being roasted, a sort of burnt smell, out onto the lane. Drawing that aroma into my lungs was like a soothing balm.

We went into a teahouse. The seating arrangement was traditional Japanese. We sat on zabutons on the tatami and were served by a girl who couldn't have been more than eighteen. She was wearing jeans and a flannel shirt. Her hair was dyed orange. She was polite and courteous but had a rebellious swagger that suggested she sought a life that was better than one in which she served tea to tourists. I imagined her future. She was the kind of girl who ends up hanging out around Shibuya Station, easy prey for adult video scouts.

When we returned to the *ryokan* after having our tea and took a bath together. The hot, sulfur water, straight from deep in the earth, loosened the tightness in my neck and back. Mizuko's face turned red. I looked at her breasts and she said, "They aren't what they were. But I'm not going to fight aging."

"I'm not what I was, either," I said.

"Yours aren't on display in a public bath."

"My balls hang down to my knees."

"Not quite. Maybe next year."

"We're getting old in spirit. The years have gone by too fast."

"We've suffered enough."

It was odd, her saying this again. I said, "That girl at the teahouse, I wonder how she'll end up."

"You've got to put an end to your guilt. Stop. Praying helps me."

"I can't help myself at times. You know how I feel about praying."

"You need something to take your mind off it."

"I'll never forget."

"But you can't keep on punishing yourself."

"I know. I know. I can't help it. But I know."

"If you don't keep busy during your retirement you'll eat yourself up with guilt."

"Okay. I'll collect seashells. We'll collect them together."

She chuckled. "That's better," she said.

We got out of the bath and dried ourselves and then lay on the futon, a sheet over us. There was a time when we couldn't have done that, just lie there together naked. But now, well, that wasn't so important to us, and I sort of regretted that, that sexual desire that had controlled us for many years.

After a while my stomach growled.

"You're hungry," Mizuko said. "Let's go to the *engawa* and sit there until it's dark before we eat."

She didn't like to eat dinner unless it was dark. It was just a peculiarity of hers. Maybe it had to do with her coming home late so often from the Keio Plaza Hotel and always eating when it was dark.

We got up off the futon and went to the *engawa*

and sat there, wearing happi coats now that it was becoming cooler. Because of the reed screen that ran around the bath, offering us privacy, we couldn't see into the town, only over the fence, in the direction of the peaks of the Northern Alps, which were a backdrop to the little town. Stars, a rare sight in Tokyo, and a harvest moon, a bit red, appeared.

"Shall we order?" Mizuko asked.

I went to the telephone and ordered dinner, a set meal—ayu, shabu-shabu (thin slices of wagyu dipped in boiling water), several different sushi dishes, *sansai*, freshly gathered mountain vegetables, and a matsutake soup. The ayu, which had a bamboo stick skewer stuck through it, had been grilled over charcoal, the traditional way to cook it. I also ordered a large bottle of Kirin lager and a flask of Nihonshu as well. We drank that warm, from small cups, only slightly larger than a thimble. We didn't say much as we ate, but only looked up now and then at the mountains and the stars and moon. The Nihonshu helped me brace myself for what I had to say. After a woman had come and taken away the dishes and bowls, I tried to speak but no words came out.

"Yes?" Mizuko asked.

"It's . . ."

"It's about Tomomi." She looked at me in a way that let me know that she'd known all along about her.

"Yes," I said.

"It was her," she said, "that girl?"

I plucked up the necessary courage and said, "Yes."

Mizuko's eyes watered but she shed no tears, which isn't how I was. I wept. It was like a pin had pricked me, letting out that secret I had been keeping from her.

"It's all right," she said. "It's all right. She was the way she was. It's all right."

We went to the engawa and sat in the chairs, looking at mountain peaks and stars and moon in an intimate silence. We didn't speak for the longest time, and then, after a shooting star blazed across the sky, Mizuko said, "You've kept the guilt in you for too long. We've suffered for too many years."

I then said, "Her killer, he's been taken care of."

She said nothing, only stared at me. Then she nodded her head, seemingly satisfied with what I'd said.

There was a long silence again that was now and then punctuated by the bellowing of a drunk in a karaoke bar. When he'd stopped and the applause had settled, Mizuko said, "We'll pack a lunch and go on a hike tomorrow up into the mountains. Tomorrow will be a lovely day."

Epilogue

The town of Abashiri is on the northernmost coast of the island of Hokkaido. The winters there are long, snowy, and harsh. Storms blow in from Siberia and the Kamchatka Peninsula across the Soya-kaikyo, in English the La Perouse Strait, that separates Hokkaido from Russia.

The Abashiri River meanders through the small town of the same name, emptying into the Sea of Okhotsk. Fishermen venture out from the protected waters of the river into the sea when the weather allows to lay down traps for crab and to search for saury, sardines, herring, squid, sea bream, and salmon, depending on the season. In the Tsugaru Strait fishermen catch bluefin tuna that are auctioned off in Tokyo's Tsukiji fish market for millions of yen, a substantial motive for the yakuza to pay off the right inspector at the market to pass off tuna of a lesser grade as premium.

The summer of the following year, Mizuko and I took a trip to Abashiri, flying out of Haneda Airport in Tokyo to Sapporo, where we spent one night in the JR Inn, near the station. From there we took a train to Abashiri.

Mizuko had booked a room in the Kitakai (northern sea) Ryokan and Onsen outside of town on Cape Notoro, which juts out into the sea like a dagger; gray rocks and pines cover the cape. The pines are bent over from the prevailing winter winds coming out of Siberia. The *ryokan* was similar to the one we had stayed in in Yudanaka, a ten-mat room that had an *engawa*, a private garden, and a natural hot spring bath. The *ryokan* was a few hundred meters from a cliff that dark waves thundered against. A trail led from the *ryokan* to the cliff, and Mizuko and I took it a few times to see the monstrous waves smacking up against it. The waves sent up a spray that blew over us. The sight of the waves striking the cliff made me think of the Japanese movie company Tohei, which has as its trademark opening, a shot of a blue wave rolling in from the Pacific and crashing onto a rock and breaking into two symmetrical halves, an iconic Japanese image of harmony.

The evenings along the northern coast of Hokkaido are cool in summer and required us to sleep under a down comforter, a pleasure. The summer days in Tokyo have become so hot that I often saw the sole prints of shoes in the asphalt of pedestrian crossings. Our trip to Abashiri was a ten-day respite from that heat, but we hadn't gone there just to escape Tokyo's intolerable heat. I wanted to visit someone in the Abashiri Prison, which is, along with fishing, one of the town's major economic engines.

The old prison opened in 1890, Japan's Meiji era, when the country rapidly developed. A new prison opened in 1984. The old prison is now, of all things, a museum that attracts tourists who want to know what life was like for prisoners during the Meiji era. The most famous prisoner is the anti-hero Shiratori Yoshie, wrongly convicted of murdering a farmer. He escaped from four different prisons. A memorial to him is at the museum. In 1961 he was released for good behavior from the Fucho Prison in Tokyo and lived out the rest of his life in his native prefecture, Aomori, where he scraped by on day labor jobs until he died in 1979, at the age of seventy-one, from a heart attack.

This fascination for prisons and prisoners has always fascinated me. No one in their right mind would want to be a prisoner, but there is this unyielding interest in crime and punishment. The first yakuza genre movie, "Abashiri Bangichi," or "The Man from Abashiri," stars Takakura Ken, the John Wayne of Japanese film. He has a strong jawline and craggy, masculine good looks. He played in many yakuza movies after that one, becoming a famous yakuza figure who lived by a code, the way John Wayne became famous in westerns for the various roles he played. I have always held that it was Takakura Ken's roles in these yakuza movies, and other actors who followed him, that did the most to recruit young, lost men. Tazu Uehara? He was a fool as well, influenced by movies. So was I.

I took a taxi from the *ryokan* to the prison. The ride was about thirty minutes. The highway ran along the coast most of the way, then the river, where there were fishing boats going out to sea. I went to the prison alone. Mizuko had wished me well and said to me, "Tell him he didn't have to do what he did."

Soon after I got into the taxi, the driver, a woman, asked, "First time to Abashiri?" It was a bit unusual for a driver to be a woman, but times are changing and more women are seeking out this job, as it provides them with a degree of freedom and independence from chauvinistic male managers in companies. She was in her mid-forties, had a round face, soft eyes, and a button nose, on which there was perched a pair of glasses in a silver, ornately decorated frame. Her hair was done up in curls. She, like most taxi drivers, was wearing white cotton gloves. She had a Kyushu dialect, which made me wonder how she had ended up in Abashiri.

"My wife and I are here to escape Tokyo's heat," I said. "We've been to Hokkaido many times, but never this far north."

Driving along the bank of the river, about to enter town, she said nothing, and then I realized what I had said didn't square with where she was taking me. I broke the somewhat uncomfortable silence by saying, "I'm a police detective."

"Oh," she said, "you don't have to explain. I take all kinds of people to the prison. It's none of my business the reasons for my passengers going there."

"You're from Kyushu," I said.

"You're a detective, all right. I was born and raised in a small town near Miyazaki. Then I went to university in Tokyo, where I met my husband. We worked in the same company. After so many years of commuting and dull company life, we decided we wanted a bit of adventure.

He makes furniture in a shop behind our house from native trees—firs and hardwoods—but some cherry from south of here."

"I think you two made the right decision," I said.

"The winters are long, but when we think of those commutes and looking at computer screens for most of the day, we know this life is for us. He sells his furniture on the internet. The internet is a wonderful thing. We wouldn't have a life here if it weren't for it. You wouldn't believe the number of orders he gets for his tables and chairs from foreigners in Europe and the U.S., Singapore, too. Now he's started to make desks. People don't mind the shipping costs either. And they're substantial, let me tell you."

"How did he transition from being a salaryman to a carpenter?" I asked.

"His father," she said. "Making furniture was his hobby. He picked it up from him. He lives in Akita. He's a carpenter."

I'd never been to Akita, but I knew, as did all Japanese, that it was famous for its Nihonshu, beautiful women, rice, and Kanto festival, in which men in *happi* coats balance bamboo poles festooned with paper lanterns on their palms and even their foreheads. The festival is held in August, and people from all over Honshu go to Akita to see it. It's been held for centuries, to pray for a good rice harvest.

The driver looked into the rear-view mirror and our eyes met. She had a hint of green eye-shadow, and her lips were a glossy pink.

"Children?" I asked.

"Two. Both in university. One in Sapporo, the other in Akita, staying with my husband's parents."

"Your children like cold, snowy places," I said.

"Yes. You're a detective, for sure. They both ski. But my son likes to snowboard now. I don't like it. It's dangerous. Too many broken bones. I have a friend whose daughter broke her leg snowboarding and had to have surgery. Now she walks with a limp. I don't like it at all, snowboarding."

"And your daughter?" I asked. It had taken me months to ask someone about their children, especially a daughter. I just couldn't listen to them speak with pride about their daughter, her education, job, accomplishments.

"She wants to be an airline pilot," she said. "I think she got the idea from a movie, or watching too many YouTube videos, those ones of women airline pilots landing planes."

I had to laugh. I told her why I'd become a police detective.

"Movies," she said. "Do you have children?"

"Two," I said, "a son and a daughter."

"How are they?"

I said, "Our daughter is well, thank you. My son is an app developer. These young women, they're head strong. Our daughter is the lead singer in a band, but she wants to move on to something else."

"You don't say? Good for her."

I had learned not to tell the truth and risk bringing an enjoyable conversation to an end. People never knew what to say in reply after I'd told them that Tomomi had been murdered.

"Maybe she'll become a police detective," she said.

"I've warned her against that profession," I said. "Too many reports to write up and too much kowtowing to seniors."

"I know what you mean there. We're not all cut out for that kind of work." She looked in the rear-view mirror again, smiled, and said, "You've got humor. Your wife must be laughing all the time."

"She's the one with the sense of humor," I said. "I just do as I'm told."

"I don't think so."

A few minutes later she stopped the taxi at the main entrance to the prison.

"Have an enjoyable visit," she said.

I thought, I don't know how this visit is going to go. It might be satisfying. It might not. I hadn't seen him since he'd walked into the Shinjuku Police Building and turned himself in, admitting that he'd killed Jiyumi Harajuku.

At the guardhouse, an old, wizened guard examined my police ID.

"Welcome to Abashiri," he then said and bowed.

I continued on through a pair of steel doors to a reception area and was met by a petite but stern woman guard in a blue uniform. I told her why I was there, and she looked at a computer screen. "I'll have a guard escort him to the visitors' room," she said. "Please sign in."

I signed a log.

"Follow me, please," she said.

We went through a door that another guard behind a pane of glass buzzed open and proceeded along a gray-tiled corridor to the visitors' room, where there was another door that a guard had to buzz open.

We entered the visitors' room. A line of gray steel chairs faced a glass wall. The glass had holes in it, to allow for a conversation between visitors and prisoners.

I sat in the chair the guard told me to sit in, the one farthest from a lawyer meeting with a prisoner.

The chair was cold, but the atmosphere was surprisingly cheerful. The walls were a sunflower yellow, and on a table behind me, which the prisoners could see when they spoke with a visitor, was a pine bonsai in a green clay pot trimmed in gold.

I braced myself for him to enter the room through a door on the prisoners' side.

Less than a minute later the door buzzed open, and he came into the room and the guard escorted him over to the chair opposite mine. He sat and looked at me. He had become a bit thinner. His hair was cropped and grayer than I'd remembered it. He was wearing a blue prison jumpsuit. He nodded deferentially, then looked me in the eyes. They were clear and bright, as if some kind of weight had freed him of all of his worries.

"Why are you here?" he asked straight off.

"I had to see you," I said.

"You got what you wanted. He's dead. What's this case to you?"

"She was someone's daughter."

"A lot of men have daughters."

"My wife and I have a daughter."

He just stared back at me before saying, "Now I understand. I'd do the same if that loser killed a daughter of mine." He looked over my shoulder at the pine bonsai. "That's a fine bonsai," he said. "It makes me proud, being Japanese."

"You didn't have to. The case was closed."

"It's how I planned it."

That came as a surprise. He was the one who'd used me, of all things.

"We had a daughter," I said. A burden of guilt dropped away.

"You said you 'have.'" Now it's 'had.' Which is it?"

"Had," I said.

"That explains things. I'm sorry for you and your wife."

"She thinks of you."

"Tell her thank you. Then you found Jiyumi's parents?"

That cut me in half.

"Yes," I said.

"She deserved a proper send off. You saw to that?"

"Yes."

"She was a nice kid who was just trying to find herself."

"Yes, she was."

He looked at me in a way that made it clear to me that he knew all about Tomomi, me, and Mizuko, everything. Then he said, "I deserve this, for her parents. The long drop is a quick death, the way I understand it. I suppose I'll shortly find out." He smiled dryly.

"You didn't have to," I said.

"I did so. I'm responsible for what happened. I had to."

There was a brief silence. I looked at the stub of his little finger. He truly had the bushido spirit. He was Japanese to his soul. I wasn't sure I could've been so sacrificial. Somehow I managed to ask, "Have you heard from your sister?"

"She writes me letters."

I thought of Ayako, wondering where she'd ended up. I knew that she'd married Mr. Murata and left Tokyo. I suppose I could have tracked her down. But what was the point? All she'd wanted was to be happy.

ABOUT THE AUTHOR

James Roth

James Roth, a writer of fiction and nonfiction, has traveled widely in Southeast Asia and has lived in Japan, China, Jordan, South Africa, and Zimbabwe but likes to say he was "Made in Japan." His parents lived there during the American occupation but he was, to his and his  mother's lasting regret, born in an American military hospital in the U.S. Golf is his game. Motorcycling in the mountains of Zimbabwe is his pleasure.

BOOKS BY THIS AUTHOR

Death Of A Gaijin

Yokohama, Japan, 1873. After almost three hundred years of self-imposed isolation, Japan has opened up to the world. Nelson Van Dorn, a former New York City police detective, sails for Yokohama, expecting to start a new life by going into the silk exporting business with his younger brother, Warren, whom he plans to meet there, only to learn that his brother has died in a mysterious fire, that he was an opium addict, and that he has left Nelson in debt. To pay off this debt, Nelson reluctantly takes on an investigation to find the nephew of Ari Markel, a mysterious elderly Jewish man. He is assisted in his investigation by Mr. Markel's beautiful Chinese mistress, Fei Wu, who has by then become Nelson's lover. During the investigation, the American consulate general threatens Nelson to end it, which only emboldens Nelson and Fei. The consulate general's wife, an exotic Hungarian, in the tradition of classic noir, also attempts to dissuade Nelson from continuing the investigation by using the only means at her disposal: flirtation and the promise of sex. But Nelson, being a seasoned New York City detective, and Fei

Wu, who is familiar with Japanese society, persevere. As they follow leads to learn about the disappearance of Mr. Markel's nephew, Nelson and Fei discover the secrets of other expatriates, Mr. Markel's real motives in wanting to find his nephew, and the secrets of other expatriates, all while their love deepens.

My Alabama Story

In 1963, Simon Klein and his family, Jews from St. Paul, Minnesota, move to the small town of Pickettville, Alabama, where Simon's father has taken a job at a nearby Army base. Simon must finish his senior year of high school there. He is as mystified of the South as Southerners are of a Jew. While gathering information for a story he is writing for his high school paper, he becomes friends with Cecilia Goodwin, a Black girl. They have much in common. While sitting together on her porch swing—a Southern tradition—they talk about the Civil Rights movement, literature, the looming Vietnam War, and, of course, football. Eventually, they realize that they are romantically drawn to each other, but they know that they must keep their relationship a secret, that is until both decide to confront the town's social restrictions by putting their romance on public display, to Simon's mother's delight, but to the angry epithets of many others. This is the year that Governor George Wallace declared, "Segregation forever!"

Told by Simon many years later, this coming-of-age Southern novel foretells the growing Civil Rights Movement, the assassinations of President Kennedy and Martin Luther King, and America's deepening involvement in the Vietnam War, all while Simon's parent's marriage falls apart, and he learns of the corruption, nepotism, and xenophobia of small-town Alabama of that era, a state he now looks back on with fond memories, as it was a time when his life changed forever.

Thicker Than Forget

With war between the U.S. and Imperial Japan looming in the fall of 1941, Colton Hancock, who grew up in Tokyo, returns to the U.S., reluctantly leaving his Japanese lover, Yasuko, an independent, free-thinking woman, behind. During the war, he serves as an interpreter in the interrogation of Japanese prisoners. Soon after Japan's surrender in September of 1945, he flies into war-ravaged Tokyo as an army lieutenant, hoping to pick up where he has left off with Yasuko, but the course of their romance does not continue in a way that he could have imagined. This tersely written love story has as is setting the destruction of much of Tokyo by B-29s, the occupation of the country by American GIs, the complexities of Japanese society, and a thriving black market, as the two lovers overcome seemingly insurmountable challenges in their effort to reunite. The title, "Love is Thicker than Forget," is taken from a poem by one of the twentieth century's most renowned poets, E. E. Cummings.

Romance Gone Wrong

Take pleasure in the sexual romps—and crimes—of

men and women in exotic locations, from South Africa to Japan to a remote island in Indonesia. Men and women meet, go off together on a sailboat, to a hotel room, to a tent on the sands of the Arabian desert. Their relationship might be for a few hours. A week. A month. A lifetime. For those men and women who are on the run from the law, the pleasures of sex are heightened by the risks they have taken to rob, murder, and smuggle, all in the mistaken belief that easy money has its rewards. Many of these stories are told in the tradition of the pulp magazines of long ago, when men were men and women were women, and they both knew how to get what they wanted from the other. For those who want stories that are erotic set in exotic locations, Romance Gone Wrong is for them.

Made in United States
North Haven, CT
10 June 2025

69682229R00186